CHILDREN'S THEATRE
PROGRAMME OF NEW PLAYS

The Ungrateful Man

*By **David Horsburgh***
*A tale from the **Panchatantra***

The Magic Drum

*From **The Magic Drum and Other Stories***
*by **Sudha Murty***

Ali Oh Baba!

*A retelling of the tale from **1001 Arabian Nights***
for a contemporary audience

The Court Jester

*Tales from **Tenali Raman***

Vitasta
LET KNOWLEDGE SPREAD
www.vitastapublishing.com

BANGALORE
LITTLE
THEATRE

COMMENTS ON THE PUBLICATIONS

"The city of Bangalore can boast of so many things. Its technical savvy, its splendid gardens, its civic discipline and so on. I salute the city for the excellent and consistent work it has done over the years in nurturing a robust theatre activity for children. As far back as 1963, the pioneering Bangalore Little Theatre had staged an original adaptation in English of the Sanskrit classic Mrichhakatika. The Group has not looked back since. Although these plays are performed in English, they are firmly rooted in the Indian soil. Even when on occasion a foreign play is selected for performance, the Indian sensibility is not lost sight of. Through the History of Ideas programme the audiences of Bangalore have learned of the lives and works of great personalities, the important historical contexts and their culture through the steady diet of quality plays staged for them by BLT. They were perhaps unaware that while being entertained, they were actually being enriched educationally. The privileged youngsters of Bangalore may justifiably be envied by children in the rest of the country. In its ongoing process of theatre activity, I have seen BLT grow from strength to strength. The group soon amassed a daunting collection of play scripts that it had staged – both plays selected from other regions, and fresh plays the group had especially undertaken. Many of these scripts have bagged prestigious awards for either the writing or their production.

Many support channels had been started in the city, to facilitate and aid play production. A publication programme has been initiated by BLT to share its vast collection of scripts ready to be staged with the world at large. Now, in 2019, on the threshold of the group's Diamond Jubilee, this programme is to see the light of day. Several volumes have been planned to reach out to theatre enthusiasts in India and all over the world. The volumes will not only contain texts of select plays,

The new publication series produced by the Bangalore Little Theatre are an important and most welcome addition to world theater knowledge. Bravo!

Arthur Giron
Founding Member of Ensemble Studio Theatre, New York, formerly Head, Graduate Playwriting Program, Carnegie Mellon University

This volume addresses the critical need for more actable and accessible versions of classic Indian plays in English. Good plays around important historical ideas are unfortunately scarce. The second admirable volume helps correct that deficiency.

Ira Hauptman
Professor of Drama, Queens College, CUNY, New York

This work is not only important for India, it also makes plays from Indian writing known across the world. It is a very important and necessary project.

Ursula Werdenberg
Dramaturg-Playwright,
Secretary General of The International Playwrights' Forum

My warmest congratulations. This is a significant milestone and a wonderful achievement that gives readers an opportunity to think about our pasts and our presents through a history of ideas.

Anuradha Kapur
Past Director, National School of Drama

ये नाम केचिदिह नः प्रथयन्त्यवज्ञां
जानन्ति ते किमपि तान्प्रति नैष यत्नः ।
उत्पत्स्यते तु मम कोऽपि समानधर्म
कालो ह्ययं निरवधिर्विपुला च पृथ्वी ॥

Those who deride or ignore my work –
let them know: my efforts are not for them.
There will come along someone who shares my spirit:
the world is vast, and time endless.

– ***Bhavabhuti***

Bangalore Little Theatre is privileged to receive a substantial grant from ***Kusum*** *and* ***Mohandas Pai*** *towards education and institutional development programmes, which include the publication of these plays.*

Published by,
Renu Kaul Verma
Vitasta Publishing Pvt Ltd
2/15, Ansari Road, Daryaganj
New Delhi 110002
info@vitastapublishing.com

ISBN 978-93-86473-85-1

MRP ₹399
First Edition 2020

Editor: Papri Sen Sri Raman
Layout: Ram Kumar
Illustrations: Ayannar C
Coordinator: Deepak Mote
Printer: Vikas Computer and Printers

CONTENTS

FOREWORD

Bangalore Little Theatre is an enormous exercise in imagination. It remains an aspiration for theatre performers and a source of inspiration for practitioners. The passion, perseverance, toil and grace is the hallmark of this intimate Institution, which has embarked on many pathbreaking initiatives, programmes and productions. If the History of Ideas programme was unique, the translation and adaptation of Indian classics in English is a huge service. In the programme Vijay Padaki has presented a pertinent model, wherein the play scripts transcend the cultural specificity and period in time to speak in a universal language that addresses our contemporary concerns. Although we read the text in English, we experience the content in the original. A truly remarkable feat.

BLT has had a strong play development programme for a long time. It is most appropriate that the plays are being published now. Several volumes of plays can be expected in print very soon. This is a huge contribution to the institution of the theatre in India. We can be sure they will be received with enthusiasm world-wide.

Feroz Abbas Khan
Theatre director and award winning film maker

SPECIAL MESSAGE

For nearly 60 years, Bangalore Little Theatre has been instrumental in promoting theatre arts in Bengaluru and across the country. The ambitious project of publishing their most successful plays in a multi-volume anthology marks a great point in their story – another marker of the tremendous success they have attained.

In translating to English and adapting the plays for the modern stage, Mr Vijay Padaki (BLT) is conserving the best of Indian theatre. Each play is especially relevant to contemporary situations, from environmental concerns to resurgent regional identities, to introspecting the carnage of wars and finally the complexities of court politics.

I am certain that such a project provides us the perfect opportunity to understand, perhaps for the first time in recent years, the sheer wealth of Indian theatre spanning different cultural and linguistic traditions in the subcontinent. In producing such plays, and putting them together in this volume, BLT has undertaken a public service, one which every Indian living in the 21st century can profit from, for a long time to come.

With this, I wish BLT the very best for this and their many future endeavours.

Shashi Tharoor
Member of Parliament for Thiruvananthapuram

PUBLISHER'S NOTE

There is a keyword for Theatre for children. Its TYA. Theatre for Young Audiences. They can be 16 or as young as 3, they are all moving towards adulthood and theatre is a representation of adulthood. Mostly. Even when children are enacting the roles, the play is usually written by an adult and directed by one. From the mouth of babes pours forth adult wisdom.

There is a catch here. Take the example of popular Nursery Rhymes. In the 21st century, we have a right to question if they were politically correct. For instance, its easy to get a child to enact the role of Humpty Dumpty or Gorgie Porgie, they are both body-shaming and one is sexist, to say the least. Most Bedtime Stories are today thought politically incorrect and anti-women. American writer James Finn Garner in 1994 rewrote stories like *Little Red Riding Hood*, the *Three Little Pigs* and *Snow White*, to supposedly represent what a 'politically correct' adult would consider a good and moral tale for children. The *Emperor's New Clothes*, for example had political overtones, even in the original. So, what is the definition of children's play exactly? Like children's literature is now a grey area, so is children's theatre. One needs to be careful and correct with this.

'As Dumbledore told Harry, "It is our choices Harry, that show what we truly are, far more than our abilities". You are poised to enter the real world tomorrow. The choices you make there will define who you become', Shikha Sharma, Axis bank CEO, told her IIM audience in Ahmedabad. As everyone knows, Harry Potter is a tale of striking out for the subaltern, the muggles, elves, dung beetle so on and so forth...magic against orthodox religion.

The latest in popular children's theatre in the West is *Nutcracker Prince, Jungle Book, Legend of Mulan, Kid Frankenstein* and several others. The concept of Frankenstein itself is adult, the Nutcracker, the eternal good vs evil battle. There are very few new ideas actually, in children's plays yet.

Theatre performed by or for children dates back hundreds of years. The first mention is seen in a 1784 entry in Madame de Genlis's *Memoirs*, in which she describes a performance by her two daughters. In the modern era, it first appeared in Moscow, when Russian actress Natalia Satz founded the Moscow Theatre for Children in 1918. In its early stages, the Moscow Theatre for Children viewed its goal as representing childhood needs, separating the struggles of childhood from those of adult life. TYA everywhere else was set up with educational purposes. With minimum props, suited to school stages.

In India, adult theatre has ancient roots. The earliest theatre for children one can connect to is perhaps the *Ramleela* of North India, improvised street plays on the story of Rama, with lots of child actors taking part, hanuman, a special favourite of children. School dramatic societies, however, also have a 200-year-old history, ever since colonial times.

Versatile playwrights like Tagore came up with a dozen children's plays for enactment first in his Jorasanko home, by his large joint family children. *The Little Big Man* is about a boy who tries on his father's shoes and begins to understand the world of responsibilities. *The Astronomer* is a futuristic tale about a little girl wanting to catch the moon, very relevant now in times of moon rovers and alien stories and films. *The Land of Cards* is a satirical tale set against the bondage of orthodoxy, possibly the most political play from Tagore for children. Marathi playwright Vijay Tendulkar's plays for children are well loved.

'Children play, make-believe and role-play. That's how their imagination soars. If allowed to inhabit a world that channels their creativity, their aggressive impulses are likely to be in check. Theatre is a powerful vehicle of creative engagement that should be a part of every child's growing up and remain so when they are adults. This is my dream', writes Sanjna Kapoor in *livemint.*

Recollecting her days with her parents Jennifer and Sashi Kapoor and Prithvi Theatre, she says: For the past 30 years, I have witnessed, first-hand, the magic that theatre can weave into a child's being. I have grown up hearing stories about my grandparents Geoffrey and

Laura Kendal travelling with their theatre company Shakespeareana, visiting schools and colleges from the 1940s-70s, bringing Shakespeare and modern classics alive with their minimalist and modern performances.

'Years later, when I was to produce my first plays for children performed by professional adult actors, I would recall my grandfather's (Geoffrey Kendal) words, "We were among the most rewarding audiences in the world; rows of intelligent Indian schoolgirls gazed at the drama with startled absorption, drinking in every word and gesture". The most honest audiences are children, and they deserve the most professionally created theatre. But, that is not always the case in India', says Sanjna.

'Almost 30 years ago, Mohan Agashe was responsible for introducing Grips Theatre in India, the highly political, socially conscious theatre for children from Germany. This began to influence new scripts and approaches to children's theatre. At Prithvi, I produced Ramu Ramanathan's *Boy Who Stopped Smiling* in the Grips style. It was a tremendous success. Never before had children's theatre heard Indian English spoken on stage, nor had children been so irreverent with adults – it was theatre that spoke with children, and not down at them', Sanjna Kapoor says.

According to aficionados following the growth of children's theatre in India, a Mumbai-based children's theatre group has staged some amazing shows in the last five years. For example, *Taoos Chaman Ki Myna*, based on an Urdu short story by Naiyer Masud, draws on elements of dastangoi storytelling and tackles difficult topics like the parent-child relationship in a way that young audiences can understand.

In this volume from Bangalore Little Theatre, Vitasta brings our readers a collection of four exceptional stories, from the east and the west, new and the old. This one is for children, not infantalising them, not discounting their intelligence and power to innovate. It also asks a very pertinent question, why is drama not in school curriculum? This is our first book of plays for children and we hope to provide some more soon.

PREFACE TO THE VOLUME

BANGALORE LITTLE THEATRE (BLT) was restructured in 2008. A public Charitable Trust was created with a non-profit status. Theatre development activities which were pursued in an on-and-off manner till then were now placed in a newly created Academy of Theatre Arts, with well-planned long-term programme thrusts. One such long term programme is titled *Work with Schools and Children* or, simply, Children's Theatre. It integrates three streams of work that were pursued separately in the past

- New play development
- Training new directors
- Promoting new talent for the stage.

When integrated, they find opportunities for presentation on stage.

The plays in this volume have all been produced in the *Children's Theatre* programme. A brief introduction to the programme should be useful for understanding the plays.

Children and Theatre in BLT

When BLT was created in 1960, it was like any other amateur non-profit drama society. The people drawn to BLT were those who either loved doing plays or watching plays. There were no public performing spaces in the Cantonment area of Bangalore in those days. The early productions were all in the assembly hall of Bishop Cotton Boys School. The stage was small by auditorium standards, but it was remarkably well outfitted for producing plays. Rehearsals for the plays were in another school, the United Mission High School behind the Municipal Corporation building at Hudson Circle. These early associations with schools were instrumental in laying the attitudinal foundation for Children's Theatre in BLT. It was a symbiotic relationship with the schools. In return for their hospitality BLT helped them in kind in many ways. The excess of income over expenditure in productions was used for technical improvements to the stage in the schools or assistance in their own drama activities.

The circumstances under which BLT produced plays in the sixties also shaped the essential character of the group, which can be called *community theatre*. It meant reaching out to the community actively in all that the group did, and not think of drama only for the group's own enjoyment. The first opportunity to understand the field of drama in education was when the Asian Education Conference was held in Bangalore in 1963. BLT worked on an original English language adaptation of the Sanskrit classic *Mrichhakatika* and produced it for the conference. The simple early learning from that period was that there was a lot more to learn about Children's Theatre! It was one thing to enjoy reading a good play meant for a children audience. It was quite another thing to actually work with children. In 1966 BLT produced the first play that can be truly classified as children's theatre, *The Ungrateful Man*. That set the group on its long term commitment to theatre for and with Children.

Very early in the Children's Theatre programme BLT hit upon a production *model* to sustain the programme that has continued till today. It is, in essence, a three-way partnership with all three parties committed to Children's Theatre:

- A philanthropy partner supporting the theatre production
- BLT as the performing partner putting up the production
- A charity partner receiving the entire proceeds from the production.

In addition, the annual production is often linked to BLT's Summer Project on Theatre (SPOT). This is an intensive Theatre Appreciation programme for newcomers. The participants of SPOT thus have the annual Children's Theatre play as an opportunity for hands-on production experience.

Terminology

Children's Theatre is an omnibus term. It includes –

- Theatre activity FOR children
- Theatre activity BY children
- Theatre activity WITH children.

They are quite different in intent, objectives, approach, methods, what is done and how it is done. Performance FOR children is important in itself, and is a major specialisation that has come to be called Theatre for Young Audiences (TYA). ASSITEJ is an international federation of artistes committed to the philosophy of TYA. It can be said that *The Ungrateful Man* is a very good example of TYA.

In reality, a lot of Children's Theatre is a mix of the three approaches – but usually with one primary thrust. For instance, in a lot of BLT's Children's Theatre productions the approach is *primarily* TYA, but may also sometimes have children on the cast or the involvement of a school in the production.

The concept of *development* appears important to recognise this view of Children's Theatre. *Development* calls for a vision of societal ideals towards which we are striving, and to see how theatre can contribute to that effort. At the Academy of Theatre Arts, the following definitions have been adopted to guide the various programmes and projects:

Theatre-in-Development

This term refers to the use of theatre techniques to enhance the processes of communication and attitude-behaviour change in social-development interventions. Among the most developed of the methods (also widely known) would be the body of work called *Theatre of the Oppressed* by the late Augusto Boal. It followed the pioneering work of a fellow Brazilian, *Pedagogy of the Oppressed* by Paulo Freire. The concept of *conscientisation* was introduced as the key to a true development process. The *Forum* is a specific technique for dealing with social realities in a here-and-now psychological space. *Street theatre* (correctly done, not as a fad) would be another way of using the theatre medium for awareness or sensitisation as part of a development intervention.

It must be clear that the theatre technique employed is neither the change objective *per se*, nor the change strategy. It is merely a useful *means* towards a clearly defined end, to be mixed judiciously with other means. It is a great pity that many enthusiastic theatre folks make an evening's entertainment out of the novelty of the *Forum*, with little or no understanding of the ideological moorings of the technique. Boal demonstrated the power of theatre methodology for initiating self-directed social change in community settings.

Another form of development intervention around theatre practice would be in efforts at revitalisation of a dormant or neglected performing art form as the vehicle for community organisation. Using that to work towards a livelihood system would be a development intervention in itself, going well beyond Theatre-in-Development.

Theatre Education

This refers to the efforts to make theatre and drama studies an integral part of educational curricula. In most schooling systems in the so-called developing countries, trying hard to accelerate economic betterment denied to them over hundreds of years of colonisation, the pursuit of the arts (as well as support for them) is either given a low priority, or denied altogether. Without grounding in a sound academic and training base, the pursuit remains largely 'amateur' – ie. not for a livelihood, but for the love of the art.

Making the pursuit of theatre arts a respectable professional option appears to require *institutional development* effort, and not isolated training inputs. At least four institutional systems may require intervention in an integrated way:

- At the level of schools – for curriculum development and teacher training
- At the level of study Boards – for accreditation of theatre studies as a curriculum subject
- At the level of Education Degrees – to enrich the teacher training courses
- At the level of Theatre institutions – to make Theatre Education a career path option for theatre professionals.

The additional challenge in most developing countries: How to achieve all of the above with a strong national-regional-local identity?

On the one hand we need to be careful not to be lost in re-inventing wheels, and be ready to learn from good experience world-wide in Theatre Education. On the other hand, we need to guard against theatre studies (and practice of theatre arts) becoming an imitation of a borrowed curriculum, without strong cultural moorings of its own.

Theatre-in-Education

This belongs to the realm of pedagogy. It refers to the innovative use of theatre techniques to enhance the learning process while teaching a curriculum subject – say, history or science.

In pedagogical theory, TIE would be categorised under *experiential methodology*. The correct use of TIE has a strong theory-methodology base and is highly developed in some societies. In India, not surprisingly, the field is poorly developed, mainly because the larger theatre *institution* is inadequately developed.

Contrary to popular belief, TIE is NOT mere *enactment* of scenes supposedly depicting the 'message' of the lesson being studied. Enactment offers a small fraction of the potential value of TIE. It does not utilise the available power of experiential methodology. Further, the novelty of such enactment wears off quickly, and it cannot be sustained.

In the recent past, BLT has developed a great deal of original material for TIE in environment-sustainability education. It resulted in a Teacher-Training Handbook for TIE. The repertoire of techniques includes short performances to stimulate alternative lines of thinking in the subject on hand. For instance, a short play titled *Thermos* provokes thinking about the root causes of global warming and climate change. The performance is followed by a study group assignment to understand the causes, as well as their inescapable inter-connectedness. The play won the Best Short Play award at the International Theatre Institute.

Children's Theatre

The emphasis here is on performance. Within this field there can be differences in emphasis. As stated above, they can be plays *for* children, *by* children, *with* children. Naturally, there can be combinations of the features above.

The overlap with Theatre Education must be obvious, with both fields convinced about the broader educational value of theatre activity. For instance, a programme of performing to children's audiences (including performances in the school), combined with interactions with the actors has been seen as a gateway for a larger programme of Theatre activity in the school.

Rationale for Children's Theatre

Ask a schoolteacher (or even the Principal) why they teach physics in the school. Or history. The chances are there will be an awkward silence. The school system never asks the *why* question. After some thinking the teacher is likely to say: 'because it is in the curriculum'. Ah, but why is physics in the curriculum? Is the school going to turn out 100 physicists a year? Or 100 historians? Of course not! Then why teach physics and history? We finally satisfy ourselves that we teach physics because we believe learning the subject *is good in itself.*

Next question. Why not teach drama? The answer, of course, is: It is not in the curriculum! So, why not have theatre studies in the curriculum? *Can drama not be good in itself?* Unfortunately, drama has a strong connotative association with 'mere entertainment', and the value-addition in the child's education is not recognised in the Indian educational system. On the other hand, cognitive scientists, developmental psychologists and personality theorists will tell us theatre activity in schools is the most effective avenue for:

- life skills development,
- cultivating multiple intelligences,
- promoting creativity and innovation,
- bridging left brain and right brain development.

The reason for the effectiveness must also be noted. It is because almost all of theatre activity is *experiential.* We are not *taught* theatre by lectures. We learn theatre by *doing* things. As convincing as this might be to the writer of this preface (and hopefully the reader) we know that the *system* is too hard and too entrenchend for any change to take place any time soon. Weekend workshops are not going to bring about the change, nor the annual school day show. It is a long haul – and an uphill journey – for the educator.

BLT has accepted that while we are waiting for the revolution to sweep though the land we must also simply keep at it. Hence the programme thrust on work with Schools and Children. It ensures the sustained effort in engaging schools and children.

Doing Children's Theatre

Not too long ago, I was invited to give a keynote talk in a national seminar on Children's Theatre. I shared some learnings from BLT's long engagement with children in the seminar. The main points are reproduced below.

1. Who should do Children's Theatre? The question was posed to the audience in the seminar. There were many responses, quite predictable – those with:

- theatre qualifications from an institution of repute – eg. NSD
- teaching-training skills
- knowledge of child psychology.

And so on.

All of the points were about knowledge and skills. I offered an alternative perspective. The most important qualification to do children's theatre is that one must love children! One must enjoy working with children. Around this basic 'qualification' are several other characteristics – patience, active listening, willingness to learn from children, ability to laugh, readiness to join their games – and so on. We will see that all of these 'qualifications' are in the realm of attitudes and values, not specialised theatre skills. A teacher-trainer who undertakes a children's theatre project without these is simply doing a job, fulfilling the requirements of an appointment, and not fulfilling the needs of the children.

We may now go on to a few simple but profound truths about the child's intellect and intellectual development and, more important, what it means for children's theatre.

2. Never talk down to children. The content of the play as well as the style of performance (especially in TYA) should treat children as intelligent participants in the act of sharing stories. Dumbing down the content or resorting to kiddie-chatter can be funny, but unhelpful for any learning objective. Children are capable of far greater levels of comprehension than grown-ups can imagine. Many educational studies all over the world have shown this again

and again. In our own country Ruth Kohn demonstrated in a year-long project in Ahmedabad long ago how even pre-primary children are capable of grasping scientific concepts reserved for textbooks to be read six to eight years later (*The Exploring Child*, Orient Longman, 1972). The play being watched actually works beautifully to raise the level of the child's comprehension – if the writer and performer is up to it!

3. Do not judge the child's capacity according to your own capacity at that age! Accept humbly that the child before you is smarter than you were at that age. And when this child reaches your age, she will be smarter than you are today. This attitudinal position is crucially important. It should also define your educational objective in the theatre: facilitating learning – different from knowledge giving.

4. That takes us to the next point. Learning theories tell us that the strongest learning takes place when the child arrives at an insight by herself – the Aha moment. 'Receiving' the idea from you, no matter how neatly packaged, is not half as effective. Your job is to *arrange things for the child to arrive at those insights*. The intelligent script and the intelligent performance are ways of 'arranging things'. This also means avoiding 'messages' and 'the moral of the story' in the theatrical engagement. This principle is valid in both TYA and TIE and, indeed, all theatre activity. The experiential value of the theatre engagement must be maintained.

In its play development programme BLT has striven hard to ensure that the content of the script is high on stimulating imagination, even as it entertains. The play is meant to create a stimulating environment. We hope the reader will discover that quality in the play scripts in this volume.

5. The theatre is a great aid for language development. That includes dealing with new languages. Even gibberish adds value in language development. The theatre brings in a lot of that! The more equivalents learnt in concept formation, the higher the abstract intelligence. Language teachers today insist on (a) getting down to speaking the language as quickly as possible, even from the very first session, and (b) *listening* to good use of the language. In the Neel

Bagh programme of David Horsburgh (author of *The Ungrateful Man* in this volume) the children in the school learnt four languages at the same time – speaking, reading, writing. They learnt songs in many more languages, with their meanings. They did not undergo any mental health problem, as feared by the city-based education policy-makers. The children were, in fact, very smart indeed because of their fluency in several languages. The 'language issue' is really a problem of the grown-ups, it is a non-issue in children.

6. A similar unhelpful grown-up way of looking at knowledge (and life) is in the arts-science divide. It actually creates a divide between left brain development and right brain development. The process of participating in storytelling in the theatre has the powerful potential to bridge that divide. If we do not attend to this in childhood it gets very difficult in later years.

7. Theatre helps in dealing with conflicting belief systems. (The *theory of cognitive dissonance* has great relevance for education, personality development, human relations.) True education should aid raising the threshold of dissonance and, through that, the ability to accommodate conflicting belief systems. It is in fact the core of the state of personality we call maturity. Good scripts in TYA, along with good performance, can get children to see dissonance as natural and normal, and to manage the dissonances in a more informed manner. The child has the inherent capacity to approach phenomena in the world with a fresh perspective. The grown-up world, on the other hand, has the conditioned response to deny the child the alternative perspective. The theatre has the capacity to allow and encourage that in the child.

8. There is a close linkage between child-like curiosity and the phenomenon of divergent thinking, also known as creativity. At the core is the facility of *imagination* – daring to think differently. All children have this nature-given capacity. A great many of them lose it through the process of school education. The theatre, more than any of the other performing arts, respects imagination, nurtures imagination, rewards imagination. We may even say that creativity is mankind's greatest natural resource.

A play in BLT's Children's Theatre programme is *Robi's Garden.* It is a tribute to Rabindranath Tagore and is drawn from a collection of his writing for children. In the opening scene we have the caretaker of *Thakurbadi*, (Tagore's ancestral home in Kolkata) meeting a group of children and giving them a mantra: '…That the first step in getting what you want in life is IMAGINATION'. That, indeed, is the core philosophy of Children's Theatre.

9. Finally, children display an eagerness for action – a readiness to experiment, an openness to new ways of doing things. This facility is lost in the process of growning up, replaced with resistance to change. The challenge in the theatre is to have grown-ups facilitating readiness to experiment! It must be clear now what we mean when we say that the qualifications to do Children's Theatre lie in the realm of attitudes!

This volume has four plays from BLT's Children's Theatre. All of them are original play scripts developed in BLT. *The Ungrateful Man* is the very first original script written specially for a schools-children audience. It was written and directed by David Horsburgh, who later became well known for his alternative education programme in rural Karnataka. The play turned out to be hugely popular as a family entertainer as well. There have been two revival productions of the play since the first production in 1966. It remains the gold standard for writing in Children's Theatre. *The Magic Drum* is a play based on a select number of stories drawn from the book by the same name by Sudha Murty. The dramatisation of the stories for the stage was with the full approval of Sudha Murty.

Ali Oh Baba is a retelling of the Ali Baba tale, but for a contemporary young audience. The play gets the audience to understand the larger context of the Arabian Nights. The story unfolds on the stage in the form of day-dreams of a little boy discovering the 1001 Arabian Nights. He and his friend, a little girl, share their discoveries with the audience through games, narratives, song and dance. In the process the key figures in the 1001 Arabian Nights are also drawn into the play, the clever Sheherezad and the not-so-clever King. The two friends manage to tell the audience the entire tale without bringing Ali Baba on stage. *The*

Court Jester has a small sample of the tales of Tenali Rama, who is sometimes known as the Birbal of the South. Considering that the reign of Krishnadevaraya was nearly a hundred years before Emperor Akbar, Birbal should really be called the Tenali Rama of the North.

There are many more plays from BLT's Children's Theatre to share with readers and performing artists. We hope to publish those too some time.

Vijay Padaki
Series Editor

STAGE DIRECTIONS

with the actor facing the audience

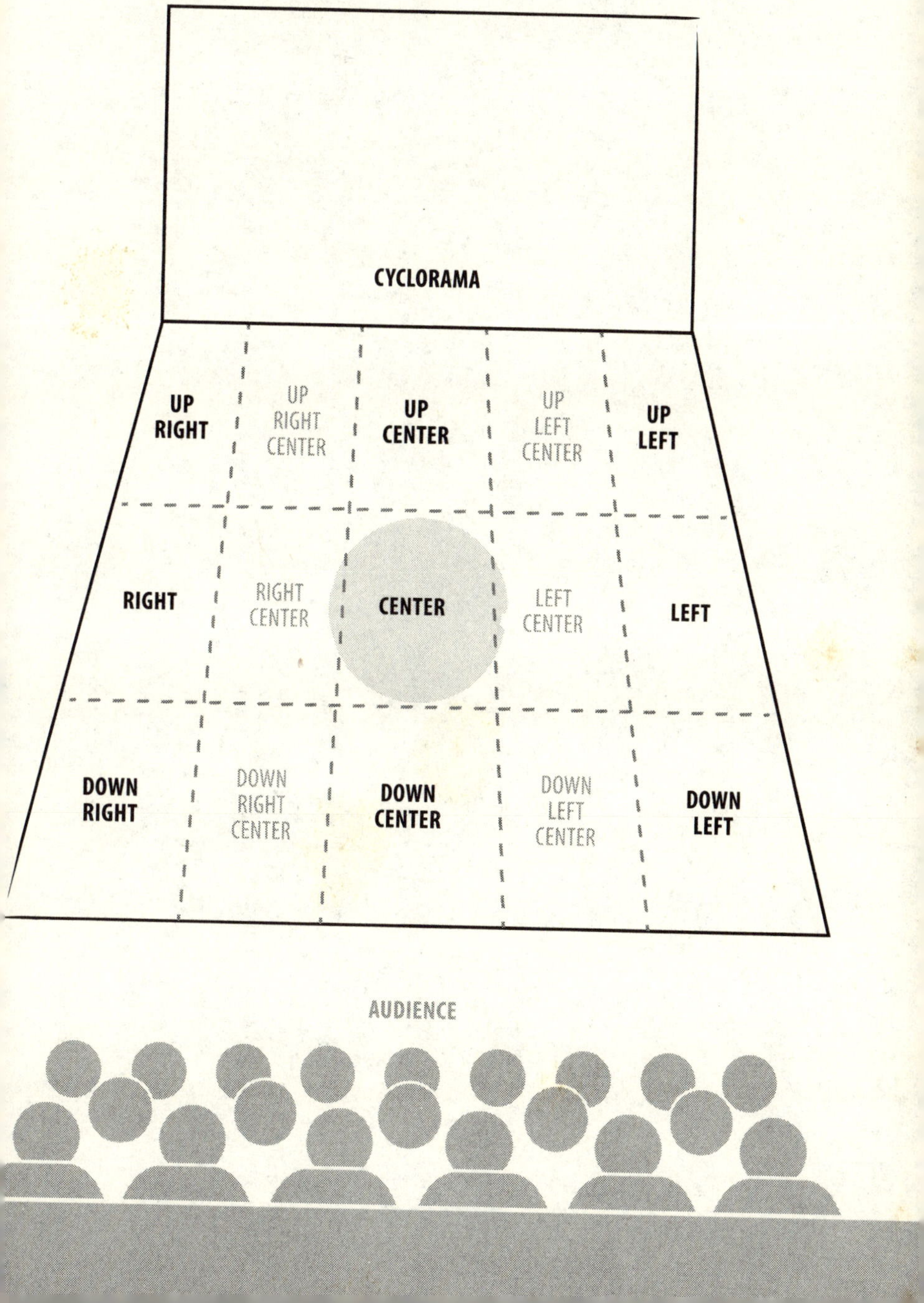

The Ungrateful Man

By ***David Horsburgh***
A tale from the Panchatantra

FOR

FOR NICHOLAS HORSBURGH

CHARACTERS IN THE PLAY

SUTRADHAR	*Nati*
YAGNAMURTHI	*Subhashini*
MONKEY	*Tiger*
SNAKE	*Village children*
ROCKS	*Spirits of the river*
SUVARNAKA	*Suvarnaka's Wife*
HINDI SPEAKING BOY	*Guards*
3RD SECRETARY	*2nd Secretary*
1ST SECRETARY	*Minister*
PRINCE'S FRIENDS	*Prince*
PRINCESS' MAIDS	*Princess*
KINGQUEEN	
STATUES	DOCTOR

Guests, visitors at the palace, guards, statues, trees, scene shifters

A men's ensemble and a women's ensemble can play multiple parts. The snake is best presented as a marionette, with a woman's voice offstage

INTRODUCTION

The Ungrateful Man is one of the tales in the *Panchatantra*. Most compilations of the Panchatantra will be done with the story in about three pages of print. With illustrations it may be stretched to five pages. The monumental play script that we have here was written by the legendary David Horsburgh, who was a life member of BLT. It has been translated and performed widely in Kannada and Hindi too. The late BV Karanth produced it in National School of Drama during his tenure as Director there. Audiences have consistently expressed difficulty in classifying the play. It is as much a family entertainer as a play for children. The 'rules of the game' for writing for children have been dealt with in the Preface to this volume. The play became the benchmark for BLT in scripting for Children's Theatre.

The story of the Ungrateful Man hardly needs explanation. A lengthy introduction is unnecessary. For readers and performers in the current generation the introduction to author that follows may be far more be important.

David Horsburgh

Over seventy years ago, World War II brought a young Scotsman to India. Fascinated by the land and its peoples, he was determined to return. He did, and made India – and Karnataka – his home. He began by teaching in a college in Mysore. He soon had to leave because he was seen to be on the side of the students, encouraging them to protest against the authorities. Having heard of Rishi Valley, which at that time was just restarted with a new principal, David joined the team of visionary teachers.

In a stint with British Council he developed the highly acclaimed MELT training course for teachers of English. (Methods in English Language Teaching) He came to Bangalore, joined BLT, and was soon at the centre of the theatre scene in the city. Actor, director, writer, designer, he was everywhere in every production. Inevitably, he became part of the Management of BLT, and contributed significantly to the directions that BLT took in the late 'sixties and early 'seventies.

But his heart was in education, school education, and in education for the disadvantaged children of the land he had chosen to make his home. He set up a school, Neel Bagh, in Rayalpadu village in Kolar District, and lived and worked there till his death in 1984. His pioneering work at the school is only now being recognised for its true significance. David demonstrated in Neel Bagh that reaching high quality education to the poor was not dependent on a high quantity budget. The principal requirements were an alternative methodology and, quite simply, love for the community.

The Ungrateful Man premiered in Bangalore fifty years ago. When produced a second time in 1979, David insisted on having all the sets built at the carpentry workshop at Neel Bagh. One cannot help wondering about the idyllic village scene in his play. Perhaps the Brahmin in the play, spending all his time with the children in the village, was really David?

The play script in this volume is a reworked version prepared for a rehearsed reading in Ahmedabad by Vijay Padaki, with the full approval of the author. It was further revised for a Bangalore Little Theatre production in 2007.

FIST PERFORMED

By Bangalore Little Theatre at Ravindra Kalakshetra, Bangalore, July 1966.

Sutradhar..............PATRICK CHASE OR REG WRIGHT
Nati..............CAROLYN MOSS
Servant..............ANNA HOOD
Yagnamurthi..............SHANKAR MENON or SHYAM RIKH
Subhashini..............JYOTI BATRA or DAISY PAUL
Monkey..............NICHOLAS HORSBURGH or MICHAEL HORSBURGH
Tiger..............JIM URE or CR SIMHA
Snake..............DOREEN HORSBURGH or MONA RIKH
Suvarnaka..............EDWARD WHITE *or* CR SAMPATH KUMARAN
Hindi Boy..............DHUN LAL
Suvarnaka's wife..............BERNADETTE DATTAREYAN *or* RAMADEVI
3rd Secretary..............RAMESH
2nd Secretary..............RAMANI RAJARAM
1st Secretary..............ANAND MATTHAN
Minister..............ALAN BATCHELOR *or* ROBERT RENTOUL
Prince's friends..............DAVID HORSBURGH, JAYADEV, UMESH BADAMI
Prince..............JOHN MOSS *or* SURESH WADHWANI
Guards..............JANARDHHAN, EDMUND EDWARD, VENKITESWARAN, VISWANATH
Handmaids..............UMA RAMACHANDRAIAH, JYOTI BATRA, MARGARET, CHOWRIYAPPAH, VALERIE DE BRAS
Princess..............SUNITA MALKANI *or* DOLLY PAUL
King..............CHRISTODOSS *or* SEETHARAM
Queen..............MARIE URE *or* PREMA SASTRI
Statues..............ELIZABETH DOVETON, DULCIE LAWRENCE

Produced by..............DAVID HORSBURGH *and* DHUN LAL
Stage Manager..............SRINIVAS
Assisted by..............RAMANI RAJARAM, JAYADEV
Sets..............CHRISTODOSS, GEORGETTE DAMEN, DOREEN HORSBURGH, ANAND MATTHAN, NAGESH, NEELI, PRAKASH, RAMESH, SATYANARAYANA, SIMHA, VIDYARANYA
Lighting..............NARAYAN SASTRI, SG RAMACHANDRA
Sound..............REG WRIGHT, MANJUNTH
Costumes..............MARIE URE, VIMALA RANGACHAR, MANGALA RAMACHANDRA

Properties........MONA RIKH
Prompt........JEAN PATTERSON, JOAN PETTIFER
Publicity........ARAVIND PRABHU, JAYADEV
Liaison with schools........JIM URE
Front of House........THELMA RICHARDSON, RONLD D'SA
Crew and assistance........UMESH BADAMI, AYESHA DAS, MARGARET CHOWRYAPPAH, ARNOLD D'COSTA, DANI, ANNA HOOD, ADI LAL, HN NAGARAJ, PADDU, DAISY PAUL, RAMACHANDRACHAR, SEETHARAM, SHIVAKUMAR, SHREE DEVI, VENKATASUBBIAH, VISALANATH, VISWANATH, VENKAT RAO, BR NAGARAJ, AL SRINIVAS, GOPI, GLORIA PETERS

ACT I

SCENE 1

Two village children, a boy and a girl, run across the stage, one after the other. The girl runs back and hides behind a prop or curtain. The boy then runs back, looking for the girl. He stops when he sees a large props basket on stage. He approaches it cautiously, opens it and peeps in. He takes out some clothes, a dress for a Sutradhar. He tries it on. It fits! He takes out more things from the basket. Through all this the girl has entered quietly and is watching the boy. She speaks.

GIRL

Is there something for me?

BOY

Got you!

GIRL

Later! What else is there inside? Is there a dress for me?

BOY

I don't know. Let's see. *(He takes out a dress for her. She holds it in front of herself. It seems right!)*

GIRL

What are these?

BOY

Things to be used in a play, I think.

GIRL

A play! Here?

BOY

Looks like it. Look, there's a programme too.

GIRL
'The Ungrateful Man – a tale from the Panchatantra.' Hmmm... Who is going to perform the play?

BOY
The usual bunch of grownups, I suppose. They will make big big eyes, and speak in that funny sing song style, and make the words syrupy. You know how grown-ups act when they do a play for children!

GIRL
Their own idea of how children ought to speak their lines on stage.

BOY
They will run training workshops in summer and teach children how to speak the way they want us to speak.

GIRL
And they will wag their fingers a lot when they speak! You know what? We should really be doing a play for the grownups!

BOY
We should do a play making the grownups do a play for us.

GIRL
You are sounding like a grownup already.

BOY
Am I?

GIRL *(Taking a mirror from the basket and holding it in front of him)*
Look at yourself!

BOY
They say that when you are on stage you become somebody else. It must be something in the clothes we wear.

GIRL *(Giggling)*
The clothes you are wearing!

BOY
It can happen to you too! Want to try it?

GIRL
Here? In front of you?

BOY

Well, you can go there and try it on.

(The girl goes into a wing. The boy takes out a moustache and pastes it on, then puts on a cap, a jacket and any other items of clothing that will make him...a Sutradhar, enjoying the transformation.)

SUTRADHAR

Oho! Is anyone there in the wings?

NATI *(From the wing)*

Yes, sire. What is your honour's wish?

SUTRADHAR

Don't you know that a play is to be performed here tonight? Look there, the audience is waiting. Where are the players?

(Enter the girl as Nati)

Are you not ready yet with the scenery, the lights and whatnot that goes to make this play?

NATI

Yes, indeed, your honour! All the whatnots are ready. Yes, indeed. The stage hands are preparing the scene. *(To someone off stage)* Hurry up! His honour, the Sutradhar, is getting impatient.

(Enter a stage hand with a paint brush and a can)

STAGE HAND

Impatient, is he? Then tell him to go and...*(Seeing the Sutradhar)* Oh, good evening, your honour. I hope your honour...

SUTRADHAR

Enough! Painting in the last minute!

STAGE HAND

But it will dry in two minutes, your honour. Before the audience has settled in.

SUTRADHAR

And what do you see out there?!

STAGE HAND *(Realising the audience is in)*

Ohh... the curtain is up! Oh my, oh my...*(He starts to go)*

SUTRADHAR

Wait! *(The Stage Hand stops)* How many times must you be told never to bring paint on to the stage! *(The Stage Hand gives Sutradhar the can and the brush and starts to leave)* Hold on! *(The Stage Hand stops, puzzled)* Take this! *(The Stage Hand takes the can and brush from Sutradhar and...waits)* Get on with the job! Hurry up! The audience cannot be kept waiting. *(The Stage Hand leaves)*

NATI

Yes, your honour. We will hurry up... the audience... shall make all haste.

(*She sees the Stage Hand out*)

SUTRADHAR *(To the audience)*

Tonight, dear friends, we play for you the story of *The Ungrateful Man*. It is the story of a kind and gentle Brahmin, and tells of his adventures in the forest and at the court of Kashi. He was a good man, but...

NATI

A little lazy. And perhaps he didn't work as hard as he ought to have done. He lived in a tiny village in South India, about a thousand years ago. There he taught the children of the village, for there were no schools in those days. And he played his flute, and he talked to his friends. Unfortunately, he had married a wife with a nature not quite so sweet as his. She was a bit like a green lime.

SUTRADHAR

Rather bitter. The Brahmin's temper was rather cool, you could say. Nothing seemed to make him annoyed.

NATI

Hers was rather hot, you might say. Sometimes she shouted at him, sometimes she frowned at him, and sometimes she stamped her foot and looked like a cloud about to burst. But it didn't worry him at all. He just played his flute, and talked to his friends, and played with the children. And he was perfectly happy.

SUTRADHAR

Anyway, enough of these domestic details. Let us start our play and you shall see for yourselves exactly what happened. I want you all to imagine yourselves in a small village...

NATI

Just like any other village in South India, but a thousand years ago.

SUTRADHAR

It is quite early in the day and the sun is just rising.

NATI

He can take over now. I will attend to a few jobs backstage.

(Nati leaves the stage. Sutradhar takes a seat at one corner of the stage, as children come running on.

A South Indian village about AD 900. Houses and a hint of a temple tank. Perhaps a temple in the background. Time: early morning.

A marble comes bouncing on to the stage. Two children enter. They rush to centre stage, and both try to pick up the marble.)

1ST CHILD *(Struggling to get it)*

I saw it first!

2ND CHILD *(Also struggling to get it)*

No, you didn't, it's mine. Give it to me, I say!

1ST CHILD

There! *(He gets it at last)* It's mine. And a very nice marble, too!

(More children enter from various directions.)

2ND CHILD

Give it to me. I saw it first.

1ST CHILD

It's mine. It's mine.

ALL CHILDREN *(Shouting together)*

>> Don't shout!

>> Give it up!

>> There's no need to fight!

>> Who saw the marble first?

(The fighting contestants for the marble are held apart by the others.)

3RD CHILD
Now, Raju, whose marble is this?

1ST CHILD
It's mine. I dropped it this morning.

2ND CHILD
No, it isn't! I dropped it this morning.
(They try to fight again. Suddenly all stop as...)

4TH CHILD
Here's Yagnamurthi. Let's ask him to settle it. *(Yagnamurthi enters and the children all run to him and surround him.)*

ALL
>> Good morning Yagnamurthi!
>> Hello, Yagnamurthi
>> At last you're here!

YAGNAMURTHI
Well, well, well! What a lot of noise! I thought the whole village was on fire. What's the trouble?

4TH CHILD
Raju and Mohan are fighting over a marble. Raju says it's his and Mohan says it's his.

1ST CHILD & 2ND CHILD *(Together)*
It is! It's mine. *(They start to fight)*

YAGNAMURTHI
That's easily settled, easily settled! *(They all keep quiet)* Sit down on the ground, all of you, and put the marble in the middle of the circle. (*They all do so.*) Now, shut your eyes and put your fingers in your ears. Like this! (*He demonstrates.*) That's right!
(The children do as he asks and he moves towards the Sutradhar and beckons him) Excuse me! Can you lend me a marble?

SUTRADHAR
A marble! *(He looks in all his pockets)*
I didn't bring my marbles today. *(He thinks)* Wait a minute.
(He comes down the steps, borrows a marble from a member of the audience and returns to Yagnamurthi) Here you are.

YAGNAMURTHI

Many thanks.

(He goes back to the circle and puts the second marble next to the first one)

Right, children! Open your eyes.

(They have their fingers in their ears and can't hear)

Hey! Can't you hear me? Wake up!

(He dances and shouts) Wake up! Wake up!

(They neither move nor open their eyes)

(To the audience) Oho, what shall I do now? They might stay like that forever. Will you help me? You will? Here's what we will do. Now, shout, all together!

(He gets the children in the audience to shout)

Come along, shout 'Wake up!' That's right.

WAKE UP! WAKE UP!

(The children all open their eyes and look at the two marbles.)

There you are! One for you, Raju; and one for you, Mohan!

CHILDREN *(All together)*

>> Thank you! Thank you!

>> Hurrah! Hurrah!

>> Yagnamurthi's magic!

>> Look! Magic!

>> Good old Yagnamurthi!

(They all dance round Yagnamurthi, laughing and shouting and pulling him round and round. After a few protestations he gets giddy. They let go and he whirls round and round, slowing down as Subhashini enters. He finishes up just in front of her, but still facing the children.)

YAGNAMURTHI

Ha! Ha! What a game. How you children worry me! Oh dear! What fun! If my wife could see me now – she'd be furious with me! Oh, she doesn't like children. They make her angry. And she doesn't like me playing the flute, either! That makes her angry too – but let her get angry! I don't care – I'm not afraid of her! Ha Ha! I should like to see her bully me. I'd tell her to...

(He sees the children standing silent and gaping. He turns slowly as he realises someone is behind him.) Keep...quiet...and...shut up! *(He sees his wife)*

Oh! *(He gives a silly laugh)* Oh! There you are.

SUBHASHINI

And there you are! What are you doing? *(Advancing, as Yagnamurthi retreats)* I told you to go to the market. Did you go? No, of course not! And why not? Because you haven't got any money?

YAGNAMURTHI

Well, my dear, I thought...

SUBHASHINI

You thought! What did you think? That I'd give you some. Well, I'm not going to. Why don't you do some work for a change? I want those things from the market. Every day I ask you to go to the market – and what do you do? You play with the children – what a nuisance they are. You play your flute – what a terrible noise – it goes right through my head. And you talk to your friends. Nothing but talk, talk, talk – all day and every day.

YAGNAMURTHI

My dear...

SUBHASHINI

Don't answer back! And another thing. I want some money. And I want some money for clothes. Look at these rags!

YAGNAMURTHI

But my...

SUBHASHINI

Not another word! Go at once and get some money.

YAGNAMURTHI

But where shall I go?

SUBHASHINI

I don't care where you go. But go! Go into the forest! Perhaps you'll find some gold under the trees! But don't come home until you've got some. I don't want to see you again unless you've got some money. *(She stalks off)*

YAGNAMURTHI *(To the children)*

Now what shall I do? Have you got any money? (*All the children look in their pockets)*

CHILDREN

No, we haven't!

YAGNAMURTHI

I know! Perhaps I can borrow some. Now, who...*(Looks for the Sutradhar who, guessing his intention, hides)* Excuse me... Now where is he? *(He looks for him but without success)* Oh, well! I shall have to go to the forest.

1ST CHILD

Perhaps you'll find gold there!

YAGNAMURTHI

Do you think so?

2ND CHILD

Everyone says there's gold in the forest.

3RD CHILD

I hope you find it, Yagnamurthi.

YAGNAMURTHI

So do I! So do I! All right, if I find gold in the forest I'll buy you a hundred marbles when I come back.

CHILDREN

Good bye! Good luck. *(They give him various bits of luggage.)*

YAGNAMURTHI

Good bye children. I'll come back...

(He begins a slow exit while the children in line wave good bye.) See you soon...good-bye...good-bye...*(His voice fades into the distance.)*

SCENE 2

Nati and Sutradhar enter and address the audience.

SUTRADHAR

And so, you see, poor Yagnamurthi had to leave his village. At first he didn't know what to do, or where to go. He wandered along the road and managed to get some food at about six o'clock that evening. But after that he didn't know what was going to happen to him.

NATI

'Where am I going to sleep tonight?' he thought. At last he found a dry ditch. He rolled himself up in his shawl and went to sleep in it. But he kept waking up in the middle of the night – that ditch was not at all comfortable. First he found a stone just in his back – Oooh! And then another – a very sharp one – just in his side – Oooh!

SUTRADHAR

And then he got an ant down his back – and then a beetle – and then a whole army of beetles! And he wriggled and jumped and scratched and slapped – and couldn't sleep a wink.

NATI

So on and on he walked, for a day, and then another day, and then a week, and then another week; and everywhere he went he looked and looked for some gold, but he didn't find any.

SUTRADHAR

At last he came to the forest. He walked through the thickets and the bushes, and he looked under every tree and behind every stone, but he couldn't find any gold. Sometimes it rained and he got wet, sometimes he was so hot he felt like bursting! But on and on he went, always looking for gold... and never finding any!

NATI

Poor Yagnamurthi! He often thought of his village and his friends, and the children – and his flute. But he said to himself, 'It's no use going home without any money'. And so he went on and on, deeper and deeper into the forest. He was getting so tired of looking for gold and not finding any.

SUTRADHAR

But late one afternoon he came to a dark part of the forest.

(A forest scene. An old, disused well is seen in a corner. It is afternoon. There is gentle music as Yagnamurthi enters.)

SUTRADHAR

He was very tired. *(He and Nati withdraw)*

YAGNAMURTHI

Oh dear! Oh dear! *(To the audience)* I don't know what to do. I think I've walked hundreds of miles in the last few weeks. Oh, I must sit down and rest.

(He is just about to sit on a rock when he remembers past occasions, and looks carefully all round the rock before sitting on it.)

Ah, do you know why I'm looking so carefully? Because I've seen hundreds of creepy crawly things in the last few weeks – scorpions, rats, frogs, bats and snakes!

Why, only yesterday I...well, I was walking along, very tired, and I saw a splendid patch of grass to sit on. I sank down on to it when suddenly...*(He mimes sinking down on grass and then jumping up)*

AAAH ! I sat on a snake. I hate snakes, don't you? (*He sees the stone well*) Why, here's a comfortable spot. I wish I'd brought my flute with me. I could have played it for a bit. Never mind, I'll rest here for a while. (*He closes his eyes and goes to sleep.*)

VOICES

Help! Help!

(Yagnamurthi wakes up and looks around, sees no one and goes to sleep again.)

VOICES

Help us, O Brahmin, help us!

(Yagnamurthi wakes again, sits up and looks round)

YAGNAMURTHI *(To the audience, looking all round)*

Can you hear anything? I'm sure somebody shouted 'Help'.

(He approaches the well and is just about to peep into it when the tiger roars.) Oh dear! *(He leaps a few feet backwards)* That sounded like a tiger!

VOICES

Help us, O kind Brahmin, help us! We're in the well and can't get out.

YAGNAMURTHI

I'll just have a look. (*He goes to the well and looks over the edge. He turns to the audience.*) There are four people in that well – a monkey, a snake, a man and...

(*The Tiger roars, Yagnamurthi gulps*) A tiger! Shall I pull them out? Yes, you say. But you see, I... Yes, you say. All right.

(*He goes to the well and pulls out the Monkey.*)

MONKEY

Thank you, O Brahmin, thank you a thousand times. I shall always be grateful to you. If ever you want my help, just call on me. I live in the forest. But ah...(*drawing Yagnamurthi to one side*) don't pull out the man in that well. He's a very bad man. He won't be grateful for your kindness. He may do you some harm.

YAGNAMURTHI

You don't say so!

MONKEY

Yes, I do. Now, good bye. Let me know if you're ever in trouble. (*Exit*)

YAGNAMURTHI

Now I suppose I must pull out the snake and the tiger.

(*He goes to the well and leans over the wall*) Are you there?

(*A terrific roar from the Tiger makes him leap back a foot or two*) Yes, I see you are!

(*He reaches down and pulls out the Tiger, and then the Snake. He moves across the stage pursued slowly by the Tiger and the Snake. They are grateful and wish to be friendly. He is scared and prefers them to be at a distance.*)

TIGER

It's all right, O Brahmin, don't be afraid. We shan't hurt you. We only want to thank you.

YAGNAMURTHI (*Backing away in fright*)

Oh, that's all right – I'm not afraid. (*Teeth chattering and quaking with fear*) It's just that I'm not used to tigers...and snakes.

TIGER (*Advancing on Yagnamurthi with a cheery handshake*)

We want to thank you.

(Yagnamurthi gingerly takes the Tiger's paw and, with great misgivings, allows the Snake to crawl around his legs.)

We shall always be grateful. If ever you're in trouble just let us know, and we shall come and help you.

YAGNAMURTHI *(Still anxious not to be too close)*

Oh, it was nothing. We should always help people in distress.

(The Tiger turns to go, then recollects something and turns back to Yagnamurthi.)

TIGER

By the way, there's a man in that well and he wants you to pull him out. Don't! He's a villain. A very bad man.

SNAKE

He won't be grateful. He might even do you some harm.

YAGNAMURTHI

Oh, indeed! Well, thank you very much for your advice.

TIGER

Good bye, O kind Brahmin.

SNAKE

Good bye, O Brahmin. *(Rearing up in front of Yagnamurthi)* Don't forget to call us if you want any help.

TIGER

No, we shall help you whenever you need us. Good-bye.

(The tiger and snake leave)

YAGNAMURTHI

I'm sure they mean well, but, you know, I can't get used to tigers and snakes for friends. *(To the audience)* Can you?

SUVARNAKA

Help! Help me, kind friend!

YAGNAMURTHI

Oh, I'd forgotten him. Now what shall I do? The monkey, the tiger and the snake – they all warned me about him. They said he was a very bad man and might do me some harm. What shall I do? *(To the audience)* Shall I pull him out? Yes, you say! Well, I'll just have a look at him.

(He creeps to the edge of the well and peers over)

Ugh! He looks a very bad man. Still ...*(walking about, pondering)* The Shastras say, 'One should always help a man in distress'. And after all, what harm can he do me? None. I'd better pull him out, I think. *(He goes to the well and pulls out Suvannaka, also known as Suvarnaka)* Suvarnaka, there you are...safe and sound.

SUVARNAKA

How very kind! How very, very very kind.

YAGNAMURTHI

Oh, it was nothing. And now, if you'll excuse me, I have a very important engagement, so...

SUVARNAKA

Wait a minute, Brahmin. Did those other three say anything about me?

YAGNAMURTHI

Yes, they did. (*Not thinking*) They told me not to trust you. *(Suvarnaka frowns)*

They said you were a very...

(*Suddenly remembering that tact and good manners are important*) A good man, and that's what I meant about not trusting you...you know...(*Confused*) a very good man...that's what they said.

SUVARNAKA

Oh! *(Still suspicious)* That's not what they said to me.

YAGNAMURTHI

A very good man. That's what they said.

SUVARNAKA

Good. I'm glad to hear it. Because if I thought you...

(He advances in a slimy, menacing way on Yagnamurthi)

YAGNAMURTHI *(Backing away in fright)*

A very good man. A very, very bad – I mean good – man.

SUVARNAKA

A good man?

YAGNAMURTHI

Yes, a good man.

SUVARNAKA

That's better! *(In a better frame of mind)* Well, O Brahmin, thank you very much for your kindness. I come from Kashi, a good long way from here. I'm a goldsmith. *(Puffing out his chest)* I make the king's jewellery. If ever you need help, just call on me. Number 105 in the Street of Goldsmiths.

YAGNAMURTHI

O thank you. Number 105, you say. I shall certainly remember.

SUVARNAKA

Well, good bye. Take care of yourself.

YAGNAMURTHI

I shall. Good bye. *(Exit Suvarnaka)*

If I don't take care of myself, who will? And what am I to do now. Go on walking I suppose – until I find the gold. Oh dear! Oh dear! (*Exit*)

SCENE 3

Sutradhar enters and addresses the audience.

SUTRADHAR

And so poor old Yagnamurthi went on walking. He got quite used to living in the forest, but even so, he had a lot of frightening adventures. One day he came to a big river with a path beside it, and he followed this path along the river for many miles.

Now, you know, if you're all alone and you've got no one to talk to, you talk to yourself. Do you ever talk to yourself? You don't! Well, I do. Sometimes my wife complains about it. Perhaps I'm sitting outside the house – no one about – and I start having a little chat with myself – Hello, my dear friend, I say – How are you today? Not very well! I reply. Or, marvellous, I'm fine today! It depends on my wife's mood.

(Nati has entered, unseen by Sutradhar, and is listening.)

And where are you going this evening? I don't know, really. Perhaps I'll go for a little walk. Or, perhaps I'll go to...and then my wife comes out. 'Who are you talking to out there?' she says.

NATI

Who are you talking to out there?

SUTRADHAR

'Me, talking!' I say. 'There's no one here, after all', she says.

NATI

There's no one here, after all.

SUTRADHAR

She says 'I'm sure I heard someone talking'.

NATI

I'm sure I heard someone talking.

SUTRADHAR

And it makes her quite cross.

NATI

Oooh! It makes me so cross. (*She snaps him out of his reverie)* Get back to the story of Yagnamurthi!

SUTRADHAR

That's what I was doing! He used to talk to himself quite a lot, you see. And then he started talking to the river. Not much at first, you know. Just 'Good morning, my dear river!' and so on.

NATI

Then he got an idea that the river was full of people. Spirits, he called them, because he couldn't see them; and he used to ask them to look after him during the night while he was asleep. Every night, before he went to bed, he would say, 'Sweet spirits of the river, guard me from all danger'. And do you know, it's a funny thing, but they always did.

SUTRADHAR

But in spite of his friends in the forest, and in spite of the spirits of the river, he still had to toil along looking for gold. And somehow he never managed to find any – not a single bit. However, one evening, just as night was falling, Yagnamurthi came to a dark, rocky place near the river.

(Yagnamurthi enters, very weary, as Nati and Sutradhar withdraw.

A river. On its bank, a jungle with large trees and rocks. The sun is about to set.)

YAGNAMURTHI

Oh dear, oh dear, my poor feet. I can't go another step. I think I'll sleep under this tree tonight. (*He looks up apprehensively*) I hope there aren't any bats...or snakes. Oh... (*Turning to the audience*) I don't like the forest at nights very much. It's so dark and frightening – especially when there's no moon. I wonder if there's any moon tonight... (*He consults the Panchangam*)...Yes, it should rise any minute now. Where is it? Wait a minute. (*The moon appears*) Ah, there it is. Still, you never know what might happen. I shall ask the good spirits who live in this river here to look after me. (*He prays to the river*)

O sweet spirits of the river! Keep me safe while I slumber here at your side. Guard me from all the evils of the night. And come to my help if danger threatens.

RIVER

We hear your prayer, O Brahmin. Sleep in peace.

YAGNAMURTHI

Ah, now I can get some rest. Someone will always look after you if you're really in trouble.

(He opens his bag and puts his personal belongings, chembu and glass, etc., on a convenient rock. He takes off his chappals and lies down under a tree. He tugs at a creeper which puts out the moon, and goes to sleep. The rocks around him advance a few feet towards him.)

YAGNAMURTHI *(Waking up and switching on the moon)*

What's that? (*He looks round, but all seems quiet. To the audience*) You didn't see anything, did you? I thought I heard a scratching sort of sound, as though the rocks were moving ... Ha ha! What a joke! Rocks don't move, do they?

(He repeats the business of sleeping, puts out the moon and goes to sleep. The rocks again advance. Yagnamurthi wakes up and puts on the moon. He looks around. He is just about to put out the moon again when he catches a rock moving. He leaps up.)

Help! Help! The rocks are moving.

(Frightening music as the rocks grow bigger and advance on Yagnamurthi.)

They're attacking me.

(At last as he is surrounded by them and calls out)

Help! Help! O spirits of the river, come to my aid.

(He faints. The river rises up and attacks the rocks: it is through dance and music. The rocks are subdued and take up their usual positions. The river flows back to its riverbed. Yagnamurthi lies still. The sun begins to rise.

Enter the Monkey.)

MONKEY *(To the audience)*

Why, what a lot of noise! It was mad! As if the rocks were on the warpath. I could hear the sound half a mile away. (*Sees Yagnamurthi on the floor*) What's this! Why, it's the kind Brahmin who saved me from the well. (*Kneels by Yagnamurthi's side*) Why, sir, what's wrong? Wake up, wake up!

(It is full daylight. Yagnamurthi groans and wakes up. He still thinks of the rocks attacking him.)

YAGNAMURTHI

Help! help! O spirits of...(*He sees the Monkey*) Hello, who are you?

MONKEY

Don't you remember me, O Brahmin? You pulled me out of the well – weeks ago. Don't you remember?

YAGNAMURTHI

The rocks are...what's that? Oh! It's you. Yes, I remember. (*He sits up*) Well, how are you, old fellow?

MONKEY

I'm very well, but how are you? You look as though you've had a long journey.

YAGNAMURTHI *(Speaking rather fast and working himself up)*

Oh, I've had a terrible time. I've walked and walked until my feet ached – I've been attacked by bats and snakes and rats – I've had no food for days – I haven't any money and last night I was set on by these rocks – and saved by the kind spirits of the river – but now I'm lost – I don't know what to do. (*He sobs on his hands*)

MONKEY *(Comforting him)*

Don't worry, don't worry. We'll help you. Come now, this won't do you any good. We'll help you.

YAGNAMURTHI

We? What do you mean by 'we'?

MONKEY

Oh, I've got all my brothers. And plenty of friends.

YAGNAMURTHI

I can't see any brothers or friends in this lonely spot.

MONKEY

Oh, I'll call them. (*The Monkey puts hands to his mouth and shouts*) Oooaaaeee! (*Monkeys come from every direction and line up in front of him*) Platoooon...Attention! (*The monkeys come smartly to attention*) Brothers! Here is the kind Brahmin who helped me. You remember I told you how he pulled me out of the well. Minister to his needs at once! (*The monkeys disperse at speed*) Now, my dear Brahmin, everything will be quite all right. Tired, you say? Hungry, thirsty? Come, we shall change all that.

(He claps his hands several times. At each hand-clap one or two monkeys run in with a variety of food, drink and comforts for the Brahmin. The Monkey introduces each of his friends. Yagnamurthi utters exclamations of delight.)

MONKEY

Water for your feet.

YAGNAMURTHI

Delightful!

MONKEY

Drink and food.

YAGNAMURTHI

Delicious!

MONKEY

Kind friends to serve you.

YAGNAMURTHI

How very kind!

(The Monkey talks to Yagnamurthi while he is being looked after and is eating.)

MONKEY

Now, my dear, sir. What is to be done with you? Food and drink – we can easily supply that.

YAGNAMURTHI *(With his mouth full)*

Yes, indeed.

MONKEY

Shelter and comfort, too.

YAGNAMURTHI

So I see.

MONKEY

But you want money. (*The Monkey ponders deeply*) I know. We shall go and visit an old friend of mine. He lives in the forest, not far from here. Come along. (*The monkeys form a procession surrounding Yagnamurthi*) This way.

(The procession follows the Monkey, past the Sutradhar who is holding a signpost marked TO THE TIGER'S HOUSE, and continues down the steps. Yagnamurthi stops the Monkey.)

YAGNAMURTHI

Do you see that signpost?

MONKEY

Yes, that's where we're going.

YAGNAMURTHI

To the Tiger's house!

MONKEY

Yes, of course. He's my friend – and yours, too. You pulled him out of the well, don't you remember? He often talks about you.

YAGNAMURTHI

Oh, yes...(*Doubtfully*)...But I'm rather scared of tigers as a rule.

MONKEY

Oh, you'll like this one. He's a very nice person indeed.

(They have now come to the steps of the Tiger's house which they ascend.)

SCENE 4

Nati and Sutradhar enter and address the audience

SUTRADHAR

Now, I wonder how many of you in the audience have ever had such experiences as Yagnamurthi. Have you? Have you?

NATI

But you know, If you're lost in the forest, you've got to find somebody to help you, haven't you? What would you do if you got lost in the forest? Would you get frightened? You wouldn't! What would you do – call the monkeys to help you? You would? Come on now, who can call monkeys? Any one of you – come along – yes, come on – up on the stage – that's right.

SUTRADHAR

What's your name? (*Gets person's name*) Good. Now, do you remember how the monkey called his friends? Show us how. (*Gets the person to call out*)

Was it like that? Try again. (*Gets the person to call again*)

No luck. Let's get some others to try. (*Gets three or four more on stage*)

All right, you try. (*None are successful*)

NATI

Well, you don't seem to be able to manage it. Let's try all together. (*She lines them up*) This is what you have to say to call: Oooaaaeee! Ready? Now, come along, one, two, three. Oooaaaeee! No luck, I'm afraid. Where are the monkeys? OK, I'll let you into a secret. I have some special sweets here. (*She takes out a box and produces the sweets*) Now, put one of these into your mouth – come along, now. These sweets have magical property. They give you a strong voice.

SUTRADHAR

Now, everybody ready? Right, let's try calling the monkeys now. All together, one, two, three: OOOAAAEEE! (*A monkey puts his head through the curtain, and they all notice him*) Once more now: OOOAAAEEE!

(Monkeys appear from all directions and introduce themselves to the people on the stage.)

There are you! No need to be frightened if you're lost in the forest now. You know how to call the monkeys. Well, off you go – it's time we got on with the adventures of Yagnamurthi. Good bye. Thank you very much indeed. Good bye.

(They see the children off the stage and return to the monkeys.)

NATI

Good bye. (*They don't move*) Good bye! (*They still don't move*) Go on now – We've got to tell these people the story of Yagnamurthi. Will you move?! Come along! (*The monkeys stand in a firm line*) What's the matter with you?

(Two monkeys unfurl a long banner with FAIR AND SQUARE – WE WANT OUR SHARE on it.)

NATI

I don't know how to get rid of these chaps, I don't...(*She turns and sees the banner*) What's all this? It looks like a strike!

MONKEYS

A hunger strike! (*All hold out their hands*)

SUTRADHARA

A hunger strike?

MONKEYS

Next step – Bangalore Bundh!

SUTRADHAR

Ah, I see what you mean.

(He takes out the sweet-box and gives each monkey a sweet. The monkeys turn the banner round and it now reads THANK YOU AND GOOD BYE. They troop off in a line.)

NATI

Well, we can now see what happened to Yagnamurthi.

(Another part of the forest. A rocky entrance to a cave. At the entrance there is a red post-box and a bell. A small garden with a gate in front. Rocks are strewn in different parts of the stage. Enter Yagnamurthi in procession with the monkeys.)

MONKEY

Here we are at last. My friend's house, quite nice, isn't it. I like the garden.

YAGNAMURTHI

Yes...yes (*Still apprehensive of meeting the tiger*) I wonder if he's in...

MONKEY

Ring the bell and see.

YAGNAMURTHI *(Approaching very carefully)*

Yes...all right...here goes. (*Rings the bell tentatively*)...Ah, perhaps he's out or asleep. Shall we come back tomorrow?

MONKEY

My dear Brahmin, that's not the way to ring the bell. Let me show you. (*He takes Yagnamurthi's hand and rings the bell violently. The sound is greeted with a tremendous roar from within.*) There you are! He's not asleep!

YAGNAMURTHI *(Shivering)*

No, he's certainly not asleep. I see that. I only hope he's not hungry. *(The tiger appears at the cave entrance, quite annoyed.)*

TIGER *(Very loud)*

Who's ringing that bell? If I catch him I'll... (*He sees the monkey*) Oh, hello! It's you. How nice to see you, and all your friends.

ALL MONKEYS

Hello, Mr Tiger. How nice to see you. How are you?

(All dance round him. The Tiger enjoys the fun.)

TIGER

Well, it's always nice to see my friends, the monkeys. You know, when I heard the bell I thought it was that devilish wild cat. He's always ringing the bell and running off. If I catch him, I'll...

(He roars and looks very fierce. Yagnamurthi, shivering at one side of the gate, lets out a gasp. The Tiger hears it and turns on him.)

TIGER

And who's this, I'd like to know...

YAGNAMURTHI

Don't you remember, I once helped you to get out of the well...

MONKEY

Surely you must recognise him. He's the kind friend who helped you.

TIGER *(Advancing on Yagnamurthi)*
Of course, I know you! You pulled me out of the well! How are you? (*He grasps Yagnamurthi in a friendly handshake, rather too hearty for Yagnamurthi's peace of mind*) How nice to see you. (*He puts an arm around his shoulder*) Is there anything I can do for you? I'm very grateful for all the help you gave me that day.

YAGNAMURTHI *(Disengaging himself with difficulty)*
Well, as a matter of fact, there is something you can do for me. I'm lost in the forest, I'm afraid. And even if I do find the road back to my village, I can't go back.

TIGER
Why not?

YAGNAMURTHI
Because I haven't any money...and my friend, the monkey, hasn't any money either...and I can't get any in the forest. Oh dear! I do want to go home and see my village again – and all my friends – and the children. Even my wife might be kind to me if I bring home some money. But I can't...find...any...(*He bursts into tears*)

TIGER *(Offering a large handkerchief from his pocket)*
Here, come now, don't cry. Dry your eyes. I can help you. There!

YAGNAMURTHI
Can you really?

TIGER
Yes, of course. Just wait here a moment. (*He goes into his house*)

MONKEY
He'll help you, I'm sure.

YAGNAMURTHI
But he won't have any money.

MONKEY
We'll see. Here he comes.
(The Tiger comes out of the cave carrying a gold necklace.)

TIGER
Here you are! What about this?

YAGNAMURTHI

Good gracious! What a magnificent necklace. It must be worth lakhs of rupees.

TIGER

Oh, it is, I'm sure.

MONKEY

Where did you get it, Mr Tiger? Surely you didn't steal it.

TIGER *(Annoyed)*

I? Steal it?! Certainly not! Listen. (*The monkeys gather at his feet*) I'll tell you. Some years ago a young prince from the North was here with a hunting party. One day he was walking along in the forest quite near this house. I was sitting up on a rock and watching him. Suddenly I saw a small black snake cross his path. The prince jumped out of the way, but he wasn't quick enough. The snake bit him and he died almost at once. (*The monkeys all look sorrowful*) Yes, it was sad. He was a handsome young prince. However, let me get on with my story. I jumped down from the rock and went over to where he was lying. He was wearing a beautiful gold necklace – this one, in fact.

I thought to myself – what will happen to this necklace – it will only get lost. I'll take it to my house and keep it. Someday, it may come in useful. So I took it. I covered up the Prince with leaves, and put a big rock at his head. Then I brought the necklace home, and it's been in my house ever since. And now it will be of some use – because I'm giving it to you.

YAGNAMURTHI

To me? Oh, no...I'm sure...

TIGER

Yes, yes, take it, my good friend. You helped me, and now I'll help you. Come along – put it into your bag.

YAGNAMURTHI

It's a wonderful necklace. But what shall I do with it? No one in my village will have enough money to buy such an expensive necklace.

(While Yagnamurthi, the Tiger and the Monkey are discussing the disposal of the necklace, the other monkeys' eyes light on the Tiger's tail and the end of Yagnamurthi's dhoti. They carefully and quietly tie them together.)

MONKEY
Then you must sell it in a big town.

TIGER
Yes; of course.

YAGNAMURTHI
But what town?

MONKEY
Yes, what town?

TIGER
Yes, what town?
(All scratch their heads)

YAGNAMURTHI
I know! The goldsmith! He'll buy it. He said he'd help me if ever I needed help.

TIGER
That villain! He won't help anyone.

MONKEY
No, he certainly won't.

YAGNAMURTHI
Oh, come now. I'm sure you're wrong. I did help him after all. He's sure to remember me and be grateful for what I did.

TIGER
Well, you can try.

MONKEY
Yes, try it and see. But I'm afraid you'll find out we're right.

YAGNAMURTHI
Yes, I'll go to Kashi and find him.

TIGER
Good.

YAGNAMURTHI

Well, then, many thanks to you both for your kindness.

MONKEY

We'll come with you for a mile or two.

YAGNAMURTHI

Oh, that is kind of you. Well, good bye, Mr Tiger.

TIGER

Good bye, Brahmin. Good luck.

(They turn to go their respective ways and both fall with a bang. The monkeys laugh.)

TIGER

Wait till I catch those monkeys!

(The Monkey unties them and the Tiger chases the monkeys all over the rocks. He retires exhausted to the house.)

MONKEY

Come on, let's walk along the road a bit.

YAGNAMURTHI

Good bye, Mr Tiger. *(They leave)*

TIGER

Well, I hope he gets to Kashi safely. But I don't trust that goldsmith...I don't trust him. I don't trust him at all.

ACT II

SCENE 1

Nati and Sutradhar enter and inspect the setting for the new scene. They address the audience.

SUTRADHAR

Well, well, well, you remember where we left Yagnamurthi – carrying a gold necklace through the forest. You remember, don't you? Good. Well, he carried that gold necklace for hundreds of miles. Everywhere he went, whenever he came to a town or a village, he tried to sell the necklace. But it was such a very beautiful necklace, and worth such a great deal of money, that no one would buy it. And he walked on and on, further and further North, until he got quite near Banaras.

NATI

He asked lots of people the way. One day he was fifty miles away, and the next day thirty, and at last he came to Banaras – or Kashi as it was called in those days. He had remembered the address which the goldsmith had given him, and he walked through Kashi looking for the Street of the Goldsmiths.

SUTRADHAR

But, you know, he wasn't used to towns and cities. He'd been such a long time in the forest that he'd quite forgotten what towns were like. In Kashi his toes were stepped on, and he was pushed from one side to the other. He had an awful time. Anyway, one morning, after a lot of trouble, he found the Street of the Goldsmiths.

(A street in Banaras. People are seen walking up and down. Enter Yagnamurthi, who is pushed about by the crowd. At last he sits down and opens a palm-leaf book.)

YAGNAMURTHI

Ah, here we are. Suvarnaka. Yes. 105, Street of the Goldsmiths, Kashi. Hey! (*Calling a boy near him*) Is this the Street of the Goldsmiths?

BOY

Kya?

YAGNAMURTHI

Is this the Street of the Goldsmiths?

BOY

Hehn? Aap kya bol rahe hain?

YAGNAMURTHI

What?

BOY

Are, swamiji – yahan Hindi mein bolna padega. Yeh Kashi hai, Madras nahin.

YAGNAMURTHI

Hindi?

BOY

Hanh – Hindi.

YAGNAMURTHI

Oh, Hindi! You speak a foreign language here! Ah yes, now let me see. Hold on a minute. (*He consults another palm-leaf book from the bag*) Yes...yes...that's right. (*He turns to the boy*) Kya, this Goldsmiths ka street hai?

(By this time the crowd has dispersed, leaving Yagnamurthi and the boy on stage.)

BOY

Hanh, yeh hi hai.

YAGNAMURTHI *(Consulting the book again)*

Number one hundred aur panch?

BOY

Woh hai. (*He points to door No. 105.*)

YAGNAMURTHI

Uska name Suvarnaka?

BOY

Hanhji hanh. Suvarnaka.

YAGNAMURTHI

Well done, my boy. You speak Hindi quite well. Now... (*He turns to the house, as the boy leaves*) I wonder if he's in? (*He knocks at the door*) Hello. Anyone at home? (*He knocks again)* Anyone at home?

(He is about to knock again ... the door flies open and a woman appears.)

WOMAN

Kya? Kab? Kidhar? Kaise? KYOON?!

YAGNAMURTHI

Excuse me, but does my friend the goldsmith live here?

WOMAN

Kya?

YAGNAMURTHI

Ohm my goodness! Don't say you speak Hindi too! (*He starts to search in the bag for the book: then thinks better of it*) Su-var-na-ka! Suvarnaka! Goldsmith!

WOMAN

Ji hanh. Bulaun?

(Yagnamurthi lifts hands in expressive bewilderment. Suvarnaka appears at the doorway.)

SUVARNAKA

Hello, what do you...Why, it's the Brahmin! How did you get here?

YAGNAMURTHI *(With feeling)*

I walked. All the way. Oooh! (*Holds a foot in pain*)

SUVARNAKA *(Coming out)*

Well, my dear friend, it is good to see you. When did you get to Kashi? How long will you be here?

(The wife returns indoors)

YAGNAMURTHI

Well, I don't know. You see, I want your help.

SUVARNAKA *(Not very enthusiastically)*
Oh! When are you leaving?

YAGNAMURTHI
Yes...You see, I've got a necklace I want to sell – and you said you would help me – so I've brought it to you.

SUVARNAKA
A necklace, eh? A good one? Let's see it.

YAGNAMURTHI
Yes, here it is. (*Empties the bag, but cannot find the necklace*) Well, that's strange. That's very funny.

SUVARNAKA (*Drily*)
Yes, very amusing.

YAGNAMURTHI
I had it this morning. (*Frantically turning over his possessions*) I remember saying to myself, 'I mustn't lose this!' Now...(*Thinks*) Ah! I remember...(*Takes it out of the waistband*) Here it is.

SUVARNAKA
Why, that's a fine necklace. Hmm! (*Examining it*) Mmm! Yes, very fine. (*To the audience, while Yagnamurthi is putting his belongings back in his bag*) I made this, four years ago, for Prince Sudarshan. Now I wonder... (*Turning to Yagnamurthi*) Where did you get this marvellous necklace?

YAGNAMURTHI
Oh, a friend gave it to me.

SUVARNAKA
A friend, eh?

YAGNAMURTHI
Yes. A tiger, as a matter of fact.

SUVARNAKA
A tiger, eh?

YAGNAMURTHI
Yes, it was good of him, wasn't it?

SUVARNAKA *(Sarcastic and unbelieving)*
Yes, wasn't it?

YAGNAMURTHI
Now, will you buy it? It must be worth a lot of money.

SUVARNAKA
Buy it? Oh, of course I will. Now, let me see...can you come back tonight? I'll have the money ready for you then.

YAGNAMURTHI
Oh, certainly. Yes, certainly. Yes, I can come back tonight. E ... your...(*Gesture of eating a meal)* dinner time?

SUVARNAKA
Yes, after dinner.

YAGNAMURTHI
Oh...all right... That's very nice of you. (*He puts the necklace carefully in the waistband.*) Good-bye then, good-bye until tonight.
(He exits, forgetting the bag, which remains lying at the foot of the steps of the house.)

SUVARNAKA
Wife! Where are you? (*The Wife comes out of the front door*) Just look at this! That Brahmin is going to give me a necklace; he wants me to buy it! And I know that necklace. I made it!

WIFE
You made it! How was that?

SUVARNAKA
I made it for the king's son, Prince Sudarshan. The poor prince went on a hunting trip to the South, and never returned. He died there. Perhaps you remember it, they said it was a snake bite or something.

WIFE
Well, wasn't it?

SUVARNAKA
Of course it was a snake bite. But wait! Perhaps it was not! This wicked Brahmin must have had the Prince killed, and stolen his necklace!

WIFE

What a wretch! But didn't you ask him? What did he say?

SUVARNAKA

As if any killer is going to say: 'Yes, sir. I killed him'. He says a tiger gave it to him. A likely tale!

WIFE

Yes, indeed! So, what are you going to do?

SUVARNAKA

I'm going to the King. Immediately. I shall tell him the whole story. And tonight, when the Brahmin comes to get the money, there'll be a warm welcome for him – The King's Guards! And then – *Khatam*! (*He makes a noise with his tongue and a slicing gesture with his hand.*) Off with his head!

WIFE

And then?!

SUVARNAKA

And then?! Why, the King will give me a huge reward! I shall become his right hand man. Ha ha ha!

WIFE

And we'll be rich! (*She cackles*)

SUVARNAKA

We shan't do any more work!

WIFE

I'll have ten servants!

SUVARNAKA

We'll live in a palace! (*He joins her cackling*)

WIFE

A huge gold palace!

SUVARNAKA

We'll have hundreds of servants!

WIFE

And the Brahmin ...?

SUVARNAKA
The Brahmin will be *khatam*! (*He cackles hideously*)

WIFE
The Brahmin will be *khatam*!

TOGETHER
(*Cackling and shouting*) Ha ha! The Brahmin will be *khatam*! The Brahmin will be *khatam*! The Brahmin will be *khatam*!

(Enter Yagnamurthi.)

YAGNAMURTHI *(Softly)*
Excuse me. (*He is not heard. Suvarnaka and his wife continue in their glee. Yagnamurthi coughs.*) Excuse me!

(The Wife sees Yagnamurthi, but Suvarnaka does not)

SUVARNAKA
The Brahmin will be *khatam*...(*Sees Yagnamurthi*) Oh! Hello... er...here you are again.

YAGNAMURTHI
I left my bag here. (*He picks it up, and starts to exit*)

SUVARNAKA
Ah, yes, your bag.

WIFE
Ah, yes, your bag. Please...

YAGNAMURTHI
Hmm. Excuse me, but what does *khatam* mean? (*Repeats Suvarnaka's gesture*)

SUVARNAKA
Khatam?

YAGNAMURTHI
Yes. You said, 'The Brahmin will be *khatam*'.

SUVARNAKA
Oh yes, *khatam*... Well...

WIFE
It's a Hindi word. It means...it means...rich. Very rich!

YAGNAMURTHI

Aha! Very good. I shall be *khatam* tomorrow, shan't I? Aha, yes. (*He laughs. Suvarnaka and the Wife join him. They are all laughing.*) *Khatam* ...Ha ha ha – *khatam*!

(Yagnamurthi exits laughing.)

Intermission here

SCENE 2

Sutradhar approaches the audience.

SUTRADHAR

Poor Yagnamurthi, he didn't realise what he was in for. He was such a sweet-natured chap, you see, that he couldn't believe anyone would do him a bad turn. He liked everyone in the world, and he thought everyone liked him. And everyone did, except a few very wicked people, like the goldsmith and his wife. They were wicked, you see, because Yagnamurthi had helped the Goldsmith when he was in trouble. Then, instead of being grateful, the goldsmith was planning to get rid of him. *(Pause. A little louder)* The goldsmith was planning to get rid of him! *(Another pause. He looks about. Louder still)* The goldsmith was planning to get rid of him. *(He strides to the wings)* Where in heaven are you?!

NATI *(Off)*

I have off stage duty in this scene. You will have to manage by yourself.

SUTRADHAR *(Controlling himself)*

Well, that afternoon, while poor Yagnamurthi was asleep by the river Ganga, dreaming peacefully of his village in the South and the happy times he would have when he returned, the wicked goldsmith went off to the Palace to see the Minister.

(The entrance to the King's Palace, the same afternoon. One of the palace guards is asleep at the foot of one of the two statues there. Enter Suvarnaka.)

SUVARNAKA *(Aside)*

Now comes the difficult part – to see the Minister. *(He coughs and advances)* Ahem! *(The Guard stirs)* Ahem! *(The Guard wakes up)*

GUARD

Hey, you! What do you want here? *(He brandishes a spear)*

SUVARNAKA

I...er...I...wanted to see the Minister. It's...er...very important.

GUARD

Certainly not! The Minister is fast asleep – the Minister is very busy!

SUVARNAKA

Oh, he'll come out if he knows it's me! I'm an old friend. I used to make jewellery for the king. I'm a goldsmith – Suvarnaka, you know.

GUARD

I don't know.

SUVARNAKA

(Handing him a coin) Surely you know me?

GUARD

Do I? Perhaps you will refresh my memory?

SUVARNAKA

Ah, yes. *(Gives him another coin)*

GUARD *(Pocketing the coin and peering carefully at Suvarnaka)*

Ah, yes, now I recognise you. Of course, you're Suvarnaka. I'll see what I can do.

(He enters the palace gate.)

SUVARNAKA

Oh dear! I'm afraid this will cost a lot of money. *(He looks at the remaining coins in his hand)* Ah, well. *(To the audience)* It's money well spent. I shall soon be rich when the King rewards me. Ha ha! And the Brahmin will...

(Enter three palace officials of three different heights)

SUVARNAKA
Oh, Good afternoon. I... er... I don't think I know you. I...

3RD SECRETARY
I'm the third Secretary to the Minister.

2ND SECRETARY
I'm the second secretary.

1ST SECRETARY *(The shortest of them all)*
And I'm the chief Secretary.

SUVARNAKA
I should like to see the Minister.

ALL
The minister is extremely busy and can't be disturbed. He has instructed me to say...*(They all look crossly at each other)* He has instructed...*(At last the 1st Secretary stares the other two out)*

1ST SECRETARY
He has instructed me to say that he is unable to see you today.

2ND SECRETARY
Exactly. He is unable to see you today.

3RD SECRETARY
Just what he told me. He is unable to see you today.

SUVARNAKA *(Aside)*
Oh dear! More money.

(He puts a coin in each outstretched hand, looking away from the officials concerned. One of the statues, too, puts out a hand and gets a coin. Suvarnaka counts three hands and four coins gone, and is mystified. The three officials confer.)

(The statue may be an actor in make up. Other innovations are certainly possible.)*

ALL
On further consideration, it may be possible...*(They stare at each other)*

1ST SECRETARY
On further consideration, it may be possible for the Minister to spare you a few moments. Please wait. (*Exit*)

SUVARNAKA *(To the 2nd and 3rd Secretaries)*
There's a lot going on at the Palace these days. What is happening?

2ND SECRETARY
Don't you know? The King's daughter is getting married next month to the young and handsome Prince of Vidarbha. He's arriving for the wedding in a few days. The Princess chose him herself. Oh, he's very handsome indeed – and rich, too!

SUVARNAKA
Perhaps the Princess will want some new jewellery. Now, I can...
(He is interrupted by the entrance of the King's Minister.)

MINISTER
Now what's all this? (*Bustling about*) Come along now, I'm a very busy man. Why should I see this Suvar...(*Looks at the paper in his hand.*)...naka?

ALL *(Together)*
The person in question has made representations...
(They stare at each other, start again all together, but the 1st Secretary eventually wins)

1ST SECRETARY *(Very officious)*
The person in question has made representations that in the event of your Honour having sufficient leisure at your Honour's disposal he is desirous of having audience with your Honour at the first available opportunity, of course in accordance with the regulations in force and pending the exercise of your Honour's discretion.

MINISTER
I beg your pardon. *(To the 2nd Secretary)* What does he say?

2ND SECRETARY
He says, your Honour, that the person in question has made representations that in the event of your Honour having sufficient leisure at your Honour's disposal...

MINISTER *(Interrupting, testily, to the 3rd Secretary)*
No, no, no! What does he mean?

3RD SECRETARY
What does he mean?

MINISTER

Yes! What – does – he – mean?

3RD SECRETARY

Ah, yes. Well, your honour, he means that (*very rapidly*) the person in question has made representations that in the event of your Honour having sufficient leisure at your Honour's disposal... (*The Minister, halfway through this speech, gives a dismal howl and clutches his head.*)

MINISTER

Ohh! *(Turns to the Guard)*

You! *(The Guard comes forward)* Do you know what he means?

GUARD *(Very laconic, pointing to Suvarnaka)*

He wants to see you!

MINISTER

Is that ... he ... me ...?

GUARD

Yes.

(The Minister firmly takes the Guard's spear from his hand, puts him at the head of the line of Secretaries, gives his spear to the 1st Secretary and makes him stand guard at the entrance. He bustles back to confront Suvarnaka.)

MINISTER

Now, my friend, what do you want?

SUVARNAKA

Well, sir, it's like this. I'm a goldsmith. Suvarnaka's my name, and this morning a Brahmin from the South brought me a beautiful necklace. He wanted me to buy it. Now I know that necklace. I made it – for Prince Sudarshan!

MINISTER

Our Prince of Kashi!

SUVARNAKA

That's right. The King's son.

MINISTER

The King's son!

SUVARNAKA

The King's son. And you may remember that the poor young prince died under most suspicious circumstances. Snakebite, or some such story – so they said. And the necklace was given to him by the King himself, before he went on his hunting trip!

MINISTER

Then how did the Brahmin get it?

SUVARNAKA

He must have – you know – had the Prince killed and then stolen the necklace.

MINISTER

The fiend!

SUVARNAKA

Yes, a fiend indeed. But...sir...listen to my plan. The Brahmin is to bring the necklace to my house tonight. If your Honour can come there with some of the palace guards, we shall be able to catch him. And then the King will reward me handsomely – I mean us handsomely. *(Touching the Minister's arm)* Won't he?

MINISTER

Yes, yes. Oh, he'll be very pleased. Yes, indeed, it's a very good plan. I'm so glad I thought of it – the King is sure to reward me handsomely. He... *(He sees the stupefied face of Suvannaka)* Ah, well... er...your plan. He'll reward us both, I'm sure.

SUVARNAKA

Yes, I'm sure he will. (*He is about to go*) Then good bye until tonight. We shall meet at my house – 105, Street of the Goldsmiths.

MINISTER

Right. I shall be there.

(The Minister exits. The three Secretaries follow him in order of precedence. The 1st Secretary tries to give back the spear to the Guard, who refuses it and firmly puts the 1st Secretary back in position, spear in hand, and follows the other two Secretaries himself. The 1st Secretary looks round and finally gives the spear to a statue. Then he enters the palace gate with a smile of triumph.)

SCENE 3

Nati addresses the audience

NATI

Well, you can see now just how wicked the goldsmith was, can't you? And while all this was going on, poor Yagnamurthi was taking a nap, rather well deserved, on the banks of the Ganga. At about five o'clock he woke up, had a bath in the river and offered a few special prayers. Then he got ready to go to the goldsmith's house and get the money for the necklace. How happy he was! But little did he know what was being planned as a welcome for him by the goldsmith.

(Dusk, the same evening. Suvarnaka's house in Kashi. Enter Suvarnaka, quite excited.)

SUVARNAKA

Wife! Wife! Open the door. (*He looks at the approaching darkness.*) Hurry up! It's getting dark.

WIFE

Well, of course it's getting dark. It always gets dark this time of the evening.

SUVARNAKA

Yes, ha ha, very amusing. This is not the time for your stupid jokes. Now, Listen. The minister and his guards are coming here very soon. You'd better light the lamps.

WIFE

Are they coming to catch the Brahmin?

SUVARNAKA

Yes, indeed! (*Rubbing hands*) Yes, to catch the Brahmin. And then...we shall get a huge reward.

WIFE

No more work!

SUVARNAKA

No more making jewellery!

WIFE

A fine, big house!

SUVARNAKA

Shhh! They're coming. I can hear them. *(The sound of men marching is heard)* Goodness – are they bringing the whole army? *(The sound becomes louder. 'Halt!' is heard off stage.)* It sounds like a hundred men. *(Enter the Minister)* Ah, here you are, your Honour. Welcome to my humble home.

MINISTER

Yes, here we are, indeed. This is your house, is it? *(Looking round)* I suppose the Brahmin will come? And he will bring the necklace?

SUVARNAKA

Oh, certainly!

MINISTER

You're sure?

SUVARNAKA

Quite sure, your Honour, quite sure.

MINISTER

Quite sure, eh? Good! *(Menacingly)* Because if he doesn't come, and if he doesn't bring the necklace...somebody is going to have his head cut off.

SUVARNAKA *(Frightened)*

Somebody will...oh, ha ha, that is so...Oh he'll come! I'm sure he'll come! But...*(thinks)* suppose he sees your Honour and the guards here...he might run away.

MINISTER

Yes, that's true. Well, we'll hide round the corner and jump out when he comes in here and nab him.

WIFE

How will you know he has arrived?

MINISTER

How will... I hadn't thought of that.

SUVARNAKA

I know! I'll get my flute. When he's ready to be caught I'll blow a few notes on it.

WIFE

I'll get it. *(She goes into the house)*

MINISTER

A very good idea. We'll be round the corner. *(The wife brings the flute and Suvarnaka blows a note or two)* That's right. We shall hear that perfectly, and as soon as we hear it, we will bound in here – on the double! *(The minister and guards leave)*

WIFE

That flute, now. You ought not to be holding it when he comes. He might suspect something.

SUVARNAKA

I'll put it in my pocket.

WIFE

No, no. Put it here on this ledge. Then, while you're talking to him, you can take it without his knowing it.

SUVARNAKA

Right you are! A good idea. *(He puts the flute on the ledge)* Shhh! I think he's coming. Go inside.

(A cheerful singing is heard and Yagnamurthi enters. He sings and looks for the house. Suvarnaka appears silently at his elbow.)

SUVARNAKA *(At his oiliest)*

Good evening.

YAGNAMURTHI *(Jumping with fright)*

Good gracious, who's that?! Oh, it's you! You gave me such a fright.

SUVARNAKA

I'm so sorry.

YAGNAMURTHI

Oh, it's all right.

SUVARNAKA

Have you brought the necklace?

YAGNAMURTHI *(Taking it out of his waistband)*

Oh yes, here it is.

SUVARNAKA *(With outstretched hands)*
What a fine necklace...a fine necklace. Thank you.

YAGNAMURTHI *(Stops as he is just about to hand it over)*
Er...wait a minute. What about the money?

SUVARNAKA
Oh, I'll give you that, not to worry.

YAGNAMURTHI
Oh, good! *(Nearly gives Suvarnaka the necklace)* But where is the money?

SUVARNAKA
Right there, in my house.

YAGNAMURTHI
Oh, that's all right then. *(Nearly gives him the necklace)* But I should like to see it... I've brought my bag.

SUVARNAKA
Give me the necklace.

YAGNAMURTHI
Well...let me see the money.

SUVARNAKA
Oh, all right. I'll get it. *(He goes into the house)*

YAGNAMURTHI
Aha! At last! I shall be able to go home, see my wife – I hope she's missed me – see all the children in the village – play my flute. Why, what's this?

(He sees the flute on the ledge) It's a flute! I wonder who it belongs to. I haven't seen a flute for months. Someone must have left it here. I'll just borrow it for the night. Then when I've got the money I can play a tune or two. I'll bring it back tomorrow. *(He is just about to try it when the door opens. He puts it hastily into his bag.)*

SUVARNAKA *(Showing a bag of coins)*
Here you are...here's the money!

YAGNAMURTHI
And here's the necklace. *(Gives it to Suvannaka)*

SUVARNAKA *(Giving him the money)*
The money.

YAGNAMURTHI
Ah! The money! *(He looks at it lovingly)* At last all my troubles are over. Ahh! (*As Yagnamurthi grows ecstatic over his thoughts of returning home, Suvannaka is groping unsuccessfully for the flute.*)

Thank you so much. I must say it was very, very kind of you to buy this necklace.

(He places the bag of money down to pick up the other bag.) Well, I must be getting along. I've got a long way to go, you know.

SUVARNAKA
Oh, wait a minute. I've forgotten something...

(*Searching frantically for the flute*) I must...you see...

YAGNAMURTHI
What's the matter?

SUVARNAKA
Well...er...oh, you must say good-bye to my wife.

YAGNAMURTHI
Well, I ought to be...oh, All right.

SUVARNAKA *(Opens the door and calls)*
Wife! Come here a moment. *(To Yagnamurthi)* She's just coming. She'd love to meet you, I know.

(The Wife comes out. Suvannaka points and whispers, but there is no sign of the flute.)

YAGNAMURTHI
Well, it was very kind of your husband to buy the necklace from me.

WIFE
Oh, it was nothing. But won't you stay a bit longer?

SUVARNAKA
Yes, do. Stay the night. Please, I beg of you.

YAGNAMURTHI
No, no. I must be getting along. Thank you very much. *(He recollects)* You know, the monkey and the tiger... well, they thought

you were a bad man. But now I know you're a very good man – a kind, grateful man. Thank you very much. Good bye.

SUVARNAKA

Oh, do stay. *(The Wife now searches frantically)*

YAGNAMURTHI

No, no, I must say good bye. And thank you, thank you. *(Moves)*

SUVARNAKA

Oh, do stay.

YAGNAMURTHI

Good bye. *(Exits, leaving the bag of money behind)*

SUVARNAKA *(To the wife)*

You fool! I told you to let me put the flute in my pocket!

WIFE

But we put it on the ledge. It was there five minutes ago. And now it's gone.

SUVARNAKA

And now he's gone, too – and our reward has gone as well. You fool! *(He starts to attack her)*

WIFE *(Standing up for herself)*

What do you mean – fool – it was your fault. I was –

Yagnamurthi enters.

YAGNAMURTHI

Excuse me, I left the money here. How silly of me!

SUVARNAKA

Oh, do stay.

YAGNAMURTHI

No, no. (*Picking up the money*) No, thank you. I must be going. (*He starts to go*) I must be going. Good bye.

(He is about to leave, but turns round once more) Oh, by the way. I forgot to tell you. I found a flute on the ledge there. I hope it's not yours. I only wanted to borrow it for a while. I do love the sound of a flute. *(He takes it out)*

WIFE
The flute!

SUVARNAKA
The flute!

YAGNAMURTHI
Is it yours?

WIFE
Oh, yes, it belongs to my husband.

SUVARNAKA
Oh, no, I don't play the flute.

YAGNAMURTHI
Oh, but I do. I play it every morning in my village. Shall I play something for you?

SUVARNAKA
Oh, that would be delightful.

YAGNAMURTHI
Well, perhaps I will.

(He sits down. Suvannaka puts the necklace on the ground and sits down. Yagnamurthi puts the money in front of him, picks up the flute and then stops.)

You know, I haven't played for along time. Perhaps another day ... *(Suvannaka rises to take the flute from him)* No, I'll borrow it for tonight if I may.

WIFE
Oh, please play something. We love music.

YAGNAMURTHI
Shall I? All right. But remember, I haven't practiced for a while. *(He plays three notes)* It's quite a nice flute, isn't it.

(He puts it to his lips again. Guards and the Minister come running in.) I'll play –

MINISTER
Stop! Guards! Hold that man! *(Yagnamurthi is pulled rudely to his feet. Suvarnaka and the Wife are pleased.)* Where did you get that necklace?

YAGNAMURTHI

Me? Oh...er...a tiger...a monkey...oh dear, now my troubles have started all over again.

MINISTER

You took it off Prince Sudarshan after you killed him.

YAGNAMURTHI

What?! Me?! Certainly not! Of course not!

MINISTER

Then where did you get it!

YAGNAMURTHI

I GOT IT FROM A TIGER – A FRIEND OF MINE.

MINISTER

A tiger!

SUVARNAKA

A likely tale!

YAGNAMURTHI *(To Suvarnaka)*

But you were there. Don't you remember?

SUVARNAKA

I was there? Do I remember what? I don't know what you are talking about!

MINISTER

Take him to the dungeons in the palace. *(Yagnamurthi is dragged off)*

YAGNAMURTHI *(To Suvannaka)*

How can you say you don't remember? You ungrateful wretch! I saved you then and now you are putting me in prison. Ungrateful wretch!

ACT III

SCENE 1

Nati and Sutradhar address the audience.

SUTRADHARA

Well, it's a sad story, I'm afraid, isn't it? The poor Brahmin was thrown into the palace dungeons and chained to the wall. He had hardly anything to eat, and only dirty water to drink. How he missed the forest, and all his friends, and the spirits of the river! It was no use calling on the spirits of the river from his dungeon cell, because they couldn't hear him.

NATI

After a few days he had some even worse news. The King had believed the story of the goldsmith about the necklace and had ordered poor Yagnamurthi's head to be cut off! His head to be cut off! Imagine that! Every day Yagnamurthi waited for the dreadful moment. Every time he heard footsteps outside his cell he jumped with fright.

SUTRADHAR

But the executioner didn't come. You will wonder why. Let us tell you. The King's daughter was to be married, and the King's wife, the Queen of Kashi, had told the King that it wouldn't be auspicious to have anyone killed until after the wedding. So poor Yagnamurthi had to wait. He sat quietly in his cell, waiting for the wedding to be over.

NATI

The night before the wedding all was great hustle and bustle at the Palace. Royal princes from all over the country had come to attend the wedding. Now, in those days there was a ceremony known as *swayamvara*, which means 'self-choice'. When a royal princess was to be married, her father announced a *swayamvara* and all the royal princes came to the appointed place.

SUTRADHAR

The princess took a garland in her hands and walked up the line of princes. When she came to the prince she wanted to marry, she put the garland over his head. Now, some months before the wedding the princess of Kashi had already chosen her husband in this way.

NATI

He was a prince, and a very handsome prince too. The evening before the wedding he was talking with his friends. Here they are now.

SUTRADHAR

This is a part of the king's palace. The prince, who will marry the princess tomorrow, is with a crowd of friends. (*To Nati)* I will see if the prince needs something. You can join the princess and attend to her.

(The prince and his friends enter. Sutradhar takes his seat at the corner. Nati exits.)

FRIEND 1

Well, my dear friend, tomorrow will soon be here – and then you'll be married.

FRIEND 2

Yes, yes. Tonight's your last night as a bachelor.

PRINCE

And, by all accounts, the princess is extremely beautiful!

FRIENDS

What do you mean 'by all accounts'? Haven't you seen her?

PRINCE

Never.

FRIEND 3

But she chose you at the *swayamvara.* She put the garland round your neck herself.

FRIEND 4

We were there. We saw her.

PRINCE

I didn't. I had my eyes shut.

FRIEND 5
You were so amazed by her beauty that you shut your eyes?

PRINCE
No, not exactly.

FRIEND 1
What happened to your eyes, then?

PRINCE
There was a gust of wind, and I got dust in my eyes. *(All laugh)*

FRIEND 2
Then...you really haven't seen her.

PRINCE
No, I haven't. But I shall tomorrow.

FRIEND 3
Hmmm...I'm afraid she's very ugly.

PRINCE
No!

FRIEND 4
Bah! Horrible! Everyone knows that her father couldn't get anyone to marry her. She has pimples.

FRIEND 3
And she's enormous in size!

PRINCE
No!

FRIEND 1
And her voice – like a crow – Ka ka ka all day! Oh, how glad I am that it's not me that's getting married!

PRINCE
You're joking!

FRIEND 2
Joking! *(All laugh)* Everyone knows what she's like – you've been tricked.

PRINCE
Tricked!

FRIEND 1

Yes, of course. Tricked! Ah well, you can always retire to the forest. A few years early.

PRINCE *(Stunned)*

Yes...Yes, I suppose so.

ALL

Well, good night. We'll see you in the morning. *(The friends leave)*

PRINCE *(Walking about slowly)*

Good heavens. Pimples! And enormous – and a voice like a crow! What on earth shall I do? Could they be joking? I must find out before tomorrow. There must be a way of seeing her somehow. And then if she really is very ugly I can run away. But how can I see her? She must be well guarded. *(He walks down and sits near the Sutradhar.)* Now let me think. *(He meditates with a sad frown)*

SUTRADHAR

What's the matter?

PRINCE

The matter! I've got to marry the ugliest girl in the world. At least I think so.

SUTRADHAR

You think so?

PRINCE

Yes. I haven't seen her yet, but all my friends say she's very ugly.

SUTRADHAR

Well, that doesn't matter.

PRINCE

Doesn't matter! How would you like to be married to an ugly wife?

SUTRADHAR

I am. I have been for twenty years.

PRINCE

Well... I don't want to be.

SUTRADHAR
Why don't you have a look at her?

PRINCE
She's the princess. She must be sitting quietly in the palace now – and I can't get in there to her to see her at this time of night.

SUTRADHAR
The princess? Why, she comes into this very garden every night.

PRINCE
What garden?

SUTRADHAR *(Pointing to the stage)*
This garden... Oh, it's not there. Let me arrange it for you. *(He gets on to the stage)* Aho! Aho there! Where's the garden?

(Music. Two men bring a bench. Then two figures come in and form a fountain. The first two men then get tree tops and stand as trees. The Sutradhar arranges everything.)

SUTRADHAR
Guards! Where are the guards? *(He goes off stage and is heard calling)* Hey! Wake up. You're supposed to be guarding the princess's garden.

(He enters pulling the guards by the shoulders) You're not supposed to be sleeping.

GUARD 1
We've been on guard duty all day... and all last night, too. Three shifts.

GUARD 2
Yes, three shows a day. This drama group drives us so hard. We're very sleepy.

SUTRADHAR
You can't sleep now. Do your duty. And don't let me catch you sleeping.

(The guards begin to march up and down, half asleep.)

PRINCE *(Walking in)*
This must be the Princess's garden. But how shall I get in? I must get rid of the guards first. I know what I'll do! *(Goes into the wings)*

PRINCE *(Off stage)*
Help! Help! Help!

GUARD 1
Did you hear that?

GUARD 2
No, I didn't hear anything.

PRINCE
Help! Help!

GUARD 1
There it is again.

GUARD 2 *(Still marching)*
I can't hear anything.

SUTRADHAR
Yes, you can.

GUARD 2
I can't.

SUTRADHAR
You can!

GUARD 2
Oh, all right. I can hear it now. *(The guards go off. The prince enters)*

PRINCE
Aha! So this is her garden. And that light *(He looks off stage)* must be her window. I'll wait here. Perhaps she'll come into the garden before she goes to bed.

GUARD 1 *(Off stage)*
I can't see anyone.

GUARD 2 *(Off stage)*
No, neither can I. We'd better go back to the garden.

PRINCE
Heavens! The guards are coming back. What shall I do now? *(He looks wildly round and at last changes places with one of the trees, who joins the second tree. The Guards enter and march up and down)*

GUARD 1

Well, it's getting late. I don't think we need stand guard any more.

GUARD 2

What will happen if the king comes?

GUARD 1

He won't.

(They sit down back to back at a downstage corner and go to sleep. The Prince is just about to give up his position as a tree when voices are heard. He decides to remain a tree. Enter the princess and her handmaids. They are in a jolly mood, she is not. Nati is one of the handmaids, but sits at a corner, weaving flowers.)

MAID 1

Well, tomorrow you'll be married.

MAID 2

Yes, how lucky you are!

PRINCESS

Lucky! But I don't know what he looks like!

NATI

How can that be! You chose him at the *swayamvara* out of all the assembled Princes.

PRINCESS

Well... I meant to put the garland on the prince of Pataliputra, but just then there was a gust of wind and some dust got into my eyes. Before I knew where I was I had dropped the garland over the head of this prince. And then his face was so covered with flowers that I couldn't see it. I hope he's handsome. I do hope so.

(She sits dejectedly in a corner, near Nati. The Handmaids gather together, excitedly discuss a plan and giggle. They approach the princess.)

MAID 1

Are you sure you didn't see him?

PRINCESS

Yes, quite sure.

HANDMAID 2

That's lucky, because I'm told he's extremely ugly!

PRINCESS
Ugly!

HANDMAID 3
Yes – and he has a huge grey beard!

PRINCESS
Not a beard!

HANDMAID 2
And pimples too – that is, on the parts of his face which aren't covered with the beard.

NATI
They could be joking.

PRINCESS
No! You're joking.

HANDMAID 1
Certainly not. It's a well-known fact that he's the ugliest man in the kingdom.

PRINCESS
No!

HANDMAID 2
Oh yes! He's been trying to get married for the last forty years.

PRINCESS
Forty years!

ALL
Ah, well. We must go. We have to make sure our clothes are ready for the great wedding tomorrow. Good night. *(They leave)*

PRINCESS
Oh my goodness! They say he has a grey beard – and he's ugly – and old – and has pimples! *(She bursts into tears. Nati gives her flowers for her hair and leaves)* What shall I do?

PRINCE *(From beneath the tree)*
Ahem!

PRINCESS
I don't know... What was that?

PRINCE

Ahem! *(He lifts up the tree. The Princess screams)* It's me!

PRINCESS

Ohh! How did you get here? Who are you?

PRINCE

I'm the prince you're to marry tomorrow. (*Looking closely at her*) They said you were ugly!

PRINCESS *(Looking closely at him)*

They said you were old!

PRINCE

They said you had pimples!

PRINCESS

They said you had a beard!

PRINCE

But you're beautiful!

PRINCESS

And you're handsome! *(They clasp hands adoringly)*

BOTH

You are different.

PRINCESS

Listen – I can hear something.

PRINCE

The beating of my heart.

PRINCESS

No, listen. It's my father. He is coming here. You must hide.

(The prince reluctantly returns to being a tree. The princess sits again. The guards wake up at the approaching sound and stand at attention. The king enters, accompanied by the minister.)

KING

Ah, my dear, there you are. Everything all right?

PRINCESS

Yes, father, everything. But you're looking worried, Father. Why?

KING

Oh, I don't want to bother you on the night before your wedding.

PRINCESS

But please tell me, father. I don't like to see you looking so worried.

KING

Well, we've caught the wicked Brahmin who killed your dear brother. You remember the hunting trip... a few years ago. We've got him now in the palace dungeons. But we shan't have his head cut off until after the wedding, I assure you.

PRINCESS

Oh, poor man! How do you know he committed the crime?

MINISTER

It's quite clear, quite clear. He was caught red handed, trying to sell your dear brother's necklace.

PRINCESS

Perhaps he got it from someone else!

MINISTER

Impossible! Quite impossible!

KING

No, he'll have to die, I'm afraid. And now, my dear, off to bed. You have a long day ahead of you. Good night.

PRINCESS

Good night, father. (*Exit*)

MINISTER

And another thing, your majesty. *(Striding up and down)* This prince she's marrying – She'll have to be very careful. I hear he's very fond of dice, and chariot racing, and hunting, and all manner of habits. I do hope he's going to be a good husband to her.

KING

Of course, minister. Now, you know we've argued about this before. I am sure he'll make a very good husband indeed.

MINISTER

I'm not so sure. I don't like some of his habits. He may not be quite the young man...

PRINCE *(From under the tree)*
He's very handsome.

MINISTER *(To the King)*
Do you think so? I thought him ugly.

KING
Oh, no! He's quite handsome.

MINISTER
Well, in all my years of public life I don't ever remember ... *(The tree puts out a foot and trips him up. He falls with a bang and lies still.)*

KING *(Not noticing what has happened)*
Well, I must be getting to bed too.

PRINCE *(Imitating the minister's voice)*
Good night, your majesty.

KING
Good night, minister. (*Exit*)
(The Prince takes off the tree-top and looks at the minister. He tries to pull the minister off the stage, but is unable to do so. He whistles to the guards.)

PRINCE
Hey!
(The Guards see the Minister and start to carry him off. They realise the Prince is not a tree.)

GUARD 1
Here! How did you get here?
(The prince runs off. The guards drop the minister and chase him.)

GUARD 2
Hey! Come back! Halt!
(The Minister lies dazed on the stage.)

SCENE 2

SUTRADHAR

Well, while all this was going on in the palace garden, poor Yagnamurthi was down below in the palace dungeons. He could hear the laughter and chatter and music in the palace, and it made him very sad. It reminded him of his village and all the children – and he knew he'd never see them again.

(The stage is in darkness, a single spot discloses a prison cell. A bedraggled Yagnamurthi, heavily chained to the wall, bemoans his fate.)

YAGNAMURTHI *(To the audience)*

Now look at me! Just see what great trouble I am in. Oh, I've had an awful time. Pulled and pushed by those villainous guards – pulled along corridors – thrown down the steps – and now, here I am, chained to the wall. And that's not all – tomorrow I die. They're going to chop off my head! Ah well, it can't be helped I suppose. What's written on one's forehead can't be rubbed out, they say.

You know, it's all on account of that wicked goldsmith. The scoundrel! Didn't I pull him out of the well? And look at what happened. The others all helped me! They were grateful. The monkey and the tiger – how kind they were too! And this wretch! Of course, he was sweet to me when I pulled him out. *(He mimics Suvarnaka)* Oh, yes, dear kind Brahmin, thank you a thousand times – so kind of you – anything I can do to help you I shall do. Any time, any time! And this is what he has done – stolen the necklace the tiger gave me, told the King I'm a villain and that I killed his son – me, imagine me, a murderer – and had me flung into prison! And now I'm to die tomorrow! Oh dear! Oh dear! *(He weeps)* Why, what's that?

SNAKE *(Entering)*

Hello, my dear Brahmin! Why, you're in a sad state!

YAGNAMURTHI *(In a panic)*

Help! A snake! Let me out!

SNAKE

Why, my dear Brahmin! Don't you remember me? You pulled me out of the well. I'm a friend of yours. *(The Snake twines itself around Yagnamurthi's legs, much to his embarrassment.)*

YAGNAMURTHI

Oh yes, a friend, yes – ha ha! How are you? Well, I hope?

SNAKE

Yes, but you seem to be in trouble. How did you get here?

YAGNAMURTHI

Oh, it's a long story!

SNAKE

Well, tell me. We've got plenty of time.

YAGNAMURTHI

You have, I haven't. I'm to die tomorrow!

SNAKE

What?!

YAGNAMURTHI

Yes. Ohhh, where do I begin? You see, I got lost in the forest. Then the monkey found me and helped me. He took me to the tiger. The tiger gave me a gold necklace. Then I brought the necklace here to sell it to that man who was in the well with you – the goldsmith – you remember?

SNAKE

Yes, he was a villain. We told you so.

YAGNAMURTHI

He was – you were right! He had me put in prison – and tomorrow I'm to die.

SNAKE

Poor Brahmin!. But never fear, I shall help you.

YAGNAMURTHI

You? How can you help me?

SNAKE

Let me think. *(The Snake lies in front of Yagnamurthi to think)*

YAGNAMURTHI *(To the audience)*
I hope she thinks hard...and saves me from dying tomorrow. Oh dear! I'm so hungry. No meals served in this prison tonight – it's Ekadasi, you know. (*Alternative:* It's the new moon tonight – a very dark night.)

SNAKE *(Rising)*
I know. I've got an idea.

YAGNAMURTHI
What?

SNAKE
I'll bite the princess!

YAGNAMURTHI
Bite the princess?! Poor thing, whatever for? She's to be married tomorrow. You can't bite her. What an idea!

SNAKE
Listen. I'll go and bite her and all the doctors in the kingdom will be called, and no one will be able to cure her. I'll use my special non-curable bite.

YAGNAMURTHI:
Non-curable bite!

SNAKE
Yes. Only you will be able to cure her, because I'll give you a small bite of the same poison.

YAGNAMUTHI:
Me!

SNAKE
Oh, only a little bite.

YAGNAMURTHI
Only a little bite! Certainly not ! You're not biting me!

SNAKE
But don't you see, you'll cure the princess.

YAGNAMURTHI
And who'll cure me?

SNAKE

You'll be all right. I'll only give you a little bite. *(Yagnamurthi grimaces)* And then, you see, you'll be able to cure the princess – just by putting your hands on her.

YAGNAMURTHI

Well, what then?

SNAKE

Don't you see? The King and the Queen – and the Prince – they'll all be so delighted that they'll pardon you. Perhaps give you a reward too.

YAGNAMURTHI

Hmm! *(He thinks)* It's not a bad idea. I suppose you can't do it without biting me, can you?

SNAKE

Oh, dear me, no! You wouldn't be able to cure her, you see. Come now, be brave, it won't hurt – not much.

YAGNAMURTHI

Well...you know...ah! Hmm. All right. *(He offers his arm. The snake bites Yagnamurthi and he yells.)* Oh! That's a little bite, is it?

SNAKE

Yes, just a nip!

YAGNAMURTHI

A nip! *(Nursing his arm)* Now, listen – don't go biting that princess too hard. You know – just enough to put her to sleep for a bit.

SNAKE *(Gliding off)*

Oh yes, I'll just give her a nip...and don't forget all I've told you about curing her. Just lay your hands on her and murmur a prayer... Oh yes, I'll be gentle...I'll just give her a nip...a little nip.

YAGNAMURTHI

That creature doesn't know her own strength. (*He nurses his arm. The Snake glides across the stage. The lights in another part of the stage go up, revealing the princess asleep on a couch. One of her arms dangles over the pure white coverlet. The snake bites her. She screams and sits up in bed, staggers a pace or two and collapses. The snake goes out. The handmaids come running in at the scream.)*

MAID 1

Whatever was that... Oh! (*She sees the princess*) What's happened?

MAID 2

The princess has fainted.

MAID 3

What shall we do?

MAID 2

Bring some water. (*Handmaid 1 brings water and puts some on the princess' face. There is no response.*)

MAID 1

Now what shall we do? Wait a minute, look here! (*She points to the princess' arm*) A snake has bitten her.

(Enter the king and the queen)

KING

What's all this? What was that scream? (*He sees the princess*) Good heavens, my dear daughter. (*He goes to her)* What happened?

HANDMAID 3

We heard a scream and came running in at once. Look, she's been bitten by a snake.

QUEEN

A snake?! Poor girl!

KING

Yes, indeed. And she's to be married tomorrow. Oh dear! Now what shall we do? All the guests have arrived. The kitchen staff –

QUEEN *(Breaking in)*

Don't think of the guests! Think of your daughter. We must get her better.

KING *(To the maids)*

Go at once and inform the minister. He must send out court messengers to scour the country. The best doctors must be brought here at once.

MAIDS

Yes, your Majesty.

KING:

They must get here quickly, before dawn.

MAIDS

Yes, indeed, your majesty. We shall see to it at once. *(They leave)*

KING

My poor, poor girl. I hope she can be cured... I do so hope so ...

SCENE 3

Nati and Sutradhar approach the audience.

SUTRADHAR

Well! You can imagine what confusion reigned in the Palace that night. Doctors were brought from far and near.

NATI

Wait, let's tell them what was happening in the palace.

Nati and Sutradhar act out the crisis scene at the palace.

SUTRADHAR

They tried everything. *(To Nati)* You tell them.

NATI

They tried pills and medicines, spells, incantations, yards and yards of Sanskrit quotations from the medical books, herbs and grasses and lotions and potions and powders and ointments and drugs and physic and aspirins and bottles of queer looking liquids and mixtures of balms and prayers and various waters and powders and patents, pink pills by the dozen and tablets and wafers and packets of soup.

SUTRADHAR

But she would not wake up! The women were crying – the King and Queen were crying – even the wicked Goldsmith was crying! But of course, he wasn't crying out of love for the poor Princess, oh dear me, no!

NATI

He was crying because he thought that somehow or the other, in all the confusion, he might not get his reward. His only interest was the money.

SUTRADHAR

All night long there was a line of doctors at work. They worked right through the night. But it was no use.

NATI

And when morning came, all the guests were standing in the palace courtyard, wondering what was going to happen.

(*A part of the palace, next morning. The guests are assembled, standing in little groups and talking in subdued voices. Suvarnaka and his doctor are also on stage.*)

GUEST 1

I have been informed that the wedding will be put off.

GUEST 2

Yes, the poor princess – bitten by a snake in the middle of the night.

GUEST 3

It must have been a cobra.

GUEST 4

It was at least four feet long.

GUEST 2

At least six feet.

GUEST 1

Last month I saw one eight feet long. It had foreign markings.

GUEST 5

I heard her scream. I woke up with an awful start.

GUEST 6

I heard it too, before you.

GUEST 1

I was the first to be informed by the palace staff.

GUEST 5

What's going to happen now?

GUEST 6

I don't know at all – we've heard nothing.

GUEST 1

Well, what I know for certain is – *(The minister enters, preoccupied)*

GUEST 5

Ah, here's the Minister.

GUEST 6

Minister, good morning. What news of the poor princess?

MINISTER

Very distressing. Bad news, I'm afraid. She hasn't opened her eyes since the snake bit her last night. The doctors are with her now. But they have no remedy. Not one of them seems to be able to cure her.

SUVARNAKA

Excuse me, your Honour, I have a suggestion.

MINISTER

Who are you? Oh, it's the goldsmith. Well, what do you suggest?

SUVARNAKA

I have brought with me a very famous doctor. He has many foreign degrees. I am sure he can cure her.

MINISTER

Does he have good references? Are his fees suitably high?

SUVARNAKA

He replaced both knees of the Prime Minister of a bygone regime. *(The King enters with his retinue. All guests bow.)*

KING

Minister, can nothing be done? She's still alive, but she hasn't opened her eyes for twelve hours.

MINISTER

Your Majesty, the goldsmith here has brought a very famous doctor, renowned throughout the land, and he swears that he can cure her.

KING *(Thinks)*

Well, all right. Let her be carried in, but very carefully. *(To the servants)* Bring the princess here at once. (*To the minister*) There's no harm in trying one more doctor, I suppose. Who suggested this man?

SUVARNAKA

I, your Majesty. It was my idea. *(Presenting the doctor)* Here he is.

KING

Good. Well, if anything... Why, here's the princess now. *(The princess, on a couch, is wheeled in, accompanied by the queen and the handmaids.)* Come, sir, come along. Cure my daughter, I beg of you.

(The doctor, a wild looking comic character, tries diverse tricks to cure the princess, without success.)

KING

It's no use! It's no use! *(Turning on the doctor)* What good are you doctors if you can't cure my only daughter? Oh, heaven prevent this tragedy! I lost my only son three years go, and now to lose my only daughter, too... (*He covers his face with his hands*)

QUEEN

My lord, I'm sure we shall cure her. See, she breaths, but her eyes are shut. I'm sure we shall find someone to cure her. (*Enter the prison guard*)

GUARD

Your majesty.

KING

What do you want? What business have you here?

GUARD

Begging your majesty's pardon, the Brahmin in the palace dungeons desires audience with your majesty. He says he can cure the princess.

KING

The Brahmin?

MINISTER

That criminal!

SUVARNAKA

We can't let him in here! He's a very wicked man! Why, he's going to have his head cut off today. He might do the princess some harm – with spells and magic. He's not a doctor, he knows nothing about medicine at all, he's just an old fool from a village. From South India too. He can't possibly cure her.

MINISTER

Yes, indeed, your majesty. It is very dangerous. And a complete waste of time. I'm sure the goldsmith is right.

KING

Yes, indeed. Guard, go back to –

QUEEN *(Interrupting)*

Stop. Let me speak. All your princes and doctors haven't cured our daughter, so why not let the Brahmin try? He may be a villain, he may be a criminal, he may be going to have his head cut off tomorrow, but as the mother of this poor girl, I beseech you to let him try.

MINISTER

But, my dear lady...

SUVARNAKA

Oh, he's a criminal, a very wicked man indeed, I don't think –

QUEEN *(Imploringly)*

My Lord! I beg of you.

KING

Very well. Let the Brahmin be brought here. (*Exit the guard*) We shall see what he can do.

SUVARNAKA

Your Majesty, I'm very much afraid...

(There is a murmur as Yagnamurthi enters in chains, with a guard on either side.)

YAGNAMURTHI

All honour to your majesty!

KING

Can you cure the princess, Brahmin?

YAGNAMURTHI

I think so, your majesty. I hope so.

KING

Let him approach the princess.

SUVARNAKA *(Coming forward)*

Your majesty, I beg of you – this man is a villain, a tried and convicted criminal, condemned to die. He knows nothing about medicine. He killed your son. Should he now be allowed to kill your daughter too?

KING

Be quiet. We shall see.

YAGNAMURTHI *(To Suvannaka)*

O ungrateful wretch! (*He goes to the princess, stands at her side and joins his hands*)

O sweet spirits of the river and all my friends of the forest, all those that run and creep and crawl and fly, come now to my aid. Cure this young and beautiful maiden, princess of the royal house of Kashi, and make her well and strong again. Come to my aid, I beseech you.

(Yagnamurthi places his hands on the princess. She opens her eyes and sits up.)

QUEEN *(Running to her)*

My daughter! She's cured!

ALL

>> She is well again!

>> She has opened her eyes.

>> The Brahmin has cured her!

(There is general rejoicing. The handmaids and the queen cluster round the princess.)

KING

O Brahmin! You have cured the Princess. (*To the guard*) Let his chains be removed. (*The guard removes the chains*)

YAGNAMURTHI

Many thanks, your majesty.

KING

You shall be released from the palace dungeons straight away – and allowed to go about freely throughout our land.

YAGNAMURTHI

Thank you, your majesty, thank you again and again.

KING

But tell me. You're a strange man. Why did you want to save my daughter when it was you who killed my son?

YAGNAMURTHI

That I never did, your majesty.

KING

You did not kill him?

YAGNAMURTHI

I swear to you I did not.

KING

How then did you get his necklace?

YAGNAMURTHI

I spoke only the truth, your majesty. A tiger gave it to me.

ALL

A tiger!

YAGNAMURTHI

Yes. I was in the forest – and out of kindness I pulled out of a well a tiger, a monkey, a snake, and...that wretch there! (*He points to Suvarnaka*)

KING

Is that true, goldsmith?

SUVARNAKA

I...well...you see...I...er...

KING

The truth!

SUVARNAKA

I... yes... Well... it's true.

YAGNAMURTHI

The monkey helped me, the tiger helped me. The snake helped me too. But that ungrateful man betrayed me to the minister with a pack of lies and had me put in prison, even though I had helped him in the past.

ALL

Ungrateful wretch! Let him die! Off with his head!

SUVARNAKA

Mercy! Mercy!

KING

Down on your knees, goldsmith, and beg pardon of the Brahmin you have wronged.

SUVARNAKA *(Prostrating before Yagnamurthi)*

Pardon, O Brahmin! Pardon!

YAGNAMURTHI

Of course, of course. I don't want anyone to die. I pardon you gladly.

KING

Since the Brahmin desires it you can be spared. But henceforth you are banished from Kashi. Never let your face be seen here again. Go! The Brahmin has saved your life.

SUVARNAKA

Your majesty. (*Creeps away, followed by the doctor*)

KING

And now – the wedding music! Come, let us rejoice.

QUEEN

And the Brahmin's reward?

KING

Ah, yes, indeed. The Brahmin's reward! Bring gifts – gold caskets – clothes – coins – and a chariot to carry them. We shall send them all the way to your village for you.

YAGNAMURTHI *(Now robed in a grand shawl)*

Your majesty, how can I thank you? I shall ever be grateful to your highness. May lifelong happiness be the lot of the happy couple. And now, with your permission, I shall return to my village.

KING

Good bye Brahmin. And may your friends of the forest keep you safe!

YAGNAMURTHI *(Going)*

They will, they will. They are always grateful, you see. They will see me safely home.

ALL

Good bye! Good bye!

(As the Brahmin moves off, the children playing Nati and Sutradhar enter. They have the costumes and props of the roles with them. The Brahmin sits at the corner of the stage.)

NATI

That's the cue, ladies and gentlemen. You must leave the scene now.

SUTRADHAR

The end belongs to us!

(The King's party withdraws from the stage. The children put the costumes and props back into the props basket and then join the Brahmin. They begin the journey back to the Brahmin's village. The tiger, the monkey and the snake join them, and the group marches triumphantly around the stage and exits.)

Close of play

The Magic Drum

From ***The Magic Drum and Other Stories***
by ***Sudha Murty***

FOR
SUDHA MURTY

CHARACTERS IN THE STORIES

The compilation in this volume has the following plays

THE MAGIC DRUM............................*Ramachandra, Rama, Kamesh, His wife, Krishnakant, Dharmashala guests*

THE SEED OF TRUTH...........*Minister 1, Minister 2, King Vidyadhara, Children from the audience, Pingala, his mother*

NINE QUESTIONS..............*Princess Suryaprabha, King, Shashishekhar, Queen, audience members, people in court*

THE WHITE CROW ....*Crow, Umasundari, Shivsundara, Satyabhama, Grandmother, Vimalavati, Minister, Villagers*

THE LAST LADDOO.....................*Dog 1, Dog 2, Devaiah, Devamma, Child, Postman, Neighbours, Milkman*

GOOD LUCK GOPALA........................*Gopala, his wife, Guard, King, Royal Barber, Royal Maid, Visitors to the court*

THE EXPENSIVE COCONUT...............*Chandrakant, Man 1, Man 2, Woman 1, Woman 2, Wife, Coconut seller, Coconut gardener 1, Coconut gardener 2, Elephant and mahout, Horse and rider*

THE EMPEROR OF ALKAVATI................*Sumant, Mithai Shopkeeper, His son, Merchant Kanakchandra, his wife, Horse, Farmer, Old man, Old woman, Grandmother, Granddaughter, Guards, King, Man with elephant*

A Chorus plays many small and linking parts

The following plays are not included in this compilation
- The Horse in the burrow
- The Cunning Fruit
- Magic in the Air
- The Two Thieves
- A Bag of Words

INTRODUCTION

AT THE VERY start of the adaptation project it was clear that the task of selecting a smaller number of stories from Sudha Murty's compilation would be a very difficult one indeed. There were three to four rounds of brainstorming before we zeroed in on fourteen stories to adopt and adapt. The two most important criteria employed for the choice were

- breadth in nature of stories
- suitability for action, rather than a reliance on text alone.

The second difficulty was an equally formidable one. There was no way all fourteen stories could be performed in the same show. A practical set would be seven to nine stories making up a performance of about ninety minutes at a stretch. An intermission would not be desirable for a production of this kind. It was then that the idea of a flexible mix-and-match design emerged. Why not have actors perform different combinations of stories at each performance? The logical extension of this idea was to get the audience to choose the stories for the evening! This idea is incorporated into the script, as will be seen in the following pages. Yet, it appeared important for the actors to have *some* control over the performance – especially in the first and last stories. This was to be accomplished with a bit of ingenuity, striking a balance between audience participation and actor discretion.

Although the adaptation project prepared fourteen scripts from the stories for performance on stage, this volume is presenting only eight of those scripts – the most popular ones from the set. Other stories to be included in other combinations are available on request.

It was recognised early that a high level of audience participation would be a key ingredient in the performance, recreating a storytelling tradition. Numerous devices were incorporated into the script (and the performance) to accomplish this. One of them was involvement of the audience in folk dancing well before the third bell, dissolving the actor-audience divide. Not surprisingly a large number took part at each show, eagerly learning the steps from the actors. Those who did not join (or could not, on account of the limited space) clapped and cheered lustily to the mesmerising rhythm of the drum.

The drum! It was a key feature of the production design. The distinct presence of a *djembe* on stage was like a storyteller itself. The accomplished drummer provided the start to the performance in the folk dance, he signalled the ends and beginnings of stories, he lent a voice to the narration in places and took the audience along all the time. It was, after all... a magical drum.

Finally, the adaptation introduced a Chorus to serve as narrators and provide links from story to story. More important, in keeping with the tradition set in BLT's Children's Theatre productions, the Chorus was a group of children – occasionally a mix of children and grown-up actors. The audience invariably found the presence of children-narrators captivating. How it enriched the rehearsal atmosphere was another story altogether – quite beyond description.

A word about casting and rehearsals. The only way to play all the characters in all the stories, maintaining flexibility in the set to be played at any time, would be by an ensemble approach – every actor prepared to play several parts, and every part to be played by more than one actor. What this does to a rehearsal schedule cannot be imagined until all are actually on the floor. Exhausting, but exhilarating.

Some guidelines for a performing group attempting the story sets should be useful.

A set of eight stories (including the opener *The Magic Drum*) is likely to take about 90 minutes to perform. That is indeed the specimen set given here. A set of six stories has also been performed in 60-65 minutes in BLT's Courtyard Theatre programme.

Courtyard Theatre works with a two-actor format. The objective of the programme is to reach a variety of audiences in a variety of spaces, rather than having audiences come to an auditorium. There are different types of material brought into the performances. For instance:

- From past successful productions of BLT – deserving a wider audience reach.

- Play scripts other than those from BLT productions.
- Converting short stories into Storytelling Theatre format – mostly from available anthologies. (Eg. short stories, folk tales.)
- There could also be fresh writing from within BLT.

There are currently seven Courtyard Theatre packages. *The Magic Drum* was one of the first productions to be converted into a Courtyard Theatre format! The name of the programme is inspired by the Courtyard in Thakurbadi, Tagore's ancestral home in old Calcutta.

Another programme thrust of BLT is aimed at education enrichment in schools through the theatre. A writing project in that programme gathered folk tales from all over India and converted twenty of them into play scripts that can be brought into the classroom. Many folk tales are rooted in the natural environment and, not surprisingly, are universal in character in having an undercurrent ecological wisdom. We found echoes of several stories in the Sudha Murty collection in tales from other lands. For instance, the play included here called *The Seed of Truth* can be heard in Nepal, Thailand, Cambodia and Laos!

We are very grateful to Sudha Murty for her ready consent for the stage adaptations. She joined us at the opening show. A while later she asked to be allowed to watch another show!

Adapted for the stage by Aliyeh Rizvi, Deepthy Sekhar, Vijay Padaki with the permission of Sudha Murty

FIRST PERFORMED

By Bangalore Little Theatre at Ranga Shankara, Bangalore, September 16-21, 2008.

As explained in the introduction to the play, the performances were with two ensembles teams taking turns on stage over the large number of shows. Members of the ensemble played several parts across the stories presented in each show.

Actors in Ensemble 1........................DEEPTI AGRAWAL, POORNIMA, AHMED SHEIKH, AMJAD PRAWEJ, ANAND RAMPRASAD, NAVEEN KUMAR, SHAMBHAVI RAJAN, SHASHANK PURUSHOTHAM, SHREE LAKSHMI RAO, SUNITHA RAJAGOPALAN, VISHAL JAIN, FIRAZ PEER

Actors in Ensemble 2...........ADIT ABRAHAM, AANCHAL SODHANI, KSHEMA SHIVAKUMAR, T RAGHAVENDRA, VIPUL SRIVASTAVA, NAVEEN MUDUNURU, SABAREESH PILLAI, REAGAN RODRIGUES, MONICA PILLAI, ATUL CHANDRA, MURTUZA KHETTY, RAMYA RAMASWAMY, VIJAYALAKSHMI CHARI, SRIDHAR RAMANATHAN, RAVI SRINIVASAN, SHILPA GAUTAM

Off stage

Sets and Property......................AANCHALSODHANI, VISHAL JAIN, SARVESH KHEMKA, MALTESH BADIGERA VIJAY PADAKI

Costumes..........................DIVYA JAIN, ALIYEH RIZVI, PRIYA RAO

Sound..ANAND RAMPRASAD

Make up.................PRIYA VENKATESH, VIJAYALAKSHMI CHARI, RAHEEM DAREDIYA, SOWMYA NARAYANAN, GUNJAN SARAF, DEEPTHY SEKHAR

Lights.................PRITHAM KUMAR AND HIS WORKSHOP TEAM

Percussion....................................GANESHAN GOVINDASWAMY

Script adaptation...............ALIYEH RIZVI AND DEEPTHY SEKHAR

Production coordinator...VIJAY PADAKI

Designed and directed by....................................DEEPTHY SEKHAR AND VIJAY PADAKI

PRELUDE

The second bell has gone. The audience is entering the auditorium and settling down. The drummer enters and takes his place DR. A group of wandering storytellers enters, placing props in the down-left and down-right corners of the stage. Some start setting up the stage. Some others start singing, striking a folk dance beat. The whole group starts a Raas dance. The audience is invited to join, and they are taught the dance steps.

At the third bell, the dancers from the audience are ushered back to their seats. The actors leave the stage. All quiet onstage. The lights dim. It is night.

THE MAGIC DRUM

The stage is dimly lit. There is the sound of something heavy being moved on to the stage. Against the cyclorama we see the silhouette of a man and a woman rolling a huge drum across the stage. They are tired and stop for breath.

WOMAN

Ramachandra, I am so happy we have come this far.

MAN

But there is a long way more to go. The palace of the minister is very far away.

WOMAN

Yes it is, but I am sure we can get there very soon. Don't worry, we will have justice. Remember what the minister said...

MAN

I do, I do. He said this is no ordinary drum. He said that it beats by itself when one speaks the truth. That is what we have done. Still, no sound from the drum. Not a single beat to save the day! *(He taps the drum from different sides)*

WOMAN

Now, now , don't lose patience...there is magic in the air. Things will turn around for us. I am sure of that.

(The man and woman step down. They are Ramachandra and Rama. The man regards the drum upstage with impatience.)

RAMACHANDRA

I am tired. *(There is a beat from the drum. Both are startled.)*

RAMA

I am tired too.

(The drum beats by itself again.)

RAMACHANDRA *(Testing)*

I am a cow! *(There is no beat from the drum.)*

RAMA

That was not the truth! Let me try now... I make wonderful chakkalis. *(The drum beats by itself again.)*

RAMACHANDRA

You are right, Rama. I think this is working. Let us tell the drum our story.

(Fade out. A dim light appears down-left to show the entrance of a dharamshala-inn. The innkeeper, Kamesh, and his wife are letting in travellers for a night's rest. Some are already asleep on the floor. Ramachandra reaches the entrance.)

KAMESH

That will be two annas per head. You can pay in the morning. Here, take this lantern. Sleep by the window there.

(Ramachandra walks past the others on the floor to the down-right corner, holding the lantern. A sleeping figure rebukes him: 'Light band kar yaar...kya batti jalata hai....'

Ramachandra sits down clutching a bag. Rama joins him.)

RAMACHANDRA

Oh Rama, I was waiting for you. Look, the nice man has given us beds near a window.

RAMA

God bless him! You know Ramachandra, I can't believe we have managed to come all this way to Kashi in North India. It has taken us a long time, but I am glad we have reached here. At last! I hear that the temple of Lord Vishwanatha is just a mile or two away.

RAMACHANDRA

It was not easy. It took us such a long time to save money for this trip. A whole lifetime of savings. Thanks to that we are able to realise this life-long dream.

RAMA

But I must tell you Ramachandra, we need to be very careful with our money. Everybody at home told me there would be many thieves on the way. We must be very careful with our belongings. Especially the money pouch. Where is the money pouch, now? *(Ramachandra pats his pouch to assure her that the money is safe.)*

So when Kamesh – you know, the kind owner of this dharamshala – when he asked us to freshen up for dinner and leave it with him, I refused. I sat with it till you had your bath. I didn't move an inch.

RAMACHANDRA

And I sat with it while you had yours. But he is the owner of the dharamshala. Where can he go with it?

RAMA *(Lying down)*

You can never trust anyone these days. Now, use the pouch as a pillow, so no one can take it away from you.

(They go to sleep. It is dark. We see the two shadowy figures of Kamesh and his wife approach the couple and take the pouch from under Ramachandra's head, replacing it with a small pillow of the same size. They tiptoe out. The lights brighten to a dawn.

Ramachandra wakes up and reaches for the pouch. He finds the replacement pillow.)

RAMACHANDRA *(Frantically)*

Pillow?? Where did this pillow come from? The money pouch... it is gone! What will we do now?

RAMA

What?! Where could it...How will we collect that much money again?

RAMACHANDRA

How will we even go back home? *(Weeps)* We have nothing... Aiyyo Mahadeva!

RAMA

Do you think we should ask Kamesh about it?

RAMACHANDRA

You wait here. I will go and talk to him.

(Kamesh and his wife appear down-left at the entrance.)

KAMESH *(Boasting)*

Oh, it was so easy to steal the money pouch! *Buss aise*, and then *vaise* – I just put my hand under the pillow, and out it came.

WIFE

Arreyji, you are just number one at this. Wah, just too good! You are the most cunning man I have ever seen!

(*Ramachandra appears. She sees him)*

Oh, the *bakra* is here!

RAMACHANDRA

Namaskar. I... have come to tell you that our money pouch got robbed last night in your dharamshala.

KAMESH

Kya? Kya bol rahe hain? (To his wife) I don't understand what this man is saying.

RAMACHANDRA

We think our... (*thinks of the word*) *paisa*...it has got...*chori*...in your dharamshala. Can you please help us find...the thief...at least find the money?

KAMESH

Stolen? In my dharamshala? *Bakwaas*! I don't know anything about your bag. You are old, you must be forgetful. You must have dropped it somewhere. This is an honest place here, for honest people.

RAMACHANDRA *(Bewildered)*

I am sure we had it with us last night. I kept the pouch under my head as a pillow when I lay down. Someone must have come in while we were asleep!

WIFE

Oji, in all our years here, we have seen nothing ever stolen or disappear like that. Do you have any money left at all? *(Ramachandra shakes his head)* Then you will not be able to even pay the dharamshala charges, right? Maybe you should find some other lodging. The free boarding houses, of course, and then think about what to do next.

KAMESH *(Smiling)*

I feel very sorry for you, but we really don't know anything about this, we don't know what to say. Besides, there is a great demand for sleeping mats in the dharamshala just now. So if you don't mind...

RAMACHANDRA

Oh, all right. Yes, yes, we will leave right away.

(Ramachandra and Rama are back in the down-right area and preparing to leave. Nandakishore, a man at the dharamshala on a pilgrimage, has been watching them. He approaches the couple.)

NANDAKISHORE

Wait! My pranam. I am Nandakishore. I am on a pilgrimage too. I could not help overhearing your talk with Kamesh and his wife just now. Something is not quite right here. I think you should seek justice. Why don't you go to the city where Krishnakant lives? He is the King's counselor. He is very wise and highly respected for the way he dispenses justice. He will surely help you. Let me take you to him. I am going the same way.

(The three of them exit.

Music: We hear a group chanting and then entering from both sides.)

CHORUS

Oh Krishnakant, hey Krishnakant, wise Krishnakant, clever Krishnakant!

We need you, Krishnakant, we need you, Krishnakant!
They are coming Krishnakant, they are old Krishnakant!
They're cheated, Krishnakant, do justice, Krishnakant!
We need you, Krishnakant! Are you ready Krishnakant?
Are you ready Krishnakant? Are you ready Krishnakant?!

(A roll on the drum as the stage blacks out. A moment later the stage is brightly lit as the drum reaches a crescendo. Krishnakant is standing UC with the group before him on two sides. Rama and Ramachandra are on one side, and Kamesh and his wife on the other.)

KRISHNAKANT

I have heard your story. I think I may be able to help you. I have in my house a drum. A large drum with magical properties. It is a very old drum, and has seen much life. If you tell the truth before the drum, it starts beating by itself.

(To the couple) Rama and Ramachandra, come here tomorrow and roll the drum to the court. On the way, tell the drum your story.

(To Kamesh and his wife) And you, Kamesh, you and your wife will roll the drum back in the afternoon. I will see how the drum behaves and then give you my verdict.

(Krishnakant exits. The group follows him out chanting 'Oh Krishnakant...'

Ramachandra enters, pushing the drum with some difficulty. The scene returns to the start of the story, with Rama and Ramachandra at the drum, against the cyclorama.)

RAMACHANDRA

I was so careful with the money pouch. Someone really must have taken it while we were asleep.

RAMA

And that is our story, oh great drum!

(There is loud beating from the drum.)

RAMACHANDRA

Aiyyo, listen! The drum is beating by itself! We may have no witnesses, but God knows we are speaking the truth. *(With renewed energy, to Rama)*

Come, let us complete the task of taking the drum to the palace.

RAMA

Oh, the drum is so light now! God must have heard us and made our load lighter.Look, there is the palace, and I see Kamesh and his wife waiting for us.

(They exit pushing the drum. Kamesh and his wife enter soon after, pushing the drum back onstage.)

WIFE

Arrey, *suntey ho*! Let us stop and rest for a while. This drum is so heavy! I don't know why we have to push it on this hot day. It is all your fault. *(They step down and argue)*

Why did you have to steal that money pouch? Now look at the mess we are in! Pushing a drum in this heat! That too in my new dress!

KAMESH

My fault? You are a smart one to talk! Who peeped in while they hid the money? Who showed me where the pouch was kept? Who tiptoed with me up to the sleeping couple?

WIFE

Hanh hanh, your hands are always clean and white!

KAMESH

Anyway, do you really believe this is a magical drum? I think it is some sort of prank. A big lie! *(Krishnakant jumps out of the drum and confronts Kamesh and his wife.)*

KRISHNAKANT

Aha! I have heard every word you said, thank you. And also what Rama and Ramachandra said just before. So, that's that! You will return the stolen money immediately, and also pay three times the amount as penalty! Wait here!

(Krishnakant claps. Rama and Ramachandra enter, along with the Chorus. They are on two sides of Krishnakant as before. Kamesh, in fright, gives Ramachandra a bag of money.)

KRISHNAKANT *(To the old couple)*

Rama and Ramachandra, complete your pilgrimage in peace, and return home safely.

(To Kamesh) As for you, don't you dare cheat anyone again, or I will have you thrown out of the kingdom!

(Kamesh and his wife slink away. The Chorus accompanies Rama and Ramachandra out, chanting 'Oh Krishnakant...' A drum roll to signify the end of the story.

Krishnakantclaps. A child member of the Chorus enters with a smaller drum. Krishnakant takes the drum and addresses the audience.)

KRISHNAKANT

In this drum are many more stories. A great collection of stories.

CHORUS MEMBER

Tales of horses and cows and goats and bananas and jackfruits and laddoos, and kings and queens and ministers and princes and princesses and clever boys and clever girls and good boys and good girls and greedy merchants and mean shop keepers and old men and old women and adventure and magic and journeys to far off lands. This drum has seen many things. It wants to tell you the stories today. Would you like to hear them?

KRISHNAKANT *(Louder)*

Would you like to hear them?? *(Krishnakant and the Chorus member get the audience to respond: YES!!*

An Actor has entered)

ACTOR

Arrey-oji! Your story is told, you are done for the evening! Time to go backstage and pack up now, and not be loitering here! We have no more to do here.

KRISHNAKANT

We do! There are lots and lots of stories in the world, and not enough people to tell them. Not just that, there aren't enough people to listen to them! Now, look out there. What do you see? We have an audience! All we have to do is pull out more stories for them.

ACTOR

Pull out stories? Just like that? From the air!

KRISHNAKANT

As long as you have this drum, you will have stories. *(He beats the drum)*

Here, take this.

ACTOR

But what do I do with it?

KRISHNAKANT

It is a magic drum. Didn't you see the story performed just now? *(The Actor is confused)* Leave it to the drum!

(He smiles and exits, rolling out the big drum upstage.)

ACTOR

So now...What do we do next? I don't know any stories.

(A drum beat. The Actor jumps.) Huh?

(Puts his ear to the drum) Oh my, oh my, this really is a magic drum! It is trying to tell us something! What...Yes...Hmmm...I

agree...What did you say? Oh...you have a hundred stories and want me to tell them? *(Looks around, goes to the audience)* But I don't know any of those stories. What? Beat the drum, you say?

(Drumbeats. The group of actors enters, joined by the Chorus. Circus atmosphere. A vigorous dance, cartwheels, juggling, noisemakers, etc. The actors function as a Chorus and share the lines below.)

ACTOR
Who are you ?

CHORUS
>> We are storytellers.
>> We travel, we sing, we dance.
>> We tell magical stories to whoever wants to hear them.
>> But we are out of work currently.
>> Not too many children listening to stories these days, you see.
>> Tuitions, karate class, tennis, art class, medals, prizes.
>> Yoga lessons, swimming lessons, Homework, prizes, prizes.
>> TV shows, X-boxes, play stations
>> Winning, winning, winning!.

ALL
Who has the time?!

ACTOR
To sit down and listen to a story! So, why are you here?

CHORUS
>> The drum called us. *(Drum beat)*
>> No, the audience called us.
>> Because no one tells them stories anymore.
>> The story will soon die.

ALL
We don't want it to die!

CHORUS
>> It will stay alive as long we have someone wanting stories.
>> And we have someone to tell stories.
>> And as long as they keep listening.
>> And asking for more.

ACTOR

So what do we do? *(To the audience)*

Should we tell more stories to keep them alive?

(The actor gets the audience to respond) YES!!

CHORUS

There is a magic chant. A mantra.

ACTOR

A what?

CHILD CHORUS MEMBER

Never heard of a Gayatri mantra?

(Whispers it into the Actor's ear and hands him one end of a rolled up banner)

They have to say it out loud.

ACTOR

The magic chant is...

(Unfurls the banner with the Chorus member: 'Tell me a story!')

All right, then, let's hear it out there...

(Reverses the banner: 'Louder')

Louder...Even louder.

(The audience chants out loud: 'Tell me a story... Tell me a story...!' The drum beats appear again.)

CHORUS

The drum is getting impatient. It's time to begin.

(Krishnakant enters with a basket which has a large number of identical-sized packets wrapped in bright colours. It also has the book by Sudha Murty.)

KRISHNAKANT

I told you! There are lots and lots and lots of stories waiting to be told.

ACTOR

Where do we go looking for them?

KRISHNAKANT

Look, this book alone has over thirty stories.

ACTOR

(Picking up the book) Hmmm... The Magic Drum and other favourite stories. Written by someone by the name of Sudha Murty. Who is that?

(Krishnakant gives the Actor a hard glare. The actor continues.)

Well, all right, so we have a basket of stories. Let's put them into this drum, shall we? Now... which stories should we listen to this evening? *(Or morning / afternoon)*

(To children in the audience) Would you like to choose the stories yourself? You would? Why not? Let's make it a lucky dip.

(The actor and Krishnakant ask children from the audience how many stories they should perform. With some bargaining they arrive at the number to be performed in the show. They move into the audience and get the children to come forward, pick packets from the basket and fill the drum with the agreed number of packets.)

Right! Here we go now! Go ahead and pick the stories for this show.

(Krishnakant and the actor get the children to pick packets from the drum. The packets are then opened at the foot of the stage.)

All right...let's see what we have here... Aha! We have... This must be a story about a... And this one? Oho, we have here a...

(And so on. The packets are opened one by one and the contents named and shown to all in the audience. The object in each packet represents the content or theme for a story. Krishnakant and the actor then talk to each other and decide the sequence in which the stories will be told, keeping the objects from the packets in that order at the foot of the stage. The Drum is placed at the down-right corner, before the drummer. Each story announced hereafter has its packet put into the drum.

A burst of drum beats again from the percussionist. Meanwhile, the Actor has become King Vidhyadhara for the play ***The Seed of Truth****.*

The Chorus advances cautiously to the objects placed at the foot of the stage. One of them picks one up, it is a small packet [or bag or bottle] of seeds.)

Link to: The Seed of Truth

CHORUS

>> What's this? What's this
>> Ooh... it's a packet of seeds.
>> Do we have a story about a packet of seeds?
>> Oh no! Not another one with an environment message!
>> A politically correct story with a moral!
>> A prize for the best essay in the end!
>> Prizes, prizes, prizes...

ACTOR

I think this story is different. It is about –

ALL

>> Stop! Don't tell them what it's all about!
>> It will come, it will come.
>> Enough to say that there is a boy in the story called Pingala.
>> And a King. His name is Vidyadhara

(A member of the Chorus places the packet with the seeds into the Drum, while another places a potted plant DC to represent the King's garden.)

CHORUS

>> Oh, here is King Vidhyadhara.
>> He seems very busy in his garden...

(Two members of the Chorus become Ministers. THE SEED OF TRUTH begins)

THE SEED OF TRUTH

MINISTER 1

There is no doubt that His Majesty, King Vidhyadhara, is the greatest ruler of Gandhara. He is just and good and believes we must all uphold the truth.

MINISTER 2

Yes. There is peace in the kingdom. The people are prosperous and happy. There is just one problem, though.

MINISTER 1

And what is that?

MINISTER 2

He does not have any children... So who will rule the kingdom after him? Will we get another just and good king like him? How do we know who is fit to be king?

KING *(Rising)*

Do not fear, Ministers. I will let nature take its course. I have a simple test in mind, and I will use my love of plants and flowers and trees to demonstrate it to you. There are great lessons to be learnt from nature. Only someone who understands this as well as I do will be king.

MINISTERS

What lessons, Oh King?

KING

A little seed grows to a mighty tree if you take care of it lovingly... *(The percussion strikes a rap beat...)*

Ta-tut-a-taa-tut-a-taa-tut-a-taa-ta-taa

Ta-tut-a-taa-tut-a-taa-tut-a-daa-daa-daa

(As the King starts on the rap below the Chorus and the rest of the cast appear at the wings on both sides, peeping in.)

KING

Uhunh...

A little seed grows to a mighty tree,
If you take care of it lovingly.
The same goes for people, that is true.
It works for everyone, me and you.

A seed takes time to become a tree,
So we learn to be patient, don't you see?
We learn to nurture, we learn to care,
About our beautiful world out there.

(The Chorus and cast chant the beat...)
Ta-tut-a-taa-tut-a-taa-tut-a-taa-ta-taa
Ta-tut-a-taa-tut-a-taa-tut-a-daa-daa-daa

KING

We learn that hard work always bears fruit.
No short cuts, no easy route.
When things grow too quickly they're really not strong.
They die too easily, before too long.

Plants have no religion, no caste or state,
No language, no border, they don't know hate.
Does a flower ever bloom for only a few?
Would a tree deny its fruit to you?

(The Chorus and cast strike the beat...)
Ta-tut-a-taa-tut-a-taa-tut-a-taa-ta-taa
Ta-tut-a-taa-tut-a-taa-tut-a-daa-daa-daa

KING

Big plants don't kill little plants for space
Each is happy to prosper in its own special place.
Plants give us plenty, they're life giving too.
The only selfish thing on this planet is...? YOU!
(He pauses, then speaks)
There is place on this earth for every little thing.
Only someone who knows that is fit to be king!

CHORUS AND OTHERS

Aaahh...
They exit with the King.

MINISTER 1

Very well then, let us announce it.

MINISTER 2

Suno! Suno! Suno! King Vidhyadhara of Gandhara has announced he will choose an heir to the throne. But he has one condition. The one who grows the biggest and healthiest plant within three months will become the prince or the princess. Here are some seeds. All children in this kingdom who are interested will get one each.

(The two Ministers distribute seeds from a bowl to children in the audience.)

Who would like a seed to plant? You? Who else? Here, take one, you take one....

(And so on. Meanwhile, two others from the Chorus distribute some pots to the same children with small plants in them. The Ministers and the Chorus members return to the stage and take positions.)

CHORUS

Time goes by.

Tick tock. Tick tock. Tick tock. Tick tock. Tick tock. Tick tock. Tick tock. Tick tock.

MINISTER 1 *(To the audience)*

Attention! Attention! The three months are now over. All the children with plants in their pots are requested to please come up to the palace gate. The King wishes to inspect the plants.

(The children with pots are guided to the down-left area. The King looks into the pots one by one. He is not happy. He sends them back to their seats with a kind gesture.)

CHORUS

>> Prizes, prizes, prizes!

>> Winning, winning, winning!

(The King spots Pingala, who is holding an empty pot.)

KING

Why is your pot empty, boy? Everyone else has beautiful flowers blooming in their pots. What happened?

MOTHER

This is my son, Pingala, your highness. He is very fond of gardening and he tried very hard to grow a plant. He took the seed home lovingly, planted it with care, gave it water and manure... the plant did not appear. Then he changed the soil and put the seed in another pot.

PINGALA

But there was still no plant.

MOTHER

He did not want to meet you, your highness, because he had nothing to show. But I brought him anyway. Just so you would know that he tried his best.

PINGALA *(Sadly)*

Me, your highness, I tried my best. I really did. I gave it the best soil and manure I had, but the plant just would not grow.

KING *(Smiles and announces in joy)*

Ministers! I have found him! This is the boy who will be king after me!

MINISTER 1

But your Majesty... he did not grow anything!

MINISTER 2

His pot is empty!

KING

Yes! That is why I have chosen him. They were roasted seeds. They would not have grown anyway! I wanted to see which child would tell the truth, and only this boy did! I now know he will rule this kingdom one day with the same honesty! *(Pingala's mother is astonished. The King embraces Pingala and leads him away.)*

CHORUS

>>Well done, boy!

>>Let your education as a prince begin!

>>Away to the palace you go!

KING

Come along, my boy! The best tutors in the land have a worthy pupil now. Pingala has become a prince today! *(He ushers Pingala away)*

Percussion and fade out to end the story.
Link to: Nine Questions for a Princess

CHORUS
And now... another story from another royal household. This time, a princess!
(An actor in a princess' costume rushes in)

ACTRESS
Arrey arrey, wait! Where are my glasses? You can't start now. I must have my glasses.

KING
Excuse me! You are an intruder in my garden.

ACTRESS
My glasses!

KING *(Lowering her glasses from her head to her nose)*
Your glasses are here...but you are not supposed to be here.

ACTRESS
I am too, according to the script. And so are you. By the way, this is not your garden anymore. It is the royal chamber.

KING
What?! What do you mean not my garden anymore? And why must I be here with you?

ACTRESS
We must be on stage together. The next story has another King in it – you! And a princess too. *(Smiling)* A clever and beautiful princess!

KING
Me... another king...but I haven't rehearsed for any other King. Which King? King who? What about his costume?

ACTRESS
Oh, never mind! Just carry on with what you are wearing now!

KING
Ohhh! *(To audience)* Don't blame me if I don't make a second good King. I have not rehearsed for this part. They're always

springing surprises on me. Surprises, surprises! One day I will quit this drama company and join TV! Then they will know how to treat their actors.

ACTRESS

All right, all right, Let's get on with it. Here's what happens. I will go off stage and come running back in shouting 'No father!' We take it from there.

KING

I don't understand. Take what from where? What do I do when you shout 'No Father'?

ACTRESS

Ohho! Just do what every father does! *(She rushes off stage)*

NINE QUESTIONS FOR A PRINCESS

A member of the Chorus picks up a packet from the foot of the stage and announces the story: NINE QUESTIONS FOR A PRINCESS. The packet is dropped into the Drum.

CHORUS

>> And so... another story from another royal household
>> A story about a princess, a very clever princess!
>> Princess Suryaprabha
>> A very clever princess called Suryaprabha!

(Half singing, to a beat)
Rajkumari, badi sayani.
Raja ki baat ek na mani.
Sundar thi, padhi-likhi bhi!
Degree-vigri, foreign ki bhi
(Spoken)
Boli shaadi? Aur ek budhu rajkumar se?

ALL

Kabhi nahin, kabhi nahin, kabhi nahin!!

PRABHA *(Offstage)*

Noooo father!

(Rushing in, the King following) No, father! Please! Not another stupid prince again! I refuse to marry someone who has nothing inside his head! I just want a man who is clever! Is there none to be found in all of this land in this age?

PRABHA *(She sings)*

I want a man intelligent and learned Not looks, not wealth, not a palace He can be black, white, wheatish or brown bread. Only in brains do I find real solace.

KING

And how will you find such a man, my darling girl? Intelligent men are not seen in this kingdom, so I suppose they must be in short supply elsewhere as well.

PRABHA

I have decided! Let any man ask me nine questions. If I am unable to answer even one of them, I will marry him!

KING *(Worried)*

And if you answer all the questions?

PRABHA

Then he will be rejected and not get another chance!

(Suryaprabha storms off to a seat down-right. The Queen enters and stands behind her. The King is stupefied.)

KING

Oh dear, oh dear, oh dear, dear, dear!
Do all fathers go through this? They tell me they do!
If there's a father in the audience, my sympathies are with you!
(The King joins the Queen behind Suryaprabha.)

CHORUS

Suno! Suno! Suno! (A drum roll)
Aaj ka mega offer!
Tho nau savaal puchhen! Rajkumari ka dil jeeten!
Aur ban jaiyen Raj Kumar ek jhatke mein! (Drum roll)
Agar aap paanchvi pass se behter hain

(The cast and chorus form a pipeline of suitors from the DL wing approaching the Princess, who rejects each one contemptuously. The King and Queen look on helplessly. A voice at the wing announces each suitor)

Suitor number 11!
Suitor number 45!
Suitor number 101!
Suitor number 420!
(And so on)

CHORUS

But the princess was very clever. She answered each one's question in no time. The king was most worried.

KING *(To Queen)*

I am most worried, my dear. This looks like the end.

Our daughter is too smart, I fear. Who else can we send?
Heads held high they come to meet
In a flash they admit defeat.

PRABHA *(Rises and screams)*
This one has dependency issues, father! And that one...wants to marry someone like his mother, he says. And that other one, he needs a course in anger management, it seems! And the one before... Ohhh! Where is a husband for me!

CHORUS
Where, oh where, is a husband for her?

PRABHA *(Singing)*
Oh, where, oh where is a husband for me ?
Someone to talk to intelligently?
A man who is clever, and equally smart
Is the one who is sure to win my heart.
(She wails)
Don't want no flowers, botany works for me
Who cares for love? I want chemistry.
No sweet words, no small talk, just philosophy,
He should readily discuss bibliography.

CHORUS
If you're too clever you scare him away,
And if you dumb it down, he won't stay anyway.

PRABHA
Intelligent, intellectual? Verbal? Cerebral, mental? Analytical?

CHORUS
Debatable! Inconceivable!! Totally Impossible!!!

PRABHA *(Singing)*
Oh, it's so hard to be a clever girl
Wanting a modern man in my old-fashioned world!

KING *(To Queen)*
If we go on like this, I fear our daughter will never marry! Will she ever find an equal? I fear not.

CHORUS

>> The King was losing hope.
>> He consulted his court philosopher
>> Who decided to send his brightest student to meet the princess.
>> His name was Shashi Shekar.

ALL

Shashi Shekhar! Shashi Shekhar hazir Ho!!

ACTOR 1

And so, the next day, they gathered again.
(Drum roll. A simply dressed, handsome young man walks in.)

SHEKHAR

I have many questions for the princess Suryaprabha. I will ask nine. *(The King points him in her direction. He approaches her.)*
May I ask them of you? *(The princess signals that he may)*
How many stars are there in the sky?

PRABHA *(Disdainful)*

Oh, there are as many stars as there are hair on a goat.

SHEKHAR

Which is the most beautiful child on earth?

PRABHA *(Confidently)*

For every mother, her own child is the most beautiful.

SHEKHAR

What is the difference between truth and lies?

PRABHA *(Thinks)*

It is the difference between our eyes and ears. Our eyes will always see the truth, but our ears can hear both truth and lies. *(The reactions of the audience in the court are building up in enthusiasm.)*

SHEKHAR

Which person has hands, and is yet considered handless?

PRABHA

A rich man who does not share his wealth.

SHEKHAR

Who has eyes, but is still blind?

PRABHA

A man without compassion, who does not see the suffering that exists in this world.

(Shashi Shekhar pauses, and takes out a picture in a scroll.)

SHEKHAR

Fair princess, may I ask what you see in this picture I hold before you?

PRABHA

What you see may be an old palace that is crumbling. *(Dropping the picture on the ground)* But this is a picture of the weakness of Man. Without a proper foundation, even a palace will crumble and fall.

SHEKHAR *(Kneeling to pick up the picture)*

Very well answered indeed. You are as clever as you are beautiful. The stories I have heard about you are most definitely true. *(Taking out another picture)*

Now, what do you see in this picture? Take a good look.

PRABHA *(Aside)*

This man is different...

What you see is an old woman with a head load of firewood picking up more twigs. What it really shows is human greed – not ever having enough.

KING *(To Queen)*

It is not working! That was the seventh question. She is too clever for him.

QUEEN *(Smiles knowingly)*

Have patience, my lord. There are two more questions.

(There is tension in the air. The court is eager. Suryaprabha is confident. Shashi Shekhar is deep in thought.)

PRABHA

Are you ready with your eighth question, sir?

SHEKHAR

I believe I am.

PRABHA

Then do not hesitate. Ask the question.

SHEKHAR

Princess, tell me...which is the one question you cannot answer?

(Suryaprabha is taken aback. She realises the implication of the question. She speaks to the audience.)

PRABHA

Ohh! If I answer truthfully, he will give me that as his ninth question. And if I don't...

KING *(Overjoyed)*

He has outwitted you, my darling daughter!

PRABHA

Yes, father. He was a worthy opponent. *(Turning to Shashi Shekhar)*

I have met my match!

(The King and Queen are delighted. Garlands are brought in on a tray. Suryaprabha and Shashi Shekar garland each other and then proceed to bow before the King and Queen for their blessings. Through this the Chorus chants and the others in court sing alternately.)

CHORUS

Rejoice! Rejoice! Rejoice!
He's a clever man indeed! It's the brain that did succeed!

COURT

Sita kalyanam vaibhavamey!
Rama kalyanam vaibhavamey!

CHORUS

Rejoice! Rejoice! Rejoice!
She's met her match, she's made her choice!
Rejoice! Rejoice! Rejoice!

COURT

Surya Prabha kalyanam vaibhavamey!
Shashi Shekhar kalyanam vaibhavamey!

Percussion and fade out to end the story.
Link to: The White Crow

(The Chorus sets up the stage, comprising two identically sized step ladders, one down-left and the other down-right. They speak as they set up.)

CHORUS
>> The next story has a crow in it.
>> In fact it is the central character in the story.
>> The story is called The White Crow.
>> In fact the crow wishes to tell the story itself.
(The packet for the story is dropped into the Drum. Meanwhile an actor has entered, flitting on to the stage and perching on the step ladder down-left.)
>> Here is the storyteller now. The crow.
>> In fact it is just an ordinary black crow.

THE WHITE CROW

NARRATOR

Now, now, now, I must tell you this story. For it is a story I must tell.

It is about a well-guarded secret of Shiva Sundara, a wise man.

There is a black crow – no, white crow – and Shiva Sundara's wife, Uma Sundari!

Poor Shiva Sundara. Although wise, he was a mild mannered man, never knowing how to deal with those who were mannered otherwise. *(Shiva Sundara is standing with another man below the second step ladder down-right.)*

MAN *(Pointing to an imagined building)*

And this is the old out-house you want knocked down.

SHIVA

Yes.

MAN

And the ground levelled, so you can grow a garden here.

SHIVA

That is right. And that will be...?

MAN

That will be two thousand one hundred and eleven rupees to knock down the old out-house.

SHIVA

Two thousand one...

MAN

And four hundred thirty two more to clear the ground later.

(The man walks away briskly. Shiva Sundara sits at the foot of the out house.)

NARRATOR

So here we are. Poor Shiva Sundara. We must meet his wife now, Uma Sundari. Aah...Uma Sundari.

(The other characters in the story, Uma Sundari's neighbourhood friends, enter as a Chorus, singing to a clapping beat.)

CHORUS

Uma Sundari? Uma Sundari? Uma Sundari, oh-ho-ho!
Uma Sundari, Uma Sundari, Uma Sundari, go gogo!
Uma Sundari...
(Uma Sundari enters and joins the friends)

NARRATOR

Everyone loved Uma Sundari. And she loved her friends. And she loved to do one thing more than anything else in the whole wide world.

UMA

GOSSIP! Oh how I love to gossip! It is the best thing to do while I'm twiddling my thumbs. No work to be done while I am dangling my feet, no one to meet. Then I love to Gossip.

SHIVA

She follows a method in her gossip

UMA

I link up incidents. Chain stitching, you could call it. I create directions.

SHIVA

Create predicaments.

UMA

I invent grand narrations

SHIVA

But there are always complications!

UMA

Just the other day, I saw...
(The women huddle. There is much loud whispering and giggling.)

NARRATOR

Nothing in the world could stop Uma Sundari from giving out her daily dose of gossip. One day it was the story of a sly Sambashiva, the next day it was about the evil daughter-in-law of Subbamma! It was as if she lived only to tell stories.

(There are more noises from the women's huddle)

But what was worse...Uma Sundari could just not keep a secret.

UMA

Oh! I feel like my tummy will burst. There is always something to tell.

In keeping secrets I just don't excel.

NARRATOR

So, as matter of routine she would pass it on to her friend Satyabhama, who had to tell her dear friend Vimalavati, who was very close to her grandmother, who simply had to share it with you know who...

And so it passed through one and all in the village and came back to... *(The crow-narrator flits across to perch on the step ladder down-right.)*

CHORUS

Uma Sundari? Uma Sundari? Uma Sundari, oh-ho-ho!
Uma Sundari, Uma Sundari, Uma Sundari, go gogo!
Uma Sundari...

UMA

Oh I simply have to tell this to someone.

CHORUS

About what? About who?

UMA

First promise me! *(The women nod readily in agreement)*

God promise, mother promise, tree promise, river promise... promise on the elephant, promise on the camel, promise on the horse, promise on the dog...promise on everything that we can promise on...

CHORUS

We promise!

UMA

You know...

(She breaks into a children's nonsense verse in Kannada, to a beat. The performing group can find equivalents in any other language.)

UMA

Manjula... Manjula muskinjola, muskinjola, aanebaala, aanebaala, kappechippu!

Kappechippu, ragihittu,ragihittu, nayibaala, nayibaala, donkubaala...

(She breaks into excited laughter.)

NARRATOR

Nothing could stop Uma Sundari, not even her husband Shiva Sundara. He was mild mannered, you remember. He did try though, in his own way.

SHIVA

Heaven help you, Uma Sundari.

NARRATOR

Uma Sundari continued to talk and gossip withturbocharged vigour as the days went by. Poor Shiva Sundara could only wait and pray for her to stop.

NARRATOR

Caw caw!

SHIVA

See, even this crow agrees. Oh, if only it could also show me a way.

NARRATOR

Caw caw!

SHIVA

Hunh...?

NARRATOR

Caw!

SHIVA

You mean...?

NARRATOR

Caw caw.

SHIVA

You think it might work?

NARRATOR

Caw... *(Shiva Sundara, inspired, goes to Uma Sundari, who is about to start on a fresh gossip.)*

UMA

Aah, there you are. You will never guess what I saw on the way to –

SHIVA *(Interrupting her)*

Uma Sundari! Wait! I have something important to tell you.

UMA

What? What important thing?

SHIVA

Shhh! Not so loud. I don't want anyone else to hear this.
(He takes Uma Sundari aside)

UMA

Something important? Is it a secret?

SHIVA

Listen carefully, Uma Sundari...
It is a secret so dear
No one else must hear
It is about a black bird
Have you heard?

UMA

About what?

SHIVA

Shhh!! Not so loud! It is about...a black...bird.

UMA

A black bird? You mean a crow?

SHIVA

A black... now how did you know? *(He points to the out-house)*
Look there. A beautiful crow is sitting on the white roof of our out-house! *(Uma Sundari is puzzled)*
Shhh! Remember, you must not tell anyone about it!

UMA

Never!

SHIVA
Nobody!

UMA
Never! Never!

SHIVA
Nobody! Never! *(Shiva Sundara leaves quickly. The crow flits off the down-right step ladder following him.)*

UMA
What does it mean, I wonder?
A beautiful crow sitting on the white roof of our out house... Is that what he said?
I wonder...A beautiful crow...sitting on the roof...our white outhouse...
A crow sitting on the roof... a beautiful crow...white house...
I must, I must-must-must keep this a secret! *(She starts to go, then stops)*
A big white beautiful crow sitting on the roof of our out-house...
And that is the secret! There is...there is a big white beautiful crow. It is sitting on the roof of our out-house. And I cannot tell this secret to anyone. Nobody, never, never!
Oh! I feel like my tummy will burst. There is always something to tell.
In keeping secrets I just don't excel.
But what about my promise? Promise? What about it? Maybe I can tell just one friend. Some one friend who won't rattle and tattle...
Oh Rama, Rama, I think I will only tell my neighbour Satyabhama. *(Satyabhama and Vimalavati enter upstage)*

SATYA
Uma Sundari! What news today??

UMA *(Glad to see her gossip group, but holding back)*
Oh, nothing, nothing. Nothing at all!

SATYA
No new story? How can that be? Are you all right?

UMA

No story today, I am afraid. *(She is restless)* There was a crow cawing, that is all. Just one...

SATYA

Yes...?

UMA *(To herself)*

Oh I know it is wrong, but I must tell her – just this once. *(The grandmother enters upstage and calls Vimalavathi to her side. Seizing the chance, Uma Sundari takes Satyabhama away from the group.)*

SATYA

What is it Uma Sundari?

UMA

Did you see our out house today? No?

(The gossip in her taking over) Early in the morning, a huge white crow was sitting on the roof of our out-house. My husband saw it too. He realised what it was – a white crow on our roof. It is a secret, of course, a very big secret. He told me not to tell anyone. But you...I had to tell you. Now you know. You will not tell anyone, will you?

SATYA

Oh, no! Never! I won't tell a soul. But what sort of a secret is... *(She returns to the group.)*

NARRATOR

But Satyabhama had the same problem. She couldn't sleep if she did not share the secret with her neighbour Vimalavati. And off she went to tell her. *(The group gathers and goes into a huddle.)*

VIMALA

Oh really? Such a big secret! What do you say, grandma?

GRANDMA

It has always been said that unusual happenings point to hidden treasure.

VIMALA

Hidden treasure! How unfair! Here I am with just one pair of gold bangles, and that Uma Sundari – just three houses away, and has hidden treasure under her out-house? I must tell my husband about this.

(The neighbourhood group grows in number. So does the agitation in the group. Shiva Sundara is seen at the down-left step ladder, with the crow perched on top, watching the group from a distance.)

NARRATOR

Now, Vimalavati's husband, Kamalesh, never did like Shiva Sundara. He rushed to his friend and whispered the news of the treasure in his ears. The number of ears could only increase. All this while, Shiva Sundara sat under a tree singing to himself.

(Shiva and the narrator-crow sing a popular Hindi verse.)

SHIVA

Kaan kon kar kutu kutu bole

NARRATOR

Kon kaan kar kutu kutu bole

SHIVA

Kaan Kon kar

NARRATOR

Kon Kaan kar

TOGETHER

Hara Hara Shambo Mahadeva

NARRATOR

This enraged the villagers even more. It was unfair for Shiva Sundara to get all that treasure. Something had to be done. It was not his treasure in the first place. So...the villagers took the news to the minister.

(The agitated village group, led by the minister, arrives at the out house. The minister bangs on the door. Uma Sundari comes out in fright.)

And before Uma Sundari knew it, the group rushed in and rummaged her entire out-house, knocking it down and turning it inside out. Nothing was found. The disappointed and angry minister turned to Kamalesh.

MINISTER

No treasure, nothing! Who told you about the treasure?

How dare you come spoiling my leisure! *(Everybody points in every direction. Finally, all hands are pointing at...Uma Sundari.)*

NARRATOR

Uma Sundari felt quite swallowed up.

UMA

I can only say I am very sorry.
I promise on everything we can promise on...
But most of all, I promise on myself, I will gossip no more!

(The village group storms out. Uma Sundari and Shiva Sundara examine the knocked down step ladder out-house.)

NARRATOR

Shiva Sundara was happy. His out-house was knocked down without spending a single paisa. He could now finally grow the garden he always wanted. Caw Caw!

Percussion and fade out to end the story.
Link to: Good Luck Gopala

(A chant is heard off stage. The narrator-crow and Shiva Sundara leave the stage carrying the two stepladders with them.
The Chorus enters chanting.)

ALL

Gopala, Gopala,
Go gogogo Gopala!
Gopala, Gopala,
Go gogogo Gopala!

CHORUS

>> Time to move on, time to tell another tale.
>> Another kind of magic this time
>> When good luck casts a magical spell.
>> Let's hear it now
>> Another chant for another man.
>> And the man's name?
(A member of the Chorus picks up the packet from the foot of the stage.)
Good luck Gopala!

(The packet is dropped into the Drum. The Chorus continues the chant, while Gopala appears against the cyclorama. His wife is seated on the floor down-right.)

ALL

Gopala, Gopala,
Go gogogo Gopala!
Gopala, Gopala,
Go gogogo Gopala!

GOOD LUCK GOPAL

WIFE
My husband is good, my husband is kind.

ALL
Gopala !

WIFE
A little simple you know, up here in the mind.

ALL
Gopala !

WIFE
Study hard, his father said! Get it into your head!
Without learning you'll be a froggie in the well.
Froggie? That did not ring a bell.
So his father called him a frog till the day he died.
One day the frog grew up and found himself a bride.

ALL
Gopala!

CHORUS
The Frog had children, one, two, three
But the one thing he did not have was...

ALL
Money! *(The Chorus exits chanting)*
Gopala, Gopala,
Go gogogo Gopala!
Gopala, Gopala,
Go gogogo Gopala!

WIFE
Listen! I have heard that our king is fond of good literature. Instead of just sitting there, idling, why don't you write him a nice poem? Who knows, he may like it and give you a reward. Then we will have some money at last.

GOPAL

Perhaps, after I have bathed in the river...

WIFE

Oh, I do hope he writes something nice. We have not eaten well for a very long time.

GOPAL *(Appearing with a leaf)*

I have written it! I have written it!

WIFE

What?

GOPAL

My verse!

WIFE *(Eager)*

And... ?

GOPAL

At the pond, I saw a pig scratching its back against a tree. The pig was scratching so hard, I thought its skin would come off.

WIFE *(Excited)*

And... ?

GOPAL

I wrote my verse. Do you want to hear it ? *(The wife nods eagerly. Gopal reads – trying to sound like a professional at a gathering of poets.)*

Don't rub so hard...

Don't rub so hard, it is not good for you...

Don't rub so hard, it is not good for you, It will put your life in danger...

WIFE *(Rising, perplexed)*

And... ? That's it ?

GOPAL

That's it! *(The wife leaves, exasperated.)*

Now I will go and present it to the king. I am sure I will get something for this. (*A palace guard appears and places a seat down-left for the King. He then sits on the floor C, sleeping against his spear. Gopal approaches the guard.)*

GOPAL

May I see the King?

GUARD

No! The King is busy. He is having a shave.

GOPAL

I have an important document for the king. Please...

GUARD

Oh, all right!

(The Guard reluctantly takes the leaf from Gopal and keeps it near the King's seat, while the barber enters and places himself up-centre, strapping his open razor. The King enters and takes his seat.)

KING

Has the royal barber arrived? Send him in! I am ready for my shave.

(He picks up Gopal's leaf) What is this ? Where did it come from?

(He reads aloud)

Don't rub so hard...

Don't rub so hard, it is not good for you...

Don't rub so hard, it is not good for you, It will put your life in danger

The barber screams in fright and falls at the king's feet.

BARBER

Forgive me, my Lord! Forgive me!!

KING *(Taken aback)*

What are you doing? What is happening? Forgive you for what?

BARBER

The minister, my lord! It was the minister, not me!

KING

Minister...not you... What are you saying

BARBER

The minister, my lord, he told me to kill you while I was giving you a shave. He threatened to punish me, if I didn't carry out his command. My lord, have pity on me!

KING

Guards! Find the minister and throw him into prison immediately! I will deal with him soon. *(Looking around)* But where did this leaf come from? Who wrote this?

(The Guard indicatesGopal, who steps forward.)

GOPAL

I did, your Majesty.

KING

You have saved my life! I will reward you handsomely for this. You are wise indeed. From this day on you will be my court astrologer! *(Gopal protests)*

No, no, I know you will want to go back to your family and your village, but we need you here! *(He turns to the barber, still prone at his feet)*And as for you, away with you! And don't let me see your face again!

(The barber crawls away. The King exits. Gopal sits C, dazed.)

CHORUS

>> Within a few days

>> Within a few days, it was the turn of the queen.

>> Within a few days, the queen lost her favourite necklace.

>> She lost the necklace, and the whole palace was turned upside down.

>> The King was at the receiving end of her wrath.

KING *(Rushing in)*

Gopal! You must find the necklace before she makes my life any more miserable! Gopal, Gopal, you saved my life with your divine powers, now help us find the queen's necklace! Someone has stolen it!

GOPAL *(Trembling)*

But your Majesty...

KING

No buts!

GOPAL

What if...

KING

Find it!

GOPAL

Your Majesty, I can look at the past and predict the future only when alone. Kindly give me a few moments to myself. I will come to you shortly with the answer.

(The King strides out. Gopal steps DC and sings.)

My village was quiet, my village was green
My village was the prettiest I've ever seen

I had my clean river, I had clean air
I had the green fields, with blue skies to spare.

I had good friends, who had time for me
To chat and gossip o'er a cup of tea.

CHORUS

You could say he was poor, that surely is true
But he was happy. You don't understand, do you?

GOPAL

I've sold my poor soul, for this wealth and power
I'm the boss's slave, working hour after hour

My wife, my children, I've left at home
I'm running this rat race while they cope alone

How rich must I get? How far must I roam?
I own a great palace, but I have no home.
This life must get over, one day I must die...
(Agonising) How can I turn back now than be living this lie?

(He takes out a picture of his wife and moans. The King enters and confronts Gopal.)

KING

Well?!

GOPAL *(To the picture... and himself – aloud)*

Oh, lady, your desires have doomed your husband! Because of you, your husband is now in trouble, and you may become a widow soon. Your husband escaped once before, but this time, alas, there is no escape.

(A scream is heard offstage. A Maid runs in and falls at Gopal's feet.)

MAID

Forgive me! Forgive me, my Lord!! You know everything! I stole an earring once. It was with the help of my husband, who is the palace gardener. We turned greedy and decided to steal the queen's necklace this time. It was I, my lord! Forgive me!! I will tell you where the necklace and earring are hidden. *(Gopal is astonished. The King snaps his finger and orders the Maid to leave. She does.)*

KING

Excellent Gopal! I knew you would not fail! Once again you have proved how great your divine powers are. I have the greatest court astrologer in my kingdom! You will be handsomely rewarded!

(A guard ushers in a messenger carrying a box)

GUARD

Your Highness, a messenger from the neighbouring kingdom has arrived.

(He reads from a scroll) We have heard much about the new astrologer in your court and his divine powers. Here is a test for him. Can he tell what is in this box?

(The King looks expectantly at Gopal. Gopal looks away.)

KING

The honour of my kingdom is at stake, Gopal. I am sure we can rely on you to come up with the right answer.

(Trapped, in shock, Gopal turns away and moans to himself.)

GOPAL

Oh Froggie, trapped... your life has indeed become very difficult!

(The messenger opens the box. We see a giant frog inside. The King claps in glee.)

KING

It is a frog! Wonderful, Gopal! Simply wonderful! Shower him with gold coins! I wonder what you will come up with next. I simply cannot wait!

(The Chorus has entered carrying trays of gifts in gold and jewels.)

GOPAL *(Quickly)*

Your Majesty, I was told I would be able to predict only three things correctly as an astrologer. I have just given you the last of the three prophecies. Kindly permit me now to return to my wife and to my village!

KING

Of course, of course! I understand. I will be sorry to see you go, but you have served me well! It is time for you to return home now.

(Gopal accepts the King's blessings. He is escorted out by the Chorus, chanting:)

Gopala, Gopala,
Go gogogo Gopala!
Gopala, Gopala,
Go gogogo Gopala!

Percussion and fade out to end the story.
Link to: The Last Laddooo

(The king, guard and messenger clear the stage. The actor playing Dog 1 in the next story picks up the packet with the laddoo from the foot of the stage and announces the story: THE LAST LADDOO. He sings a verse about Devanna picking up a laddoo and thinking it was a cricket ball, before dropping the laddoo into the Drum. He then picks up the mask of a dog from the props corner down-right and begins introducing the story.)

THE LAST LADDOO

OPTIONAL: The story has a little boy or girl in it. It can be a rehearsed part. On the other hand, it can also be an impromptu appearance by a child from the audience. If so, the following preparatory scene can be included.

DOG 1

Well, let me begin. Oh, before I forget, we need a child to play a small part in this story. How about somebody from out there in the audience? Anybody? *(The actor chooses a child and briefs her or him about the part.)*

Let me tell you what to do. You will go into the wings now, and be given a box of laddoos. No, you can't eat the laddoos! Not just now, maybe later. At the right time you will have to come on and give the laddoos to people on stage, as needed in the story. Nice job, hunh? Giving away laddoos? OK? Off you go now. We will see you soon. Remember, no eating laddoos backstage! *(He leads the child into the wings. He then sets the scene for the story. From the wings there are sounds of dogs barking, all by the actors. Dog 1 responds.)*

Woof! *(Barking responses off stage. Dog 1 responds in turn.)* Woof woof!

A village, a beautiful little village, in Karnataka. A little square. People. *(As he speaks the characters referred to come on stage. Dog 1 greets them with barks excitedly. The people respond affectionately.)*

A milk man with his bicycle...a vegetable vendor...a woman selling flowers...a postman...*(He stops, listens)*

Woof! *(There is a barking response off stage)*My friend! Woof woof! *(Another response)* Woof woofwoof!

(Dog 2 runs in with food in his mouth, happy. The two exchange happy barks and nuzzling. They carefully divide the food into two parts and begin to eat.)

DOG 2

We love food. We make it our job to eat three times every day. We are very very organized. One of us goes looking for food, and the other stays back to take care of the neighbourhood. If I go looking for food on Monday, he goes on Tuesday. Wednesday me – Thursday he – Friday – Saturday – Sunday –

DOG 1 *(Cutting in)*

Alternate days! Odd number, even number! That's right, people in big cities have copied our method.

DOG 2

We came here when very young. We have been here ever since. Everyone in this colony feeds us. Even the newcomers who move in...like the little kid there.

(The child enters, feeds the dogs some biscuits, strokes them playfully, and exits. Meanwhile Deviah and Devamma have entered their kitchen area down-left.)

DOG 1

Everyone except... *(Points towards Deviah and Devamma's house)*

Deviah and Devamma. Oh! I can't tell you how kanjoos they are. They are the ultimate kanjoos couple in this colony. Makkhichoos!

DOG 2

You know what that means, don't you? Yes? No? Let us tell you.

(The two of them break into a rhythmic beat, alternating the Kanjoos-Makkhichoos with little stories about Deviah and Devamma.)

Kanjoos, Makkhichoos!
One day Deviah was drinking some tea
A fly dropped into the tea.
Devamma pulled out the fly before heating the old tea anew
But Deviah licked the fly to save the brew!
Now you know how they got their name. Makkhichoos!
One day Devamma opened a packet of sambar powder
When the powder stuck to her hands
She did not wash them...oh no!
She dipped her hands into the sambar she was stirring
Washing hands is wasting the powder, she said.
Kanjoos!
But Deviah was not glad, oh no!
He was livid...

He said, Devamma, that was stupid.
You could have dipped one hand in today
And the other tomorrow!
Kanjoos!

(They build up the tempo chanting Kanjoos, Makkhichoos. As it builds up, Deviah rushes out in anger. The dogs freeze.)

DEVIAH

Shoo shoo! These dogs – such a nuisance! Always barking and howling!

I know, I know, you want my biscuits. Well you are not getting any! This neighbourhood, bah! You have been spoilt! Get out from here! Shunakas!

DOG 1

The house belongs to Deviah and Devamma, the misers. Nobody knows who is the bigger miser. But it never matters. People just look at them and say: Ah, what a couple! Made for each other!

(We see Deviah placing pots to collect drops of water from leaks in the ceiling.)

DOG 2

Their house is falling apart. They have never repaired the leaks. The poor couple –

DOG 1

Why do you call them a poor couple? You can't say Deviah and Devamma did not have the means. They did not have the mind. It was not in them to spend their wealth – not for others, not even for themselves.

(We see Deviah taking off his shirt. Underneath is a torn and tattered vest.)

DOG 2

That's right, exactly! They never spend any money even on themselves for anything. All day long they sit at the window, looking at people coming and going, going and coming, coming and going –

DOG 1 *(Cutting in)*

Same thing!

DOG 2

Never talking to anyone in the neighbourhood. That was their life!

DOG 1

Until one day...

(The child comes running in. The two dogs rush up to greet the child, who plays with them. There is much barking and laughing. Deviah and Devamma are disturbed. He steps out.)

DEVIAH

Hey, you! Who are you? What are you doing here?

CHILD *(Going up to Deviah)*

Uncle, it is my birthday, and my mother has sent these laddoos for you and aunty.

DEVIAH

Two laddoos? For us? Thank you, my boy (girl)! May we have many more laddoos...birthdays. May you have many more birthdays like this one. Thank your parents from me. *(To Devamma)* Look Devamma, the new neighbours have sent us laddoos!

DEVAMMA

One each? How extravagant of them! *(They eat a laddoo each with great relish, picking at every grain on their palms and lips)* Mmm... delicious! Oh, look! What is that boy (girl) doing?!

(The child has taken out another laddoo and tossed it to the two dogs. The dogs catch it, split it in half, and share it, playing with the child all the time.)

Foolish boy (girl)! Giving laddoos to those dogs! How wasteful!

(The child exits. The two dogs settle down in a corner. Deviah and Devamma cannot get over the experience of the delicious laddoo.)

DEVIAH

Devamma...

DEVAMMA

Deviah...

DEVIAH

You know...

DEVAMMA
I know...

DEVIAH
The laddoo is over... Don't you feel like another one? Do you think you can make some laddoos for us to eat?

DEVAMMA
Yes, yes, I can. I learned to make laddoos from my mother long ago. But listen, we will make only two laddoos – one for me and one for you. *(Thinks)* Oh, if I make the laddoos at home the neighbours will get to know about it. They will want a share.

DEVIAH
I know what to do. Let's close all the doors and windows. No one will find out then. *(They close windows and doors and begin preparing to make the laddoos.)*

DOG 2
You know what the cat thinks? If I close my eyes and drink the milk, no one can see me...Foolish Deviah and Devamma! Everybody in the village knew their plan – from the grocer who sold them the ingredients to the postman who could smell the laddoos on his beat.

DOG 1
But that was not the problem, no sir! The real problem was something different. They had never made laddoos before, you see. So, not knowing the correct measures, they ended up with three laddoos instead of two! Now... the big question was who should get the third laddoo. Yes, you guessed right. There was a quarrel.

DEVIAH
So, you want two, and I have to take only one, hunh?! It was my idea, and I went to the market and got things to make them. So I must get two, and you get one.

DEVAMMA
Who prepared the laddoos? I did! So I get two, and you can have one.

DEVIAH

You would not have made them if I hadn't asked for them.

DEVAMMA

And you would not get to eat them if I didn't make them.

DEVIAH

Mine!

DEVAMMA

Mine !

(They struggle with the laddoos, chasing each other.)

DEVIAH

If you take the third laddoo I will never speak to you again.

DEVAMMA

Fine! I don't want to speak to you anyway.

DEVIAH

Very well then, don't! *(He stops in his tracks)*

All right! Here is how we will decide on the third laddoo. You say you will not speak, right ? Well, if you do, you lose! Then I get the third laddoo.

DEVAMMA

That goes for both of us. Whoever speaks first is the loser, and will get one laddoo. The winner gets two.

DEVIAH

Fine! Ready? We start...

DEVIAH AND DEVAMMA *(Together)*

Now!

DOG 1

What?! A mouna-vrath competition? Over a laddoo? This must be the first of its kind. Let us see how long they remain silent.

(The two dogs take a nap. The postman walks across on his beat. Dog 2 wakes up.)

DOG 2

Oh ho ho, it's four hours now, and not a sound from their house. Do you think we need to find out what's going on?

DOG 1

All right, let us try see. *(They approach the house and howl)* Hellooo!!!

DOG 2

Anyone at ho-o-o-me???

(Deviah is agitated, but cannot shout at the dogs. He tries to make Devamma shoo them off. Neither of them succeeds in making the other break the silence.)

DOG 1

Ohho! We have a problem now. Since they have stopped talking, this story will end here. What do we do? *(They think)*

DOG 2

I know! Let's call the neighbours!

(They rush out barking and bring in the postman.)

POSTMAN

The dogs are barking and howling in front of Deviah's house... there must be something wrong. Deviah! Devamma! There's no reply. Maybe I should get help.

(The postman rushes out with the dogs barking and returns with a small group.)

NEIGHBOUR

Deviah! Deviah, Dervamma! Open the door! What has happened? Oh my, there is no response. Somebody get a ladder!

(One of them rushes in with a ladder. The neghbour climbs on it and peeps in. Deviah and Devamma are lying down, quite still.)

NEIGHBOUR

Deviah! Devamma! Oh no! They are lying there on the floor – no sound, no movement. I think they are dead! *(The group is alarmed)*

ANOTHER

Can you smell the unwashed dishes? They must have died a while ago!

ANOTHER

Let's break down the door!

(The group tries to break down the door with the step ladder. There is a second try with more joining. A third try with a larger group... and they barge in.)

NEIGHBOUR
They are surely dead.

ANOTHER
Poor couple! Come on, let us take them to the cremation ground.

NEIGHBOUR
It is enough if we have just one pyre. They were a kanjoos couple anyway. They can both be cremated on the same pyre.

(The neighbours carry Deviah and Dervamma in a funeral procession to the upstage area chanting 'Kanjoos Makhi-choos' and stand around them. Meanwhile, the two dogs enter Deviah and Devamma's house.)

DOG 1
Hey, I found the laddoos! There are three of them.

DOG 2
We can share them.

There are two alternatives to end the story from here.

OPTION 1: *The dogs howl in glee and settle down to eat. Just then Devamma sits up at the pyre and screams.*

DEVAMMA
Deviah! There are dogs in our house! The laddoos!

DEVIAH
I won! I won!! You spoke first! I get to eat two laddoos!

DEVAMMA
Only if we hurry! The dogs may get at them first!

(The village group is enraged. They attack Deviah and Devamma, who run towards the house. The neighbourhood runs after them. The entire group runs off stage. The dogs pick up the remaining laddoo and scurry to the DC area.)

DOG 1
Ah, one more laddoo! What do we do with the third laddoo?

DOG 2

Share it of course! Here, you eat one half of it, and I will eat the other half...fair and square.

DOG 1

Sounds a good idea. And remember the little kid who started it all...?

DOG 1 AND DOG 2 *(They sing together)*

Happy birthday toooyooo!!!

OPTION 2: *The cyclorama turns red with the cremation fire. Just then Devamma sits up at the pyre and screams.*

DEVAMMA

I can't stand it! The flames are licking at my feet! I must get back home to my laddoos!

DEVIAH

I won! I won!! You spoke first! I get to eat two laddoos!

DEVAMMA

Yes, but let's hurry! The house is left open!

(The village group is enraged. They attack Deviah and Devamma, who run towards the house. The neighbourhood runs after them. The entire group runs off stage. The dogs pick up the remaining laddoo and scurry to the DC area.)

DOG 1

Ah, one more laddoo! What do we do with the odd laddoo?

DOG 2

Share it of course! Here, you eat one half of it, and I will eat the other half...fair and square.

DOG 1

Sounds a good idea. And remember the little kid who started it all...?

DOG 1 AND DOG 2 *(They sing together)*

Happy birthday toooyooo!!!

Percussion and fade out to end the story.
Link to: The Very Expensive Coconut

(The actor playing Dog 2 rises and takes off his mask.)

DOG 1
What's up? Where are you going?

ACTOR
Time for the next story. This time I play a human... a promotion!

DOG 1
Human? A demotion! I will look for more animal parts to play.
(Dog 1 exits. The Actor picks up the next packet and announces the story: THE VERY EXPENSIVE COCONUT. As he is dropping the packet into the Drum he notices a box of burfis in the props area. He picks it up, shows it to the audience and stealthily sneaks out.)

THE VERY EXPENSIVE COCONUT

The Chorus, comprising two or three men and two or three women enter from different directions and go about their business – as a couple, a businessman, a flower seller, and so on. There is a loud exclamation off stage, and all are startled.

VOICE

Where did it go?!!

(The actor playing Chandrakant enters agitatedly and runs about the stage asking everybody: 'Have you seen it?' 'Did you see it?' The Chorus improvises responses and actions to the questions. Finally they get the intruder to tell them WHAT he is looking for.)

CHORUS

Who are you? And what is all the shouting about?

CHANDRA

I am Chandrakant. I have just lost a boxful of –

CHORUS

Full of what? Money? Gold? Frogs? Jewellery?

CHANDRA

No! No nono! Oh, you materialistic lot! It was a box full of –

CHORUS

Full of...?

CHANDRA

Burfis!

CHORUS *(Puzzled, disappointed)*

Burfis?

CHANDRA

Yes, yes, burfis! I managed to pinch some from the props box there. I put them carefully in my bag, and now... it's all gone.

CHORUS

Oh, come on! They were just burfis!

CHANDRA

Just burfis?! What do you know?! Those were no ordinary burfis... they were heavenly burfis, made of fresh white coconut flakes, and the sugar oh, the crisp, rich, bite that broke into a million pieces of heavenly grains in my mouth!!!

CHORUS

>> Oh, I know exactly what you mean!
>> The sugar dust just clings lovingly to your tongue
>> And the fragments of coconut remain as dreams for hours

CHANDRA

Now you've got it! Yes, that's the true burfi!

CHORUS

>> Hey, I want some now!
>> My grandmother used to make burfis like that!
>> I want some too!
>> I want them now!

CHANDRA

So, come on, help me find them!
(They all break into song...)

Burfi burfi, burfi burfi
Burfi burfi, burfi burfi
Kahan gaye mere burfi burfi
Burfi burfi, burfi burfi
Burfi burf, burfi burfi...

(Choreography. The groupchants and looks for burfis all over the stage, ending in a row on their knees stage-centre, still chanting. They stop abruptly when they see another actor entering with a box of burfis and munching one by himself down-left. The group rises as one and chases the actor, who drops the box and rushes out, followed by the others. Only Chandrakant remains. He picks up the box. It is empty!)

CHANDRA

Empty! Oh, what rotten luck! I suppose this is what they mean when they say,'Hath ko aaya, muh ko naa lagaa'. But god! I will eat a burfi today! By hook or by crook. But how will I get one? I know, I shall ask my wife to make me one! Why didn't I think of that before?! Wife! Oh wife!! Oh wifeeeee!!!

(An actor is pushed on to the stage up-left. He tries to rush back. He is pushed on again.)

ACTOR

But I don't want to play this part! I don't want to play the wife!!

(Too late. The backstage crew has tossed him a dupatta. Chandrakant has started to address his wife. The actor covers his head with the dupatta and clears his throat.)

CHANDRA

Oh wife...you look so beautiful today! *(The wife responds with a coy gesture)*

I feel like eating a coconut burfi today! Made with a nice fresh coconut and pearly white powdered sugar! Will you make some for me?

WIFE *(In one continuous burst, with Chandrakant shrinking steadily to the ground)*

What?! You are such a miser. You hide every rupee you get! You hardly give me enough to make even daal and rice, how will I make you burfis? I have never seen a man more stingy than you! Do we live in a coconut grove? Go and buy a coconut at least, and then I will think of making some burfi for you. What are you waiting for? No coconut, no barfi!!

(Chandrakanth rises and exits into a wing. The actor playing the wife whips off the dupatta, wraps it as a sash around his head and takes his place down-right as a coconut seller. He peddles his coconuts in Kannada. The actors may choose to use any other vernacular language.)

ACTOR

Yelneer, yelneer!! Yelneer, yelneer!!

What a day for some cool yelneer!

(Chandrakant enters, still smarting from the wife's dressing down. He sees the coconut seller and goes up to him.)

CHANDRA

Ah, coconuts! Do you have coconuts for cooking.

ACTOR

Keep them in the sun. They will be ready soon.

CHANDRA

How much for one?

ACTOR

I know you Chandrakant. These are not for you.

CHANDRA

But they are. They are coconuts, are they not? I want one.

ACTOR

No they are not. You can't buy them.

CHANDRA

I can! I want one for making burfi. I will give you... five rupees for one.

ACTOR

Five rupees?! You see what I mean when I say these are not for you? These coconuts cost much more.

CHANDRA

How much? Seven?

ACTOR

Just for you, because I know you Chandrakant, I can give you one for twelve rupees.

CHANDRA

What?! Twelve rupees a coconut? That is daylight robbery!

ACTOR

Then these are not for you. You can walk ahead. About ten kilometers down you will see a coconut grove. You may get one there for five rupees.

CHANDRA

Five rupees a coconut at the grove? Good! I will walk right ahead. Actually, I think even five rupees is a bit too much. Let's see if I can get it there for less.

(Chandrakant exits. The Chorus enters with step ladders and forms a coconut grove. The song 'Burfi burfi' is heard as a refrain as they set up.

The Actor climbs on to one of the step ladders and becomes a coconut plucker. Chandrakant enters and goes up to him.)

CHANDRA

Hello, my man! I want a coconut! Will you give me one?

ACTOR

Certainly, sir. But these coconuts are for sale, sir.

CHANDRA

Will you give me one for...three rupees?

ACTOR

What? Three rupees?! Silly! Look sir, I am very busy and have no time to waste on this kutchkutch. Ten kilometers from here is another coconut grove. You may get it there for one rupee.

CHANDRA

Wonderful! I will save two more rupees! Here I go!

(Chandrakant wanders about as the Chorus rearranges the step ladders to form another grove. The Actor is now on another rung on the stepladder, in another location. The 'Burfi burfi' refrain is heard again.)

CHANDRA

Hello! Hello there! These coconuts –

ACTOR

Are for sale.

CHANDRA

Ah, yes. Will you give me a coconut for one rupee?

ACTOR

What?! Do you take me for A fool? I'll tell you what – walk down that way for ten kilometers. You will reach the seaside. There are lots of coconut trees there. Lots of coconuts on those trees. All free. You will get a coconut there free!

CHANDRA

For free? Free!! I will walk to the ends of the earth to get anything for free! Free! Free! Buy none, take ten! All free!!

***OPTIONAL:** A song by Chandrakant.*

Oh, the lovely taste of FREE!
Oh, the lovely smell of FREE!
Give me a discount, jaldi, jaldi
No full price for me!

Buy two, get one FREE!
Mega offer? Definitely!
Guaranteed gifts, Diwali!
Dinner guests? BYOB!

Fridge with toaster FREE!
Clearance sale? immediately!
Old for new? kyon nahin?
Can I exchange my biwi?

They may call me miserly.
I save money carefully.
No living wastefully!
Every paisa counts for me.

Oh the lovely taste of FREE
Oh the lovely smell of FREE
The most beautiful word in the dictionary!
Is FREE !

(The Chorus rearranges the step ladders to form another grove. The 'Burfi burfi' refrain is heard again.)

CHANDRA

Walking, walking, no beach I see...Oh, there it is...the coconut tree! Oh, there are plenty here. I can take whichever one I want!

(Chandrakant tries throwing stones at them. It doesn't work. He tries shaking a tree trunk. It doesn't work. He finally decides to climb a tree – with the help of the stepladders that form the grove. He moves from the lowest to the tallest stepladder. He reaches the top. He is shaky.)

CHANDRA

Oh, it's so windy! Help! Help! I am going to fall! Someone save me!!

(An Actor enters as an elephant, with its owner behind.)

CHANDRA
Help me, please! Sir, will you help me, please?!

MAN
What? Who? What are you doing up there?

CHANDRA
What do you think? Chilling out! Please help me get down!

MAN
I am in a great hurry! But I will do it if you give me a hundred rupees.

CHANDRA
A hundred rupees? No!

MAN
Well, then...

CHANDRA
All right! All right! Here, bring your elephant below this tree.

(The Man gets on to the second step ladder and holds Chandrakant's leg. Just then the elephant wanders off and they are both left hanging there, screaming. A second Actor enters as a horse with its owner behind.)

CHANDRA
Sir! You on the horse! Will you please help us get down?

MAN 2
No!

MAN 1
Sir, please! You must help us!

MAN 2
A thousand rupees.

CHANDRA
A thousand...?! No!

MAN 1
Yes!

CHANDRA
No!

MAN 1
Yes!!

CHANDRA
Well... yes! All right...

MAN 2
Strictly cash.

CHANDRA
Here, sir, bring your horse below this tree.
(Man 2 gets on to the first step ladder and holds Man 1's leg. Just then the horse trots off and all three are left hanging there. There is much frightened yelling by all three. Finally, they all fall from the step ladders in a heap. They pick themselves up one by one, groaning.)

MAN 1 *(To Chandrakant)*
You! You will now pay the doctor's bills!

MAN 2
And the hospital billsl!

CHANDRA
How will I face my wife now?Ohh! What a very expensive coconut!
Chandrakant faints. Man 1 and Man 2 are left holding him.

Percussion and fade out to end the story.
Link to: The Emperor of Alkavati

(Two members of the Chorus enter and get the cast of the previous story to clear the stage. They shout instructions into the wings that the elephant and the horse must stand by, as they are needed for the next story.)

CHORUS
Abbah! We can get on with it now.
(One of them picks up the last packet and drops it into the Drum, announcing...THE EMPEROR OF ALKAVATI)

Introducing...Sumant, the young man in a hurry
To make it to the top. He simply cannot stop.
Sumant, from Vidhishanagara in ancient India

SUMANT *(Entering)*
I can introduce myself, thank you – if that is all right with you.

CHORUS
>> It says in the script that we must introduce you
>> And tell the people out there of your cleverness
>> And the kings and emperors that come into your life.

SUMANT
Kings, I tell you! Ponderous dunderheads! Your people out there are like people everywhere – with this addictive fascination with royalty. Now, please...

(Sumant shows the Chorus groups the way out.)

THE EMPEROR OF ALKAVATI

SUMANT

I am Sumant, a young man of exceptional talents, as you might have heard, who lives in Vidhishanagara. I am an orphan, but don't look at me with pity. I am extremely clever because I have had to look after myself from a very, very, very young age.

(By now a mithaiwala and his son are at their shopin the up-left corner.)

SHOPKEEPER *(As he moves offstage)*

Arrey beta, it is very hot, and I have had a heavy lunch. I am very sleepy. Look after the shop and I will take a little nap. Call me only if something very important comes up. *(Sumant is listening, getting an idea)*

SON

Ji, Pitaji.

SUMANT *(Going up to the son)*

Hello, boy ! My, my, how big you have grown. *(The Boy looks puzzled)*

I am your father's best friend's son. I will take some of the best sweets in the shop *(He picks up two boxes, but does not pay. The boy is suspicious.)*

BOY

What is your name?

SUMANT *(Stepping down and eating a sweet)*

Makkhi. My name is Makkhi.

BOY *(Calling off)*

Pitaji, Pitaji, Makkhi is eating our sweets! What do I do?

FATHER *(Off)*

Arrey, how much can a makkhi eat? Let it be! Now, leave me alone and let me sleep! *(The boy packs up the sweet shop props and exits. Kanak Chandra enters and moves to centre. Sumant sees him.)*

SUMANT

Ah, Kanak Chandra, the miser. *(Going up to him)*

Good afternoon, Kanak Chandra! Here is a present for one of Vidhishanagara's greatest men! I am just a poor man. I have nothing more to give you. Please accept this. *(Kanakchandra sees the two boxes of sweets and is delighted)* Sir, I have just one request. May I have the two boxes back, please?

KANAK

Of course, of course. Please go to my house and tell the wife to give you two vessels to put these sweets in. Then you can take back the empty boxes.

(Sumant goes to the wings and speaks off)

SUMANT

Chachiji, your husband has asked you to give me two gold coins.

WIFE *(Off)*

What?! Are you out of your mind? My husband would never say such a thing!

SUMANT *(To Kanak Chandra)*

Your wife is refusing to give me what you asked for.

(Kanakchandra is busy eating the sweets and is annoyed.)

KANAK

Arrey, just give him what he wants, will you?!

(We see the wife giving Sumant two gold coins at the wing. Kanak Chandra exits and Sumant moves down-left, talking to the audience.)

SUMANT

I decided to bury the gold coins in a bushy patch outside the city. Just then...I heard a horse approaching.

(An actor appears as a horse and stops next to Sumant. Sumant busies himself, waving his cane along the ground.)

Oh, it is a soldier with a moustache. A big moustache. He asks, 'What are you doing?' I say to him, 'My magic cane leads me everyday to a hidden treasure buried under a shrub. Today it led me here, and I am looking for the treasure. Sshh! Don't disturb me.'

(He starts digging and takes out the two gold coins)

The soldier does not believe his eyes. 'Give me your magic stick', he says. 'You can take my horse in return.'

'Oh, no, no, no! This stick is my life. I cannot part with it.'

'Please!'

'No, No, No!'

'PLEASE!'

'NO!'

We struggled, of course. I finally gave in. Of course. So, he took the useless stick... and I took the useful horse.

(Sumant waves a goodbye to the imagined soldier. He leads the horse around the stage to the down-right area. A farmer is seated on the floor with a winnow.)

I rode till I came to a farmer's house. *(He dismounts and speaks to the farmer)*

I am a weary traveller. Could you please give me and my horse shelter for the night?

FARMER *(Without looking up)*

No! *(The horse neighs and nudges the farmer. He looks up and sees the horse.)*

All right... you can sleep in the stable there with this beautiful horse. *(Sumant starts to go, but stops to ask the farmer...)*

SUMANT

May I borrow your winnow?

FARMER

What for?

SUMANT

For a little puja. *(The farmer gives Sumant the winnow. Sumant stands the horse in the stable UC and goes behind it with the winnow. The farmer, suspicious, watches from the side. Sumant produces a gold coin, sees the farmer, and feigns fright.)*

FARMER

Tell me about this horse! Only the truth, now!

SUMANT

Th-this h-horse h-has m-magical powers. Once a d-day it produces a g-gold coin in its dung. *(He holds up the coin)*

FARMER

Give me the horse! I will give you a hundred gold coins in exchange.

(Sumant hesitates, then takes the money. The farmer leads the horse away down-right, as Sumant laughs and steps down-centre. He takes out a little green bottle and talks to the audience again.)

SUMANT

Time for a little swig. No, it is not what you think! This is one hundred percent impure ganga jal. The rich folks pay a fortune for it. *(An old man and woman position themselves up-left. Sumant spots them.)*

Ah, there is the house of the old man and old woman. I slept there last night. In the morning, they asked me what this bottle was. 'It is a magical medicine to make people young', I said. *(He moves to them)*

I found it while wandering in the Himalayas.

MAN

It is not possible. Do you have any proof of it working?

SUMANT

I can show you the proof, but only if you pay me in gold.

(The old woman nods approval. Meanwhile, another old woman has entered the stage down-right, sweeping the floor, In tow is her pretty young granddaughter. Sumant goes up to them and whispers something, showing them a gold coin. They agree and exit. He goes back to the old couple and asks them to watch. Soon the second old woman enters down-right alone, sweeping, moving very slowly. Sumant goes to her and offers her a cap full of the drink from his bottle. She drinks it and goes in. Moments later the granddaughter steps out and sweeps the floor with great vigour. She exits with a flourish. The old couple is stunned.)

OLD MAN

Give us the medicine! I am going to be young again!

(Sumant turns aside, adds some herbs to the bottle, and goes back to the old couple. He holds out his hand. The old man puts a gold coin in his palm. Sumant gives him a capful of the drink. The old man shivers and drops unconscious. The old woman is alarmed.)

SUMANT

Don't worry, he is only sleeping. He is so old, you see. It will take some time for the medicine to work. He will be a young man when he wakes up. I will give you your dose tomorrow.

OLD WOMAN

No! I want my dose now. If my husband wakes up looking younger and sees me as I am, he will go looking for someone younger. I want my medicine now!

(Sumant holds out his hand. The old woman puts a gold coin in his palm. He gives her a capful of the drink. The old woman shivers and drops unconscious. Sumant exits laughing. The Chorus enters and carries the two bodies out – or rolls them out.)

CHORUS

So, that was that.

But that is *not* the end of the story. *(The Chorus sets up the down-left area for the King, who enters and takes his seat.)*

KING *(To guards off stage)*

Guards! For many months now I have heard tales about this cunning young cheat roaming free in my kingdom. Finally, we have arrested him. I cannot have him cheating innocent people anymore. Put him in a sack, and when the sun sets, throw him down the mountain cliff.

(Two guards enter the down-right area with Sumant, put him into a sack and tie it up. They decide then to go and get a little drink, and leave the stage. A man enters on an elephant and passes by. He speaks to the elephant.)

MAN

Come on, Jumbo. Time to get home. Never go near a coconut tree again.

(He sees the sack, stops, and opens it in curiosity. Sumant jumps out.)

SUMANT

Thank you sir! Thanks ever so much for letting me out of the sack.

MAN

But what were you doing in there in the first place?

SUMANT *(Hesitates)*

Our king, you know... he has no heir. This morning his elephant happened to touch me with its trunk. So, he decided I should be king after him. I protested and said I was just an ordinary man. But his guards tied me up in this sack and left me here till I agreed. *(The man thinks to himself)*

MAN

If you don't mind...I could take your place in the sack... and you can take my elephant. It's no problem at all. You don't want to be in the sack anyway.

(Sumant agrees after some hesitation. He ties up the man in the sack and exits with the elephant. The two guards enter and drag the sack off stage.)

GUARD *(Off)*

Off the cliff he goes!

(A voice screams off stage: Aaaaaaahhhh. The guards re-enter.)

GUARD

And that's the end of the cheat! The king will be very happy with us.

KING *(Angrily)*

Guards! The soldiers at the palace gates reported seeing Sumant enter the city on an elephant! I told you to throw him off a cliff in a sack! How dare you disobey my orders!

GUARDS

We threw him off with our own hands, Sire! We swear it!

(Pointing to audience) Even they will swear to it!

(Sumant enters, striding. The guards are stunned.)

A ghost! Ghost!

KING

Quiet! Tell me, Sumant, how did you escape from the sack?

SUMANT

Sire, When I was thrown off the cliff, I landed on a great big mound of feathers. It was in a beautiful kingdom called Alakavati Valley.

(The entire cast appears little by little from the wings through Sumant's story to form a town square group. They form a large, composite Chorus.)

KING
Alakavati?

SUMANT
Alakavati!

CHORUS
Alkavati?

SUMANT
Jadoo nagari.

CHORUS
Alkavati?

SUMANT
Sab crorepati

CHORUS
Alakavati!

SUMANT
Buss, ekdum pretty!

CHORUS
Alakavati

SUMANT
Chalo jaldi! The streets are paved with *sona*, everybody rich
sone ke windows, *chandi ke* doors, You just can't believe it!
Alakavati!

The flowers have rubies, emeralds on trees,
Diamonds stuck on every leaf. What a mast place to see!
Alakavati!

There was just one *afsos ki* thing
This rich Rajya had no raja-king.
So when I dropped there from the sky
Shah Rukh was a lesser hero than I.

Now here I stand, most royally,
His Highness...yes, tan tarraa, the new king of Alakavati!
(Sumant strikes a grand pose. The King rises and goes up to him.)

KING

Sumant, you have told many stories in your life, and taken many people for a ride. But this one will just not pass. I know that valley well! There is no Alakavati there!

(The Chorus murmurs in anger. The King silences them... then laughs)

But since you are so clever, why don't you use your wits for the good of this kingdom, and not just for yourself? You will study under the best pundits in the land, so one day you can be my Prime Minister!

SUMANT *(Overwhelmed)*

Your Majesty...

KING

I would rather have you as a friend than match my wits against you!

SUMANT *(To the audience)*

I think I must take back what I said about kings!

(There is much rejoicing. The Chorus carries Sumant and showers him with flowers.

A grand procession is followed by the curtain call.)

Close of play

Ali Oh Baba!

A retelling of the tale from ***1001 Arabian Nights*** *for a contemporary audience*

Adapted for the stage by ***Vijay Padaki***

FOR
VIJJI CHARI

CHARACTERS IN THE PLAY

LITTLE GIRL
LITTLE BOY
LEADER OF STORYTELLER TROUPE
DUH-KING
SHEHERAZAD
ALIYEH
KASIM
BEGUM
DON
MARJI
CEO
THIEVES 1, 2, 3, 4, 5, 6

Ensemble-chorus for
BAND OF THIEVES, STORYTELLER TROUPE, TOWNSFOLK

INTRODUCTION

THE PLAY WAS developed in 2009 at the annual Summer Workshop on Theatre (SPOT) for newcomers to the experience of theatre. This workshop was started by BLT in the late seventies. Since the mid eighties it has been institutionalised as an annual event. The training programme through the summer culminates in a performance project in which all participants are engaged on stage or off stage. A great many of the theatre community in Bangalore have been through BLT's SPOT.

In some years the annual production from SPOT is a play fitted into BLT's long term programme of reaching children and young audiences. Additional shows are always held for adult audiences. Not surprisingly, many grown-ups enjoy the plays as well, with children often making the grownups attend. The Children's Theatre productions are in collaboration with a reputed NGO, as a fundraiser for their programmes for and with disadvantaged children.

The play has a built-in flexibility to satisfy a variety of audiences, playing between 85 minutes to 115 minutes. The points at which the performing team can choose between options are shown in the script.

SPOT 2009 chose to work on a retelling of the Ali Baba tale, but with a SPOT of originality. The play gets the young audience to understand the larger context of the Arabian Nights. The story unfolds on the stage in the form of day dreams of a little boy discovering the 1001 Arabian Nights. He and his friend, a little girl, share their discoveries with the audience through games, narratives, song and dance. In the process the key figures in the 1001 Arabian Nights are also drawn into the play, the clever Sheherezad and the not so clever king. The two friends manage to tell the audience the entire tale without bringing Ali Baba on stage. It might well be the little boy himself! And who knows the clever maid in Ali Baba's house might well be the little girl! As can be expected, they engage the audience actively in all of the storytelling and it is done with much contemporary humour. The India-Bangalore context in a few places will be obvious to the reader-player. They are also explained at the end of the script. Otherwise the play can be performed in any language, and anywhere in the world.

The play has songs. In the Bangalore performances, the songs are printed and distributed to the audience. Groups of students are heard singing the songs lustily as they leave the hall, after every performance.

Bangalore Little Theatre is delighted to share its ideas and experiences with any group wishing to perform the play.

FIST PERFORMED

By Bangalore Little Theatre at Guru Nanak Bhavan, Bangalore, opening on 30 October 2009

Little Girl..................MAHATI SUNDAR, AISHWARYA MURTHY, REHA CHANDRESH
Little Boy..............................PRITHVI KUMAR, PRANAV RAO, SAHIL SHAILESH
Leader......................................SHILPA ALUR, TANU KULKARNI
Duh-King...................................ARVIND BALAKRISHNAN, BIBHAVASU MISHRA
Sheherazad.......................................VIJAYALAKSHMI CHARI, NANDINI RAM MOHAN
Aliyeh...................................PARUL AHLAWAT, TAHERAJABEEN
Kasim.................................MAYANK RUNGTA. SHAMIKMAITY
Begum......................................POORNIMA SUKUMAR IYER, KRUTHIKS DUTTA NARAYAN
Don....................................RAVI SRINIVASAN, NITHYA DAVID
Marji...............................PUSHPA MURTHY, SONALIKADUGAR
CEO..KARTHIK KRISHNASWAMY
Women's Ensemble.......................SATABDI DAS, RAMA R KUMAR, DIVYA AT, SHIPA GAUTAM, NEHA KUMAR
Men's Ensemble.........CHANDRA MAHESH, PRASHANTH NATARAJ, SHREEKANTH L RAO, AMOGH KUMAR
Sets........................PREPARED BY STUDENTS OF ASSOCIATION FOR THE MENTALLY CHALLENGED
Property............MAYANK RUNGTA, POORNIMA SUKUMAR IYER, SHREEKANT L RAO, SONALIKA DUGAR, NANDINI RAM MOHAN, SHREELAKSHMI RAO, RAVI SRINIVASAN, PRIYA RAO, VIJAY PADAKI
Costumes.........................PRIYA RAO, REMA BAIS, INDIRA KATTI
Make up...PRIYA VENKATESH, VIJAYALAKSHMI CHARI, DEEPTHY SEKHAR
Lights................................NAVEEN KUMAR, AHMED ZAHOOR
Music-lyrics..VIJAY PADAKI
Percussion..KRISHNA VASAN
Backstage...............................RAGHU T, NAVEEN MUDUNURU, SUNITHA RAJA, SHREELAKSHMI RAO
Production Coordinator..PRIYA RAO

Directed by......................................SHASHANK PURUSHOTHAM, PRIYA VENKATESH

PROLOGUE

An almost bare stage. A drum is seen standing in the down-right corner.

At the second bell, as the audience is settling down, a quiz show begins. It is a quiz show with a difference, as there is no quizmaster on stage.

From catwalks above the stage we see a large, attractive placard descending. It has a question on it. It gets the audience to respond. Another placard descends. And another. Many placards, many questions, all of them getting the audience to respond. Full throated responses, please. If the stage does not have a catwalk, any alternative arrangement may be considered, including choreographed placard-carriers. A Power Point projection is also possible. A sampler:

CARD 1: Ready for the show?
CARD 2: What kind of show?
CARD 3: How about a quiz show to get going?
CARD 4: Yes?
CARD 5: Can't hear you louder please
CARD 6: Okay, shall we start? Ready for question 1?
CARD 7: Who has a sketch pen in the audience?
CARD 8: Whose dress has a safety pin on it?
CARD 9: Who has smelly socks?
CARD 10. Whose birthday is it today?

And so on. About eight to ten questions about things the girls and boys might have on them, fun things too.

The GIRL enters. She carries a stick in her hand that might be a magic wand. Or a conductor's baton. She is wondering about the noise in the auditorium, as the next card descends.

CARD

Who is this pretty girl?

(The audience has guesses. Girl cuts in and gets them to be quiet. Positioning herself DC, she prepares to 'conduct' the show.)

GIRL

One...two, three...

(She makes a grand gesture with the baton.

The drum DR starts to beat by itself, trembling as it does.

Girl gestures 'stop'. The drum sound stops. So does its trembling.

Girl gestures 'start' again. The drum starts to beat again.

She gestures 'stop'. The drum stops. So does its trembling. She does this a few times, at different speeds, with different lengths of time.

She speaks.)

GIRL

There is magic in the air. Oh, yes, definitely, there is magic in the air. Let's try that again, shall we? (*To audience)* Shall we?

(She positions herself DC again, and repeats the grand gesture)

One...two...three...

(There is a single, loud beat of the drum. Tight spot C. Nobody comes in. Spot off. Girl tries again. Spot on. Nobody enters. Girl strides L exasperated and shouts into the wing.)

GIRL

Aho!

VOICE *(Off)*

Yes, madam?

GIRL

Where is he?

VOICE

Who, madam?

GIRL

Him!

VOICE

Oh, him, madam...

GIRL

Yes, him, that good for nothing –

VOICE

But he is always with you, madam. By your side, madam. Always doing what you tell him to do, madam.

(By now, the Boy has entered from R and positioned himself Centre.)

GIRL

Always goofing off! Who is going to bring a seat for Her Highness, the Queen? Who will seat her? Where do we get a Queen? How on earth... (*She turns to Centre and sees the Boy waiting there. She takes him aside.*) Goofing off, as usual!

BOY

I got a seat for Her Highness, the Queen.

GIRL

You got a seat! How about a Queen? Have you got one? We can't start without a Queen!

BOY

In the right wing.

GIRL

In the...? Ah, yes, I see!

BOY

She is all dressed and ready.

GIRL

I can see that too. About time! Gosh, isn't she lovely?

BOY

Deliciously plump, if you ask me.

GIRL

Boys! You have no idea about these things. I wonder what story she has for us today. Shall we ask her in now?

BOY

Her mind is elsewhere. She is wondering about the audience tonight (this afternoon/ morning). Are they up to it?

GIRL

Why not find out?

BOY

Are they up to it?

GIRL *(To audience)*

Ladies and gentlemen, we have with us today a lovely Queen...

BOY

Deliciously plump...

GIRL

A lovely Queen who is unwilling to come on stage until she is assured that you, our gracious and respected guests gathered here, can satisfy the requirements of venerable tradition and make suitable gift offerings to her.

BOY

She means the Queen loves presents.

GIRL

Notwithstanding the prevailing custom of personalised, voluntary contributions in cash or kind, high in value or modest, the princess has the predisposition, in a manner of speaking, to seek from a gathered audience...

BOY

She means: the Queen asks, you give. She knows what she wants.

GIRL

The Queen has graciously consented to subject the audience to a test before she reveals the story to be performed here today.

BOY

Are you up to it? Yes? *(To Girl)* Can you hear them?

GIRL *(To audience)*

Can't hear you! Are you up to it? That's better! Now...

(Girl positions herself down-centre again, and repeats the grand gesture. The drum down-right starts to beat by itself, trembling as it does. At the same time a troupe of performers enters from all wings, juggling, cart-wheeling, prancing...using costumes and masks from a play. One of the props is a drum – perhaps the 'magic drum'. The Leader wears a turban and kurta.)

BOY

Who are you?

CHORUS

We are storytellers!

Song 1. The troupe chorus sings a short song

LEADER

Ging gang gooli gooli hey nanny ho
Come closer, come now, here we go!

SINGER
Heaps of stories we have to tell ya!
Some to excite ya, some more to tickle ya!

SINGER (SPOKEN)
But sadly, badly, very ungladly
Work for us now is hardly, hardly.

SINGER
Binga-banga-binga-bonga you can sing-along
We can tell ya stories all day long.

SINGER
But no one to listen, what can we say?
No time to be children, laugh and play.

SINGER
(Spoken) Babies turn grown-ups even yesterday
For that MS in the US, got to start from today!

LEADER
Shakalaka-makanaka page 3 fame
A world without stories, oh what a shame!

SINGER
(*Slower)* Tuitions, coaching, dawn to dusk

SINGER
(*Repeat, slower)* X-Box, Play Stations, dusk to dawn

TOGETHER
(*Chanted)* Win, win, win is the name of the game!

SINGER *(Spoken)*
So... no more work for us you see,
Which child has time for stories?

LEADER (*Sadly, half sung)*
Ging gang gooligooli hey nanny ho
Come closer, come now, here we go!

ALL
We are storytellers...
We sing and we dance...
COME ON NOW, WILL YOU GIVE US A CHANCE!

* * *

GIRL *(Cutting in)*

Wrong play! Wrong play!!

(The troupe is snapped out of it)

BOY

All this is from last year's play. Where were you when we started on the new play?

CHORUS

>> We took a little break

>> A little snack

>> A little nap.

GIRL

You have slept for three hundred days.

ALL

Ohhh...

BOY

We are doing a new play now. All these old props are useless here. And why is everybody wearing donkey masks?

CHORUS

>>Oh, we just thought, you know

>>For a change, you know

>>We thought they might come in handy

>>Aren't they cute?

GIRL

And look at your clothes!

BOY

You simply can't be seen here like this.

GIRL

You have to get off stage. Out!

CHORUS

>> You mean we are not needed anymore?

>>Not wanted?

>>You know how that feels

>>Not being wanted.

BOY

Oh ho! It's nothing like that. We have to get the new play started. The audience is waiting. Her Royal Highness, the Queen is waiting in there.

LEADER

Deliciously plump, if you ask me.

GIRL

And we have to set up the game for her.

CHORUS

Game?

BOY

She is testing the audience.

LEADER

Aahhh...we can help with that!

GIRL

You can?

LEADER

Of course we can. (*Taking charge, to Chorus*)

Right! All of you, off you go backstage, and get set for the new play! Of course you can do it! Get going. I will join you in a minute. And you! GET ME THAT DRUM! Jump to it!

(The chorus disperses. The last member picks up the 'Magic Drum' and brings it to the Leader. He waits. The Leader signals that his job is done and he must leave the stage. He does.)

GIRL

Please...hurry. It's late. The Queen is cross.

LEADER

She looks prettier when she is cross! Ah, here it is, just what we need for the game! And you thought you could do without us! *(To audience)* Does this look familiar? Of course! That's what it is, the Magic Drum. Let's see what we can do with it today.

(To Girl and Boy) Let Her Royal Highness in!

(Boy rushes off into the wing. Girl positions herself DC again, and repeats the grand gesture. The drum down-right starts to beat by

itself, trembling as it does. Boy wheels the Queen in to C, seated on a decorated stool or chair. Girl, Boy and Leader make suitable respectful gestures to her.)

LEADER

We will form two teams here on the stage. A team of eight on the left of Her Highness, the Queen, and a team of eight on her right. How do we form the teams, you ask?

BOY

How do we form the teams? (*The Leader gestures)* You mean...

GIRL

Of course, from the audience!

BOY

Who will make the teams? You?

LEADER

This drum will do it for us! You want to know how, of course. Now, listen carefully. *(He shakes the drum)* What do you hear? What do you think is inside this drum?

That's right! Marbles! Now...the drum is going to offer you a lucky dip. My friends here will go around the hall, and you can pick up a marble from inside the drum.

But ah-ha-ha, there's a condition! You must close your eyes when you put your hand in to pick a marble. Got that? Ready? Set? Go!

(Girl and Boy take the drum to as many parts of the hall as possible, getting kids to pick a marble each – eyes closed. They return to the Leader. The play can also use an alternate device for the lucky dip – not necessarily the magic drum.)

LEADER

What colour are your marbles? Blue? Green? More green? More blue? How sad?! The Queen likes only black and white. Does anybody have black marbles? White marbles? Ahhh... there they are. All those with white marbles, on this side, please, on the left of the Queen. Those with black marbles on the other side, please, on the right. *(The two teams are formed. Leader speaks to audience.)*

LEADER

Presenting...Her Royal Highness, the Queen of...
(To Girl and Boy) Where shall we say she is from?

BOY

You could say...Baghdad. *(Taking over)* The Queen of Baghdad!

LEADER

And now, with your kind permission, I will disappear backstage and make sure the others are on their job.

GIRL

And haven't fallen asleep again. Thank you.
(Leader exits. Girl and Boy continue.)

BOY

Lovely Queen of Baghdad, your wish is our command...

GIRL

Their command...*(Pointing to audience)*

BOY

What rare gifts do you wish your loyal audience to place before you? *(The Queen gives Girl a scroll. She unfurls it and studies the list.)*

GIRL

Thus, it is written, thus it shall be done! Her Highness, the Queen, not only wishes to be presented the gifts she has listed, she wishes to see which team is quicker in meeting her demands.

BOY *(to the two teams)*

We shall announce the gifts to be brought before the Queen, one by one. The team that succeeds in bringing and placing the gift at her feet first shall win one point. After all the gifts asked for have been placed at her feet, we shall see which team has the larger number of points scored.

GIRL

Is that clear? Are you ready?
(Girl and Boy conduct the game. They take turns to call out one item at a time from the scroll: 'And now, the Queen of Baghdad wants... smelly socks!' And so on. They are all fun things, and include the items from the opener 'quiz show': sketch pen, safety pin, a birthday girl, and

so on. The teams scamper all over the auditorium to get the objects for the princess.

At the end of about ten items – or about 4 to 5 minutes at most – the Winning Team is declared. 'And the winners ar... White Marbles!' [Or Black]

An actor [Duh-King?] enters with a tray and a box of sweets. He is about to present it to the winning team, when the Queen [Sheherezad] rises and interrupts him.)

SHEHEREZAD

Wait! (*She steps forward and addresses the winning team)*

Tell me – have you really won?

(Some replies. She turns to the losing team) Have they won?

(Some replies. She turns to the first team again) How can anybody win, unless...there is somebody who has lost? So...? You must thank them for your victory. You won only because they helped you by losing...

And what is the best way to thank the people who helped you win?

(Some replies) That's right, you must share the reward with them!

(As the winning team is sharing the sweets with the others, Girl and Boy get the two teams to leave the stage.)

DUH

And now, by your leave, your humble servant will also withdraw from this august ceremony.

BOY *(To Sheher)*

Your Royal Highness...

SHEHER

I am not the Royal Highness *(Duh-King stops in his tracks)*

GIRL

Your Highness...

SHEHER

Not yet! The day has not dawned for such a title yet.

BOY

Not yet, my lady? I don't understand...

SHEHER

You will, by and by. And he – he is no humble servant.

DUH

I am not?

SHEHER *(To Duh-King)*

In this play...he is the king.

DUH

Duh...king?

SHEHER

And I am...for the moment...a simple woman, neither here nor there, not wife not mate, neither queen nor slave. Just a storyteller by night, invisible by day.

(With quick turns in their dresses the servant and the Queen have become Duh-King and Sheherezad. He moves the seat to a corner position and seats himself royally on it. He claps three times. Sheherazad goes up to him. Girl and Boy exit.)

DUH

Is it night!

SHEHER

Has the sun gone down, my lord?

DUH

Has it not? It had, an hour ago.

SHEHER

Have the lamps been lit in the courtyard, my lord?

DUH

I believe they are lit.

SHEHER

And inside the chambers, my lord?

DUH

Hmmm...inside, inside...ah, yes...they are lit.

SHEHER

Well, then, it must surely be night once more.

DUH

Surely, surely.

SHEHER

As surely as the day shall follow this night.

DUH

As surely as the next story shall follow the last one.

SHEHER

My lord, a thousand nights have passed since you commanded the very first story. It will be one thousand and one nights when the cock crows at dawn tomorrow.

DUH

What? A thousand nights already? That means, let me see...

SHEHER

Two years, eight months, twenty-seven days...and nights.

DUH

And a thousand stories? That's a lot of stories, what? Hmmm... an award seems to be in order here. A little reward thrown in...

SHEHER

After the cock crows, my lord. After the next story, on this, the one thousand and first night.

DUH

Very well, then. You may begin.

SHEHER

My lord, it has already begun.

DUH

It has? What is the story about?

SHEHER

It is about winning and losing. And rewards.

DUH

Ah, I know, you win some, you lose some.

SHEHER

That is so profound, my lord.

DUH

Are you going to act out the story before me? As usual?

SHEHER

Better still, we have a company of actors with us today. They will help me act it out.

DUH

Is there a part for me?

SHEHER

We shall see...

DUH

Where is the story from? Some interesting place, I hope.

SHEHER

Shall we say...our enchanting city of Baghdad?

DUH

Ahh... the place they call Bag-dad nowadays.

SHEHER

Once upon a time... we don't know how long ago, it feels just like yesterday, or even today... *(Fade out)*

SCENE 1

Boy is lying down-left, enjoying a lazy afternoon, reading a book. Voice of Aliyeh off.

ALIYEH *(Off)*

Ali! Where are you? Aa-lee! Somebody please go and find that Ali and bring him here! Goofing off again! Just when there's such a lot of work around the house!

(Leader enters, looks about the stage, sees Boy DL and goes up to him. He watches for a few moments and then sits down next to Boy.)

LEADER

She is calling you.

BOY

Who is?

LEADER

The one they call Aliyeh.

BOY

Aliyeh? That's the name of the wife in the story here.

LEADER

Aliyeh, a beautiful name, meaning *noble born*. A beautiful name given to a beautiful woman.

BOY

But she is a quarrelsome woman in the story.

LEADER

True, true. Many beautiful women of noble birth turn out that way.

BOY

And she nags him all the time.

LEADER

Ah, yes. That's the one. She is married, isn't she? And her simple minded husband is...?

BOY

Ali. Ali Baba.

LEADER

Why do you think she nags him?

BOY

Because she wants things for the house, and there is no money.

LEADER

Why is there no money in the house?

BOY

Because Ali... well, Ali doesn't... he is just a woodcutter.

LEADER

And she wants him to go and do some work, and bring home some money.

Didn't you hear her call?

ALIYEH *(Off)*

Ali! Where are you? Ohh baba-re-baba, that husband of mine... !

LEADER

There! Didn't you hear her?

BOY

Hear what? Who are you talking about?

LEADER

Ali, Ali, Ali, that was your wife Aliyeh calling. She wants you home instantly.

BOY

There must be some mistake. I am not Ali. And I certainly don't have a wife called Aliyeh. I am not married!

LEADER

But you are!

BOY

I am not! I am just the boy you put into this play to get it started. I have done that already. Now I am taking a break and reading a story book. And if you don't mind, I want to get back to the story.

LEADER

The story of...

BOY

Ali Baba.

LEADER

Ahhh...your story.

BOY

How can it...how can I...?

LEADER

Tell me how far you had come in the story. What is happening in the story just now?

BOY

Well, Ali Baba has just done what Aliyeh asked him to do, a lot of dusting and cleaning and washing around the house, and he decides to take a break, and he goes to the pond outside the town and he lies down there...getting his breath back.

LEADER

And...?

BOY

And he falls asleep.

LEADER

And...?

BOY

And Aliyeh calls for him. She wants to remind him that it is time to go into the forest and get some firewood for the house.

LEADER

And...?

BOY

So he slips into the house, picks up his axe, gets his faithful ass from under a tree, and slips out of town before Aliyeh can catch him.

LEADER

You need an ass! *(He claps)* One smarty-pants coming up.

(An actor with a donkey mask in hand comes on stage and waits to be instructed.)

LEADER *(To actor)*

Well, put it on!*(He does)* There! Ali Baba and the ass are all set to go into the forest to collect firewood!

ACTOR

I am not an ass! I am a donkey!

BOY

What's the difference?

ACTOR

Donkeys are smart. They are handsome too. Asses are dumb.

LEADER

Let's say Ali Baba has a donkey. What the others have are asses. Right?

ACTOR

And I have a name. Ali's best friend has a name.

LEADER

Of course! You must be... Don. Ali's best friend, Don.

ACTOR

This is where we have the woodcutter's song, ably assisted by Ali Baba's donkey.

Song 2. Don and Ali

DON

Hee haw, baba-re-baba, Ali now has a new master,
I must give him a push everyday, 'coz he can't work any faster.
Spends all his time dreaming away, *(To Ali, spoken)*
How much wood have you cut today?
Hardly enough to buy me some hay! How much more do I bray and bray!
A lazy boy turned man is he. *(To audience)*
I have to take care of him delicately,
Sleeps every afternoon under a tree, and I have to stand around patiently.
(Spoken) My friends say he's dumb, it sounds harsh to me,
Not everyone's born a clever donkey.

ALI *(Slipping into it)*

I'm off to the forest, off to cut wood, just as any good woodcutter should,
I'll be a rich man, with sacks of gold, then I won't have to work even when old.
(Dreamily)
A huge big palace it will be, for my wife and me...and my favourite donkey.
Ah how grand it's all going to be, with everything going just honky tonky.

DON *(Spoken)*

See what I told you? The man's a dreamer! I've been with him ever since I was this high. Kept him safe, and always in sight.

(Singing) But although he gives me so much stress, I ought to remember, I must confess. *(Leading Ali out)* That it's only thanks to this fuddy duddy.

I'm no ass in this tale, but his donkey buddy. *(They exit dancing)*

LEADER

It's only thanks to this little Ali, he's no ass in this tale but his bada buddy. *(Leader exits)*

SCENE 2

Girl is at the seat DR. Leader stands above her. Girl continues the story.

GIRL

So.... A thousand nights are done. The one thousand and first story is on. And it is all about what? About a lazy husband who is never even seen.

LEADER

But there's his hardworking wife, Aliyeh.

GIRL *(Rising, to audience)*

Why can't the story be about Aliyeh?

LEADER

Well, it is about Aliyeh, isn't it?

GIRL

Is it?

LEADER

Isn't it?

GIRL

Poor Aliyeh! She deserves a few good things in life herself.

LEADER

I agree, it is time the good lady Aliyeh had a new collection of jewellery.

GIRL

How do you know she wants jewellery?

LEADER

Among other things. She needs new clothes, new carpets, a new washing machine, fully automatic, and a new gas cooking range. How long will she go on with firewood?

GIRL

Firewood!

LEADER

Isn't that what her husband is going to get from the forest?

GIRL

Has he left already? Aliyeh was about to send me to look for him. She is terribly cross with him.

LEADER

The one they call Ali.

GIRL

The one who is never there when she wants him.

LEADER

His name means *sublime, elevated, exalted.*

GIRL

She thinks it's more like lazy, good for nothing, *kaamchor* (avoiding work).

LEADER

Where is she now?

GIRL

With the begum, admiring her jewellery.

LEADER

And the begum only too happy to show them off.

GIRL

For the hundredth time.

LEADER

What an unlucky woman, to be married to a poor man.

GIRL

While her husband's brother turns out rich.

LEADER

And the begum only too happy to show off her rich husband.

GIRL

Poor Aliyeh! All she can do is wish that the begum will continue to entertain her in her rich home.

LEADER

Tch tchtchtch! While Ali Baba is all by himself in the forest, his tummy empty, his bones weary, but about to stumble upon the most marvellous secret ever revealed to any man in any story, in any land.

GIRL

At this point you know what I really want to do?

LEADER

I can guess, little lady, but perhaps you should inform the people gathered here what that is in your own words.

GIRL

That's it! I want to be there, I want to watch the play with my friends there.

LEADER

Ah, but who will tell them the rest of the story then?

GIRL

You are doing well enough. Do you really need me?

LEADER

And if I say I do?

GIRL

I'll say let me go and sit there, and you can always call me when you think I should be here.

LEADER

Hmmm... Sounds fair enough. Just one little service before you leave us. May I?

GIRL

Yes?

LEADER

Tell me the name of the begum.

GIRL

Is it important? Just call her Begum.

LEADER

And her husband? The rich brother of the poor Ali Baba?

GIRL

His name is...hmmm...what shall we call him?

(Kasim, Begum and Aliyeh enter from up-left, snaking their way in. Aliyeh carries Kasim's seat, following the other two. The Chorus – as the neighbourhood – peeps in from wings L and R and from behind the house sets. Kasim, Begum and Aliyeh – K-B-A – stop Centre. Kasim striking a pose.)

Song 3. Kasim and Begum

The Chorus starts a chant to a beat that will be taken up by K-B-A as a rap beat.

CHORUS

Ta-rut-a-DAA...Ta-rut-a-DAA...
Ta-rut-a-daa- tut-a-daa- tut-a-daa- tut-a-daa-tut-a-daa...
Ta-rut-a-DAA

KASIM

The name's Kasim...
Ta-rut-a-daa-tut-a-daa-tut-a-daa-da-daa
Ta-rut-a-daa-tut-a-daa-tut-a-DAA-DAA-DAA

K-B-A

Ta-rut-a-daa-tut-a-daa-tut-a-daa-da-daa
Ta-rut-a-daa-tut-a-daa-tut-a-DAA-DAA-DAA

CHORUS

Ta-rut-a-DAA...Ta-rut-a-DAA...
Ta-rut-a-daa- tut-a-daa- tut-a-daa- tut-a-daa-tut-a-daa...
Ta-rut-a-DAA

K-B-A

Ta-rut-a-daa-tut-a-daa-tut-a-daa-da-daa
Ta-rut-a-daa-tut-a-daa-tut-a-DAA-DAA-DAA

CHORUS

Ta-rut-a-DAA...Ta-rut-a-DAA...
Ta-rut-a-daa- tut-a-daa-tut-a-daa- tut-a-daa-tut-a-daa...
Ta-rut-a-DAA
Ta-rut-a-daa- tut-a-daa-tut-a-daa- tut-a-daa-tut-a-daa...
Ta-rut-a-DAA

(Kasim, Begum and Aliyeh are positioned C. The chorus is watching.)

KASIM
They call me Kasim, that's me
Kasim the rich, that's me.
There's only one Kasim, that's me.
Kasim, that's right, that's me.

BEGUM
That's you!

KASIM
That's me!

BEGUM
My rich husband!

KASIM
That's me! *(Pause)*

KASIM
I love my money! *(Singing, moving L)*
There's money in my blood
There's money in my head
There's money in the sacks, right under my bed.
(Aliyeh moves L to Kasim with seat)

CHORUS
Ta-rut-a-DAA...Ta-rut-a-DAA...
Ta-rut-a-daa- tut-a-daa- tut-a-daa- tut-a-daa-tut-a-daa...
Ta-rut-a-DAA

BEGUM *(Fawning)*
And gold....

KASIM *(Moving to L of Begum, singing)*
In my mouth, there's a gold tooth
One gold tooth for now
Diamonds in mah ears, and pearls on mah cow.
(Aliyeh moves to Kasim with seat. Kasim moves R.)

BEGUM
Our hens are gold, our goose is gold
The eggs they lay are golden gold.

Gold dust in our butter, on golden toast
Our breakfast is richer by far than most.

CHORUS
Ta-rut-a-DAA...Ta-rut-a-DAA...
Ta-rut-a-daa- tut-a-daa- tut-a-daa- tut-a-daa-tut-a-daa...
Ta-rut-a-DAA

ALIYEH *(To Begum, spoken)*
Such a golden voice you have, lips of reddest ruby
Eyes like sparkling sapphire, none more beautiful than my lady.

KASIM
I've got it all, yeah I've got it all,
Everything to get, big and small.
Dinar and dollar, euro and pound,
All in a Swiss bank, safe and sound.

CHORUS
Ta-rut-a-DAA...Ta-rut-a-DAA...
Ta-rut-a-daa- tut-a-daa- tut-a-daa- tut-a-daa-tut-a-daa...
Ta-rut-a-DAA
(Aliyeh starts to move R to Kasim. He starts to move back to Begum at C. Aliyeh follows him back.)

KASIM
They say the name Kasim rhymes with sim sim,
If there's a joke there somewhere, it's rather dim dim,
They know I'm the boss, no one in mah way.
(Spoken) The name's Kasim. The richest man today.
(Aliyeh places the seat C. Kasim sits.)

CHORUS *(Dispersing)*
Ta-rut-a-DAA...Ta-rut-a-DAA...
Ta-rut-a-daa- tut-a-daa- tut-a-daa- tut-a-daa-tut-a-daa...
Ta-rut-a-DAA

* * *

KASIM
And where is that fool husband of yours at this moment?

ALIYEH
At this moment, dear brother-in-law, he must be deep in the forest.

KASIM

In a forest? Dear me. Taken to hunting, has he?

BEGUM *(Guffaw)*

Hunting? Ali Baba and hunting? He is out there chopping wood for Aliyeh's kitchen.

KASIM

What? No gas cooking range yet? Dear, dear me. What is the model you have, Begum?

BEGUM

Well, the gas comes piped from I-Ran...

KASIM

I-Ran?

BEGUM

We call it I-Ran now. It was Iran in those days. And the range itself is I-talian. Fully imported.

ALIYEH

Oh...I...we...you know what? They say that food cooked with a wood fire is tastier – and healthier. It's the way our grandmothers used to cook.

KASIM

What about the disappearing forests, my dear?

BEGUM

What would happen if all of us insisted on food cooked on wood fires? We must also think of the environment, you know.

ALIYEH

Ah, yes. I suppose the gas piped from Iran is much better for the environment. I must tell Ali about it.

KASIM

You must. Just imagine the whole nation insisting on food cooked on wood fires. There'll be only two kinds of people in that kind of nation – those cooking on wood fires, and those cutting wood in forests to keep the fires burning.

BEGUM

Heavens! A nation of woodcutters! It won't do. It won't do at all.

ALIYEH

I will tell Ali. We will scrape and save. We will beg, borrow and steal...no, just beg and borrow...we will get that gas stove into our little home one day. Inshallah, not too far from today.

KASIM

Meanwhile, wipe the tears from your eyes.

ALIYEH

Meanwhile, I will pray...

BEGUM

Pray that the smoke from the wood fire brings you less tears than the wretched poverty Ali keeps you in.

ALIYEH

He is a lazy *kaamchor,* but he is a good man.

KASIM

A woodcutter still. *(To begum)* Time for my hourly snack, my dear. Will you fix me something nice and light to lift the mood a bit. All this talk about wood cutters leaves me depressed and hungry. Do you have those Dutch troop waffles still? And the English marmalade?

BEGUM

I have just the right snack for you today. It is from India, and is called a sa-mo-sa. You can have it with the marmalade.

(Song 3 refrain. Begum and Kasim exit singing.)

KASIM *(Singing)*

There's money in my blood, there's money in my head
There's money in the sacks, right under my bed.
They know I'm the boss, no one in mah way
The name's Kasim. The richest man today.

(Aliyeh picks up the tune and sings a verse at slower tempo, bemoaning her fate and also...wondering about Ali's fate in the forest.)

ALIYEH *(Singing)*

There's money in his blood, there's money in his head
There's money in the sacks, right under his bed.
We know you're the boss, no one in your way
What's there tomorrow for the richest man today?

SCENE 3

The stage is transformed into a forest area. Boy and Don enter and halt.

DON

This should do, master. It is close enough to town, and deep enough to be out of sight from all townspeople. And there's a nice withered tree with lots of dried up branches. Just what you need.

BOY

They say the forest has all kinds of hidden treasures. But nobody has seen them.

DON

I have.

BOY

You have? What kinds of treasure?

DON

I am not allowed to tell you.

BOY

Come on! You can tell me, I am sure.

DON

Uh unh.

BOY

I won't tell anybody else. It will be a secret, I promise.

DON

Sorry. It is a matter of honour, you see. Code of conduct, and all that. I am sworn to it. I have taken an oath of secrecy of office.

BOY

Who gave you this – what do you call it – code of conduct?

DON

The International League of Donkeys for Worldwide Peace.

BOY

You have an international league?

DON

We have an anthem too. Have you heard the Donkey Serenade? *(He sings a bar)* No? Well, you can google it when you get back.

BOY

So...there is a treasure here somewhere, and you won't tell me where it is.

DON

You know, little master, you are a bit impatient. Clever and well-read and all that, but impatient. And that's not good for you. You will learn soon enough that everything comes in truckloads to those who can be patient.

BOY

I am going back! It is much more fun reading about it in my book! What can I expect from a donkey?

DON

Those who know not, know not they know not.

BOY

Enough! Will you show me the treasure, or do I leave you here and get back? *(Pause. Don ponders over it.)*

BOY

Well?!

DON

Well... since you really are clever and well read and all that and, more important, you are so important for the rest of this play, I can agree to a little compromise.

BOY

And that is... ?

DON

I can show you a teeny weeny bit of the treasure as a sampler. Not all of it. Is that all right?

BOY

I suppose it will have to be. Where is it kept?

DON

Follow me.

(Don leads Boy through a winding path in the forest and brings him to a corner where there is an old props trunk of the theatre company. It is covered by a rock prop from another play.)

BOY

Is this where it is hidden?

DON

This is it! Here, help me move this rock...this way...there! *(The trunk is revealed)* Go on, open it!

(Boy opens the trunk. It is full of props from other plays, some familiar, some not so familiar, but all make-believe things.)

BOY

But...these are...These are just useless props from plays!

DON

Useless? There is jewellery too, you know.

BOY

Fakes! Useless!

DON

But they were real enough when you used them in the play the last me.

BOY

But it was a play!

DON

But real – for you and for all of them out there.

BOY

You are confusing me! I want to go back!

DON

Go back where?

BOY

To my story book!

DON

This is the story! It is happening right before you!

BOY

But I don't see anything of the story here. I started on it long ago. Nothing has happened after that.

DON

It will. You will see everything. You do not see it now, because you are not allowing it to happen.

BOY

What should I do to see the rest of it?

DON

I can tell you. Will you listen?

BOY

All right, but are you sure it will work?

DON

Are you sure you are listening?

BOY

I am listening!

DON

Let me see if you are. *(He claps once. There is sound of distant hoof beats)*

What was that?

BOY

Horses, I think. Many riders.

DON

Good! *(He claps again. There is sound of a men's chorus singing.)*

BOY

A song! Many men singing.

DON

You are doing well. *(He claps again. Sound of an old gigantic fortress door opening with a groan.)*

BOY

A great big door opening.

DON

It is meant to be a great big boulder, but the boys in the sound room couldn't get it. Right, a great big door will do.

BOY

And now...

DON

And now, I must give you the sacred mantra for your awakening.

(Don draws the boy near, covers both their heads with a cloth– sheet/ shawl and whispers the Gayatri mantra to the pupil.)

DON

To discover the secrets of the universe you must first learn...
...to put aside everything you now believe
...and believe in what you want to believe
...the trunk beside you has real gold, real jewellery
...there is more of it there, lots and lots more, waiting for you
...you will find it soon
...because it is written
...Ali Baba will find a great big mountain of hidden treasure
...and you are...Ali Baba.

(The stage gets darker through the mantra. At the end there is sound of hoofbeats approaching, soon combined with the chorus of men in song.)

DON

Come along, little master. We cannot be seen here. We must hide.

ALI

Hide from what?

DON

The band of thieves coming this way. They are a ruthless lot. Their leader – the one they call the CEO – he is no Robin Hood. He loots and plunders and kills with sheer joy.

ALI

A hard criminal, is he?

DON

Ready to stand for elections now.

(Boy and Don slip away to a corner down-left and watch... as the band of thieves enters, led by the CEO, riding – stick horses and singing with great gusto).

Song 4. The gang of thieves

The song is choreographed with a 'riding' dance.

Clip Clop Clip Clop Clip Clop rubba-dubbah
Clip Clop Clip Clop rubba-dubbah-day

Gotta be gotta be getting on our way now
Who do we who do we rob today?

Ziggety-gang ziggety-gang ziggety-piggety bang bang
Ziggety-gang ziggety-gangrubbah-dubbah day.

Gotta be gotta be getting on our way now
Who do we who do we rob today?

They call us evil, call us mean, we know just how they hate us.
Hurram-ho! We're never ever seen, you're better off dead if you met us!

Huptidibuptidihuptidibidibidi
Huptidibuptidirubba-dubbah-day

Gotta be gotta be getting on our way now
Who do we who do we rob today?

Snakes and toads and rats and bed bugs
Keep us company everyday

Gotta be gotta be getting on our way now
Who do we who do we rob today?
We're baddie boys, we have no shame, got kicked out of school at seven
The boss came along and taught us the game, now hurram-ho it's heaven!

Ziggety-gang ziggety-gang ziggety-piggety bang bang
Ziggety-gang ziggety-gang rubbah-dubbah day

Gotta be gotta be getting on our way now
Who do we who do we rob today?
(The song ends. The thieves chant in chorus.)

THIEVES
All hail the CEO!
(The CEO motions all to be silent. There are a few stylised-choreographed moves, the band crouching and taking position as in an infantry attack. Finally, the CEO barks the command.)

* * *

CEO

OPEN UP...SIM SIM!

(To the accompaniment of the sound of an old gigantic fortress door opening with a groan, a part of the set opens to reveal a dark area of the stage. There are many twinkling lights, in many colours, as in a dark room full of fireflies. The CEO and his band enter the 'cave' and disappear. From off stage we hear the CEO's voice commanding the cave to shut.)

CEO *(Off)*

OH-SHADDUPP...SIM SIM!

(The sound of the door closing with a groan. The set closes.

A tight spot picks up the drum down-right. It beats and trembles. The Leader steps in.)

LEADER

He may appear a little baba, but the lad is taking to the part of Ali really well! And we must thank Don for that. They are getting along just fine. A little boy is a donkey's best friend, they say. So,where do we go from here? We can go fast forward and see Aliyeh in Ali Baba's house, deliriously happy with the gold Ali Baba has brought from the forest...

And, of course, the jealousy that it kicked up in Begum and Kasim! But I suppose you want to see the band of thieves and their CEO leaving the magical cave, and then have Ali Baba entering the cave himself?

(To audience) You do, don't you? Ahha, I know you do. All right, let's have it.

From off stage we hear the CEO's voice commanding the cave to open:

CEO *(Off)*

OPEN UP... SIM SIM!

(The sound of the door opening with a groan. The set opens. The twinkling lights in the cave come on again. The CEO and his band appear out of the cave. They take their positions. The CEO barks the command.)

CEO

OH-SHADDUPP... SIM SIM!

(The sound of the door closing with a groan. The set closes.

There is a loud hurrah from the band. They break into their song in chorus, 'mount' their horses, trot around the stage in song and gallop away.)

Song 4 refrain

Ziggety-gang ziggety-gang ziggety-piggety bang bang
Ziggety-gang ziggety-gang rubbah-dubbah day

Gotta be gotta be getting on our way now
Who do we who do we rob today?

(Repeat as needed) Gotta be gotta be getting on our way now
Who do we who do we rob today?
(Sound of chorus and hoof beats receding.)

SCENE 4

Spot on Leader down-centre.

Don ambles along and greets Leader with a friendly bray.

LEADER

I suppose Ali was suitably impressed.

DON

Impressed? Stunned is a better word. Dazed, stupefied, knocked out of his wits. Took all I had to snap him out of it.

LEADER

What did you do?

DON

I sang to him. *(Breaks into melodious braying)*

LEADER *(Cutting in)*

Poor Ali!

DON

Well, not so poor anymore! What do you think he did when he regained his senses?

LEADER

Let's ask them. *(To audience, getting them to fill in)* What do you think Ali did then?

(The Leader and Don prompt the audience to say what happens next, step by step –

>> Ali tries opening the door to the cave himself

>> The secret command

>> The cave opens and he goes in

>> Wow! All that gold and all those gems

>> What gems? What else? What else?

>> He loads up and comes out

>> He uses the secret command to shut the cave

>> He goes home to Aliyeh excited)

LEADER

And they lived happily ever after?

DON

No! Their troubles had just begun!

(The sound of the drum beating by itself down-right. Crossfade to Duh King and Sheherazad at the seat).

DUH

I don't understand. They should be happy. All that gold after all those years of having nothing.

SHEHER

My lord, remember your words of wisdom? 'You win some, and...'?

DUH

And you...uh...I say...I said what?

SHEHER *(Prompting, miming taking a nap)*

And you... rhymes with snooze...

DUH

That's right! But this is no time for a nap!

SHEHER

You are getting there, my lord. You said 'you win some and you...'? Try again, my lord... la-la-la-

DUH

I give up. You win, I lose.

SHEHER

Excellent, my lord! You win some, you lose some. You had the answer all the time.

DUH

I had the answer? I did, didn't I? Of course, I had the answer! Uh...what was the question?

SHEHER

We were wondering how you can have a lot of wealth and be in a lot of trouble as well.

DUH

I am in trouble? What kind of trouble?

SHEHER

The trouble, my lord, is that we cannot go on with the story of Ali Baba without Ali Baba on stage himself.

DUH

And why is he not here?

SHEHER

He says he doesn't want to. He doesn't feel like it.

DUH

Well, we should knock some sense into his head, shouldn't we?

SHEHER

We will need some help. *(She claps)*

(Crossfade to down-left. Boy is absorbed in his book. At the sound of the claps Girl rises from her auditorium seat and goes up to Boy.)

GIRL

What happened then?

BOY

Ali reached home with a sack of gold coins loaded on the ass...

(Loud protesting brays from off stage. Boy continuing)

On his donkey. When he reached the front door he called out to his wife.

VOICE *(Off)*

Aliyeh! Open the door!

ALIYEH *(Off)*

Ali, you are back! Have you got the firewood?

VOICE

Actually, no.

ALIYEH

Well, you are not coming in here then. I don't want to see your face till you get me that firewood. And you get no dinner either!

VOICE

No firewood, but I have brought a little surprise for you. If you don't want to see my face, open the door for our donkey. He willshow you what I got for you. I am going up to the pond for a snooze. It has been a tiring afternoon.

(Lights come up on Ali Baba's home area. A bare floor, with a large sheet spread on the floor. Aliyeh is standing, arms akimbo. Don ambles in with a large sack on his back. He pours the contents of the sack on to the sheet. Aliyeh is stupefied.)

ALIYEH

Gold! A sack full of gold coins!!

(Crossfade to Girl and Boy.)

GIRL

And Ali?

BOY

He went back to the pond to be by himself again.

GIRL

Should he not be there as part of the story?

BOY

He says there is no place for him in the story anymore. All he had to do was find the treasure. The fun starts now, with all the others jumping into the story. Lots of *masala* at every step.

GIRL

You'll tell me about it?

BOY

Sure.

(Crossfade to Duh and Sheher DR. Girl joins them.)

GIRL

It's all right. We can do without him.

SHEHER

Thank you. We may go on, then?

GIRL

It seems perfectly all right to do so.

DUH

She means...?

SHEHER

We may go on, my lord.

GIRL

Aliyeh decides to take charge at this point.

SHEHER

Who else is needed?

GIRL

There's Aliyeh, there's Begum, then we have Kasim... that should do for now. Then there's the servant girl, Marjeena.

SHEHER

Also known as Morgiana in English speaking lands.

GIRL

We'll call her Marji. She is the servant girl in Aliyeh's house.

SHEHER

She may be a servant girl, but she is very clever.

DUH

As clever as me? No? As clever as Sheherazad here, then.

SHEHER

We'll find out a little later, my lord.

GIRL

She comes in a little later.

DUH

Do you have somebody for Marji?

GIRL AND SHEHER *(Together)*

I think I do.

SHEHER

Your call.

GIRL

So...we may proceed. *(Girl joins Leader down-centre.)*

GIRL

I think Sheher wants to play a part in the play.

LEADER

I think Duh-King wants to play too.

GIRL

What should we do?

LEADER

Give them some parts to play.

GIRL

But she is supposed to be telling the story.

LEADER

To whom?

GIRL

To Duh-King, of course.

LEADER

She can still do that.

GIRL

What do we do, then?

LEADER

Tell the story to them, out there.

GIRL

So, whose story is it anyway?

LEADER

Our story, of course! And our story has within it another story, in which there is a clever woman called Sheherazad, who tells stories to a king. She does her job, we do our job.

GIRL

You know, I think Sheherazad thinks this is her story. And that her story has within it another story, in which there are clever people who tell stories to an audience. She gets us to do her job.

LEADER

Too many storytellers! We must get on quickly with the story itself.

GIRL

I know what to do. Let's get Duh-King and Sheherazad on our side. What do you say we get them into our story.

LEADER

You mean give them parts in our play?

GIRL

Of course! We must do that as quickly as possible. Now!

LEADER

You know, you should really be the one leading us all in this story.

GIRL

Thank you, but I want to get back there with my friends. Call me if you need me again.

(Girl steps off stage into the auditorium. Leader continues)

LEADER *(To audience)*

Smart cookie, don't you think? I wonder which school she goes to! Do you know? Can you guess? *(Gets some responses)*

Thank you...you could be right... (*Etc.*)

And so we move on...

SCENE 5

Leader remains down-centre and describes interim scenes with short narrations, as the characters move in the upstage areas in fast-forward mode.

LEADER

Well, there she was, Aliyeh, the poor woodcutter's wife, turned into Aliyeh, the rich woodcutter's wife... or was it the poor woodcutter's rich wife? No matter, it was a magical transformation, and it was all in the twinkling of an eye. There she was, standing in front of a huge pile of... ?

ALIYEH

Gold! A sack full of gold coins!!

LEADER

What do you think was the first thing she did? What is the first thing you would do if you had a pile of gold coins dumped on the floor in front of you?

(He gets responses from the audience)

Ah, but Aliyeh was different. She wanted to know exactly how much gold she had got. So... it had to be measured. Have you ever seen how piles of rice and wheat and sugar and dal and other grains are measured in the market? What do they use to measure the quantity? *(He gets responses from the audience)*

That's right. She decided to use a grain measuring jar with the pile of gold. But she didn't have a measuring jar herself. So she went to... ?

(He gets responses from the audience)

That's right. She went to Begum... and asked if she could borrow her grain measure. Begum agreed to lend her the grain measure... but couldn't help wondering what on earth a poor woman like Aliyeh would want to do with the measure.

So...when Begum went in to get the measuring jar, she took out the imported American chewing gum from her mouth and stuck it at the bottom of the measure, then came out and gave it to Aliyeh.

Aiyeh rushed home and measured all of the gold lying in a heap on the floor. There were nine hundred and ninety eight jars of gold coins. She was overjoyed. She measured again...no, there were nine hundred and ninety *nine* jars of gold coins.

She rushed back to Begum and returned the grain measure, thanking her profusely. Before Begum could ask what it was all about Aliyeh had rushed back home, bolted the door, and started to dig a hole in the backyard to bury the pile of gold coins. It had to be kept a secret.

(By now Don has joined Leader.)

LEADER

And Ali? Where is Ali? *(Don shrugs)*At the pond, day dreaming as usual? *(Don shrugs)* Poor Aliyeh! She had to take care of the treasure all by herself. Anyway, remember it is a secret. A very special secret. *(Don shrugs)*

(Leader is joined by Begum and Kasim. They are agitated.)

BEGUM

You think we don't know?

KASIM

She thought she could keep a secret from us?

LEADER

You talking to me?

KASIM

No, we have a habit of talking to ourselves. A touch of the sun, you see.

LEADER

Oh dear, one of those...

BEGUM

Two of those!

LEADER

I think I should be on my way. If you'll excuse me...*(Exits hurriedly)*

BEGUM

I knew there was something fishy going on.

KASIM

You think it had something to do with this ass going there with a sack on his back ?

(Don brays aloud, kicks him and makes an exit.)

BEGUM

Look at this! *(Showing Kasim a gold coin)* A gold coin!I found it at the bottom of the measure, stuck on the chewing gum.

KASIM

Hmmm... It has the seal of the Doddamallya empire, a kingfisher.

BEGUM

If she needed a grain measure for the job, and if she didn't miss this gold coin, can you imagine how much of it she must have?

KASIM

Let me see...yes, I can imagine it.

BEGUM

The size of the pile?!

KASIM

I suppose you could sit on it. It would make a fine bean bag.

BEGUM

And what are you going to do about it?

KASIM

Get a seat like that for myself.

BEGUM

Fool! A lifetime of peddling your wares has only made that skull of yours thick as brick. What do you know about Ali?

KASIM

Baba?

BEGUM

The liitle Baba called Ali.

KASIM

Well, everybody knows he is a day dreamer. And lazy.. And a general good-for-nothing.

BEGUM

And a Chhupa Rustom. You can add that.

KASIM

Could be, could be. I never understood the boy.

BEGUM

So... what are you going to do about it?

KASIM

Ask him for some of it. He is my kid brother after all.

BEGUM

How much will you ask for?

KASIM

I don't know. I suppose it depends on how much he has.

BEGUM

That is the first thing we must find out – how much of it they have. Be firm with them.

KASIM

'Oy little baba Ali, gulli-walla Ali, turned out a Chhupa Rustom Ali, henh? Tell us now, how much of it do you have? The truth, or else...'

BEGUM

And then we must find out where they got it from.

KASIM

'Oy, this didn't come from under the tail of your ass, did it? Tell us now, where did it come from?'

BEGUM

They are not as dumb as they appear. You must get the secret out of them.

(Begum and Kasim exit. Leader and Don enter and go down-left, where Boy is seated, absorbed in the book.)

BOY

And so...Kasim and Begum dropped in on Aliyeh and Ali for a little social visit. They were caught unprepared.

LEADER

'Ahh, what a pleasant surprise! Come in, do come in...'

DON

What unusual weather we are having now. All on account of the climate change, they say...

BOY

Begum took out the gold coin and held it in front of Aliyeh's nose. Kasim came to the point quickly.

LEADER

'Oy, this didn't come from under the tail of your ass, did it?'

(Don complains with a loud bray)

Begum had Aliyeh cornered, and Kasim had Ali in a bind.

BOY

And since neither of them could find a way to wriggle out, they had to tell them everything – all about the forest, the cave, the secret password...everything.

DON

And they had to drag me into the story.

BOY

That was it! Kasim begged Ali to lend him –
(Don cocks his ear) – the noble donkey.
(Satisfied, Don ambles along offstage)
He took directions from Ali for the exact location of the secret cave, and off he went into the forest.

LEADER *(To audience)*

And you know what happened next, don't you?
(Gets responses)
You do? You don't?
Should we do this scene, or skip it? Are you sure you want it?
You don't mind seeing blood being spilt?
Ughh... all that tomato ketchup... (*Etc.)*
Well... if you insist...

SCENE 6

The forest scene as before. Don narrates the happenings as they unfold.

DON

There I was, dragged to the forest against my will. I went along simply because Ali asked me to. Imagine doing this for that greedy Kasim! Oh, well, ours not to question why... Heh hehheh, *theirs* to do and die!

I know the way to the cave, of course. But I let him think he is in charge. He has all the facts, all the answers. Or so he thinks. No sooner has he reached the tree beside the cave, he jumps down off my back – that is some relief – and crouches like a drooling hyena behind the tree, he croaks in feverish excitement...

VOICE
OPEN UP... SIM SIM!

DON
He leaps into the cave without a second thought, leaving me behind. Heh hehheh. How is he going to carry all that loot out of the cave? He needs me, you will see. First, a moment of stunned silence. Then a loud gasp. That is followed by...

VOICE
AAAEEERRAAAHWWOOMMPPAAHYAAHHOOO !!!

DON
Rushing in to get his hands on the gold and the mountains of jewels he commands the cave to shut behind him.

VOICE
OH-SHADDUPP...SIM SIM!

DON
He dives into the pile of jewels, rolls in them, tosses them about himself, like a little boy splashing in a pool of water.

Right, enough of the joy bit. We have to get home quick and celebrate. Of course he needs that noble donkey to help with the logistics business. So, let's get that cave opened.

VOICE
OPEN UP... RIM JHIM!

DON
Heh heh, no go.

VOICE
OPEN UP RIN TIN TIN!

DON
Let's give him a few more tries.

VOICE
GIN AND TONIC!
DIM DIM!
DIM SUM SOUP!

DON
None of this works.

VOICE

PLEEEASE OH CAVE! LISTEN TO ME! JUST OPEN ONCE MORE! SIM – SIM – SIMPLY OPEN UP ONCE FOR ME! PUHLEEEZE!!

DON

Too late!

(Don slips away to a corner and watches... as the band of thieves enters, led by the CEO, as earlier. The thieves chant in chorus.)

THIEVES

All hail the CEO!

(The band takes position as earlier. CEO barks the command.)

CEO

OPEN UP... SIM SIM!

(The CEO and his band enter the cave and disappear. From off stage we hear the CEO's thundering roar followed by Kasim's death cry in quick succession.)

CEO *(Off)*

AAAYYEEEAAAAHHH!

KASIM *(Off)*

AAAGGHHHH!

DON

Please don't ask me to show you the scene. There, on the floor of the cave...oohh...I can't stand the sight of blood...strict vegetarian that I am. Let's just say that he acted swiftly and decisively, as every CEO is expected to, and dispatched the intruding Kasim to...well... a permanent state of retirement. It had to be done, keeping the interests of the shareholders uppermost.

(The CEO and his band appear out of the cave. They take their positions. The CEO barks the command.)

CEO

OH-SHADDUPP... SIM SIM!

(The set closes, as earlier. There is a loud hurrah from the band. They break into their song in chorus, 'mount' their horses, trot around the stage in song and gallop away. Sound of chorus and hoof beats receding.)

DON *(Emerging)*

With a heavy heart I must now tell you about a little detail in the last scene. How was Kasim actually dispatched, you might wonder? He was... oh dear...I suppose I have to tell you...He was hexed. Do you know what that means? *(Gets a few responses)*

You don't? You want me to explain? Are you sure you want it? You don't mind?

Ughh...all that tomato ketchup!

Well, all right. Here goes. It is a bit like keeping a cake or a pizza pie in front of you and dividing it into six parts. Hex for six...that's right, as in hexagon. You have a nice, large, sturdy, broad blade knife to slice it into six parts. Well, that's what the CEO did to poor Kasim – with his nice, large, sturdy broad blade sword. And you know what? He did it in just five sweeping strokes – one to chop off the head, two chops for the two arms, and two for the two legs. Gory, right? Don't say I didn't warn you.

(Leader joins Don)

LEADER

Anyway, this is better than letting you see it happen there.

DON

Took the words out of my mouth.

LEADER

Back in town, when there was no sign of Kasim's return, Begum begged Ali to go and look for him in the forest. Maybe the poor man had lost his way.

DON

Lost his way! Hee haw!

LEADER

Ali approached the cave quietly, cautiously. When he saw Don standing there all alone, he knew Kasim was somewhere nearby.

DON

Somewhere nearby! Hee haw!

LEADER

Perhaps in the cave still. Fallen asleep perhaps. He decided to go in and look for Kasim.

DON

Wait! Let me turn away. I am not sure I can go through this again.

LEADER

We don't have to go through that Open-Sim-Sim-Shut-up-Sim-Sim business all over again, do we?

(Don ambles into the cave area).

So, Ali went into the cave, his faithful donkey in tow. What he saw there left him speechless. His own brother, lying dead on the floor of the cave. Not just dead. Hexed. What was he to do? Could the band of thieves and their CEO be somewhere near, watching? He was frozen stiff in fear.

(Don comes out carrying a large sack.)

DON

Now, it was left to me to carry the six pieces of Kasim's body back into town. Ah,well! Another day, another sack load on my poor back.

(Don exits, carrying the sack. Leader signals to Girl to join him. She does.)

GIRL

I know! You are wondering how to get rid of the body.

LEADER

Not me. It was the Begum. And Aliyeh and Ali too. They had to give Kasim a decent burial.

GIRL

But how? What do you do when you have a body in six pieces?

LEADER

Hexed.

GIRL

You know, I don't think I am going to enjoy my geometry lessons anymore.

LEADER

They had to find a really clever way to do it.

GIRL

And... there had to be a really clever person to carry out the plan.

Crossfade to Duh-King and Sheher

DUH

Marji! Of course, Marji! Who else could think up such a clever plan? And carry it out too!

SHEHER

Let me show you how she did it.

DUH

Is there a part for me? A teeny weeny part? Please!

SHEHER

Well, all right. You can play the old cobbler.

DUH

An old cobbler?! Me?!

SHEHER

My lord, it is much more than a teeny weeny part. It is a very important part in the story.

DUH

Hmmm...all right, then.

SHEHER

A small part –

DUH

Small part?!

SHEHER

But a very important part.

DUH

Oh, well...

SHEHER

He doesn't have to speak a single line –

DUH

What?! No lines?!

SHEHER

But a very important part!

DUH

A part to suit my status as Duh-King, I hope.

SHEHER

A part made just for you, my lord. The cobbler does not see anything around him.

DUH

The man is blind too?!

SHEHER

Not quite. He simply cannot see. *(Duh-King tries to protest)*

It is a part that demands very special talent, my lord. There is a long line in the actors company begging to play the part...

DUH

Put the thought out of your head! I will play the part.

SHEHER

A wise decision, my lord. You will not regret it. Here...*(Giving him a gown)*

Put on this gown. Ah, how noble you look in the humblest clothing! And now...

(Sheher claps three times. Marji enters and positions herself before Duh-King and Sheher obediently.)

MARJI

Marji, the housemaid of Aliyeh and Ali, at your service, my lady.

SHEHER

Proceed! *(She exits)*

MARJI

Oh, dear old cobbler, prepare now for the greatest feat of sewing you have ever undertaken in your whole life.

(She holds out a blindfold. Crossfade to Leader and Girl.)

GIRL

Marji had heard about an old cobbler who lived in another part of the town. This cobbler had worked on every kind of skin from every kind of creature in all of god's creation. He had made sandals, shoes, slippers, purses, bags of all shapes, bags in all sizes, bags with buttons, bags with strings, bags with folds, bags with pockets, pockets with bags, saddlebags, handbags, carpetbags, waterbags, winebags, baggy pants, baggy eyes, baggy waistlines, bags within bags, bags without bags, export bags, import bags, asli bags, nakli bags, bags for wheat, sugar, basmati rice, bags for horse feed, horse dung manure, bags for kings, slaves, rich man, poor man, cowboy, thief.

LEADER
And one more.

GIRL
And bags for cooking oil. Huge quantities of oil, tub-fulls. Hahaha, you are wondering about that, aren't you?

LEADER
She found him out, the clever old cobbler. She challenged him to take on a very different and very difficult cobbling job, saying it was something he had never ever done in his whole life.

GIRL
And never have another chance if he missed this one.

LEADER
The old cobbler laughed, and said there simply was no cobbling job he could not do. But he was too busy, and was sorry he could not take up Marji's challenge.

GIRL
A gold coin exchanged hands. The old cobbler was tempted.

LEADER
But no, he was too busy with another job, a customer in Alaska wanting a bag to keep ice cubes.

GIRL
Another gold coin, pressed quietly into his palm.

LEADER
Well, nothing would happen to the ice cubes if they went without bags for another month. He asked to be told what to do straight away.

GIRL
Ahh, said Marji, I will have to blindfold you first, you see. The folks in the household are rather sensitive to these things.

LEADER
Protest, protest...

GIRL
Another gold coin... and it was all settled.
(As they speak, we see Duh-King and Marji enacting the scene. Duh-King [as cobbler] is led blindfolded by Marji through a long, winding path to inside Begum's house. A little later he is led out, returning to Sheher.)

LEADER
And all done. The body was sewn up neatly, as if nothing had happened, and there was a decent burial for Kasim, and everybody slept in peace that night, Begum, Aliyeh, Ali, and even Don.

GIRL
And, of course, the old cobbler. Little did he know then that his little part in the story was not the end of it.
(Duh-King and Sheher in their corner.)

SHEHER
Little did the old cobbler know that his little part in the story was not the end of it.

DUH
One more time? You mean I can play the part again?

SHEHER
Did you like playing the part, my lord?

DUH
I think I need to get the age right – maybe stick my neck out a bit, and bend my knees, like this.

SHEHER
You will get it, my lord.

DUH
You can find out if that drama company has any summer workshop.

SHEHER
They do, my lord, for newcomers. Not for seasoned players.

DUH

Ah, well, their loss then.

SHEHER

Let's see, now, we want the cobbler to come on again, so that you can play the part once more.

DUH

You can get Marji in again, if you like.

SHEHER

I might have to do that.

DUH

What can you do with your story to get the cobbler on again?

SHEHER

That should not be difficult.

DUH

You don't have to do it just for me, you know.

SHEHER

But the whole story is just for you, my lord.

DUH

There can always be other parts for me, my dear. I must work on extending my range.

SHEHER

My lord, you really were good as the cobbler.

DUH

Ah, well, hmmm...

SHEHER

That is why you must stick to the part now. Trust me!

DUH

You know, I think we make a good pair. What do you think?

SHEHER

Now that you mention it, my lord...

(The sound of hoof beats and the chorus approaching)

Hush, my lord.

SCENE 7

The forest area. The band of thieves enters, led by the CEO, as earlier. The thieves chant in chorus.

THIEVES

All hail the CEO!

(The band takes position as earlier. CEO barks the command.)

CEO

OPEN UP... SIM SIM!

(The CEO and his band enter the cave and disappear. From off stage we hear the CEO's thundering roar.)

CEO *(Off)*

AAAYYEEEAAAAHHH!

(The band rushes out, led by the CEO. He is livid. He rants, raves, waving his sword in all directions. He stops, and gathers his men in a tight huddle. There is a buzz.

Crossfade to Duh-King and Sheher.)

SHEHER

The time has come. The CEO will ask one of his men to go into town and find out about anybody dead recently, any body found that was not quite in one piece.

(Sheher gets Duh-King to become the cobbler again, and slips out.

In the forest area the buzz reaches a crescendo and stops. The CEO rises out of the huddle, walks around it slowly, pauses, and taps a thief on the shoulder with his sword. The thief rises and kneels before the CEO, who assigns him the mission by tapping him on the two shoulders and his head. The thief mounts his horse and rides away. The rest of the band melts into the forest.

Duh-King, in the cobbler's gown, awaits his cue. The thief, enters on foot, goes up to Duh-King and addresses him)

THIEF 1

Oy, there! Look sharp!

DUH

How dare you...

THIEF 1

Chhup! You are not supposed to speak! I do all the talking. You only nod your head. You nod up and down to say Yes, or you nod left and right to say no. All right, if you are from the land of Hindustan, you can nod left and tight to say Yes.

THIEF 1

Now, listen carefully. Has there been a death in this town recently? *(Nod)*

Anything unusual about the death? *(Nod)*

Yes? *(Nod)*

Unusual in what way? Can you tell? *(Nod)*

Do you know the house? *(Nod)*

Can you give me the address? *(Nod)*

You can't? Why not? You've been there, haven't you? *(Nod)*

So, why can't you tell me?

(Duh takes out blindfold and shows it to the thief)

What's this? A blindfold? *(Nod)*

You want me to blindfold you? *(Nod)*

And now you can show me the house?

(Duh, as the blindfolded cobbler, leads Thief 1 through a long, winding path to Aliyeh's door. Thief 1 is amazed, but pleased. The blindfold is removed.)

THIEF 1

Wah! You found the house blindfolded! Now, are you sure this is the house you came to? *(Nod)*

Did you see the house when you came the last time? *(Nod)*

You didn't? *(Nod)*

But this is the house. *(Nod)*

No goofing up? *(Nod)*

There better not be! And you went in there and...

(Nods and half mimes sewing up the body)

Good! You can go now. (*Duh doesn't move)*

Go on, now. Away with you! *(Duh doesn't move)*

Ah, you want a tip for the service. Here... *(Gives him a banana. Duh is annoyed. He half peels the banana and stuffs it into Thief's mouth, and strides off yelling.)*

DUH

First they give me a non-speaking part! Then they want to make a monkey out of me! Where is that woman? SHEHERAZAD!!

THIEF 1

The trouble with actors these days – goes to their heads! He thinks he is a king or what? Anyway...back to work.

(Thief 1 takes out a stick of chalk and marks Aliyeh's entrance with a large and prominent 'X' Just then Marji walks by. Seeing her, the thief hides the chalk sheepishly. A double take from Marji. She returns to Thief 1 and asks for the chalk. He gives it to her reluctantly.

Marji immediately adds two more lines to the large cross and makes it into the frame for a game of crosses and noughts. She enters a cross and gives Thief 1 the chalk, who cautiously enters a nought. Marji enters a second cross. The thief enters a nought. Too bad, Marji enters the third cross, and the game is up. She gives the chalk back to Thief 1 and goes on her way. Thief 1 is stunned, but relieved. He wipes out the crosses and noughts, leaves the double-cross on the floor, and steals out of the scene.

Crossfade to Girl and Boy seated in their corner.

She has a notebook and two sticks of crayon, and is trying to get Boy to play crosses and noughts. He is not interested, absorbed in his book. Finally he agrees.)

BOY

You know how to play crosses and noughts?

GIRL

Yes!

BOY

Will you teach me?

GIRL

Sure.

BOY

It's what Marji does in the story.

GIRL

Here, you first draw two long lines up and down. And then two lines across those lines, like this.

BOY

She got the thief to play, see?

GIRL

You get nine windows, see?

BOY

She knew there was something fishy about him marking the floor in front of Ali's house with a cross.

GIRL

And you are ready to start.

BOY

She got him to play. He did. And lost too. And then, she just walked away – as if nothing had happened.

GIRL

I'll begin. Here, I put a cross in this window.

BOY

I put a nought here.

GIRL

A cross.

BOY

Nought.

GIRL

A cross – and...

BOY

Nought... oh, no...

GIRL

Too bad! Try again.

(As they speak, we have a choreographed scene played through the rest of the stage. Marji is teaching the crosses and noughts game to all and sundry in the neighbourhood.)

Song 5. The game.

Marji begins by explaining with a large figure on the floor, as Girl is explaining to Boy, and then everybody is playing it with figures on the road in front of their doors.

***Optional:** We can show Sheher explaining the game to Duh-King at the same time.*

MARJI
Okay!
You put a nought nought here, then put a cross cross there
You put a nought nought here, they cross another place
Then they go and cross it, and take away the game
That's what it's all about.

SHEHER *(To DUH)*
Let's play noughts and crosses, come on, come on, let's play
I'll do the noughts and you do the crosses
That's what it's all about.

CHORUS
It looks real easy, but there's no second chance
You think very carefully before you make a plan.
Then you might just block it, or you might just cross it
That's what it's all about.

GIRL *(DL to BOY)*
Let's play noughts and crosses, come on, come on, let's play
I'll do the noughts and you do the crosses
That's what it's all about.

MARJI
You have to use your brains, you have to be real quick
You keep your eyes wide open, and you stick your nought right in
Or you cross to crossing crosses, and you cross your crosses in
That's what it's all about.

CHORUS
Let's play noughts and crosses, come on, come on, let's play
I'll do the noughts and you do crosses
That's what it's all about.

(Gradual fade out. The stage is empty. Night. The CEO and four thieves enter stealthily. They make their way to Ali's house. Thief 1 from the earlier scene stops and points out the gate with the marking. At the same time the CEO and the other thieves point to other gates in other directions – and then in all directions. The CEO is not pleased.)

CEO

AAAYYEEEAAAAHHH!

(He stomps out, followed by the other thieves.

A general alarm. Lights come on. The townsfolk come out to see what happened. Nothing seen. They go back. Marji remains.)

* * *

Song 5 Refrain

Marji sings or hums– as she 'cleans up', wiping off the crosses, first in front of her gate, and then from the rest of the road in the neighbourhood.

Crossfade to Girl and Boy.

BOY

The thief goofed up.

GIRL

Not making sure Ali's house had been marked right.

BOY

No other house but Ali's.

GIRL

No such goofing up by the CEO.

BOY

One swift stroke of his large, sturdy, broad blade sword, and...

GIRL

Khatam.

(Don enters flustered and settles between Girl and Boy.)

BOY

Poor Don! Can't stand the sight of blood.

DON

Ugh! All that tomato ketchup!

GIRL

There was another try. Another thief was sent into town to find out Ali's house. He chipped out a little slice of stone from the wall, placed it neatly in front of the gate pillar, and slipped back into the forest, rather pleased with himself.

BOY

But Marji's sharp eyes noticed the chip lying there as she returned from the market. Not taking any chances, she got everybody in the neighbourhood together, and started to teach them another game.

(As they speak, we have another choreographed scene played upstage. Marji is teaching a hopscotch game to all in the neighbourhood.

Everybody is hopping all over the stage to background music.

Gradual fade out. The stage is empty. Night. The CEO and four thieves enter stealthily. They make their way to Ali's house. Thief 2 stops and points out the gate. At the same time the CEO and the other thieves point to other gates in other directions – and then in all directions. The CEO is not pleased.)

CEO

AAAYYEEEAAAAHHH!

(He stomps out, followed by the other thieves.

A general alarm. Lights come on. The townsfolk come out to see what happened. Nothing seen. They go back. Marji remains. She smiles.

Crossfade to Girl, Don and Boy. Don is covering his eyes and ears.)

GIRL

Another goof up.

BOY

Another thief bit the dust.

GIRL

Khatam.

BOY

Two down, thirty eight to go.

GIRL

Thirty seven plus one. The CEO.

(Leader joins the group.)

LEADER

The CEO. It was up to him now. The buck stopped there. When the going gets tough, and all that. The tough only get rougher.

BOY

And more determined than ever.

DON

And that usually means big trouble for others around.

(CEO has approached the group. He barks to them.)

CEO

Oy! Whose ass is this? *(Don is about to protest. The others stop him)* I want him for an hour. Get him up!

(Don is raised by the three others) Follow me!

DON *(To audience)*

Why me? *(The CEO leads Don off stage)*

LEADER

He was set on finding out Ali's house.

BOY

He was going to do that himself.

GIRL

Disguised as a merchant carrying all his wares on a donkey, he entered the town...

(The CEO is seen entering with Don.)

CEO

New lamps for old! New lamps for old! *(Girl and Boy are puzzled)*

LEADER

He was not the type to bother about copyrights and sticking to the text and things like that. He went ahead with his own business model.

CEO

New lamps for old!

BOY

First he gets friendly with his customers.

GIRL

Then he gets them to talk about happenings in the town.

BOY

Very soon, they are telling him about Ali...

GIRL

And showing him Ali's house.

(We see several people in the neighbourhood gather around CEO. There is a general interest in his wares. Presently, all of them are pointing to Ali's house. Fade out.)

LEADER

We are ready now for the last part of the story. *(To audience)* Are you?

BOY

We are going in there to help out.

GIRL

They need lots of help for the last scenes.

LEADER

And we must find poor Don. They must not drag him into... *(CEO crosses the stage beaming, dragging Don along. Exits.)* Too late!

SCENE 8

Weekly market scene in front of Ali's house. Men and women peddling goods and services. Lots of noise.

Among the peddlers is CEO, in disguise. In tow is Don with a large leather oil cask. It has a large sunflower painted on it. We see the CEO approaching Aliyeh and striking up a conversation. He lifts the lid to the cask, and Aliyeh peeps in. She points to the courtyard of the house upstage. CEO is thankful, and whistles to the band of thieves in the wing. The rest of the peddlers start dispersing... as the Chorus enters. They are all donkeys, each with two casks, one on either side, a large sunflower on each cask. They all follow CEO and Don upstage and wait in a huddle. CEO addresses them.

CEO

Remember the signal. I tap the floor with my boots seven times like this. *(Demonstrates)* That's the time to spring out of the oil cask... and then... heh hehheh... it will all be over! Finally!

VOICE 1

Seven taps on the floor, master, with your boots.

VOICE 2

At the right time, master, seven taps.

CEO

I am going out for a while now. A liitle snack and drink. I will be back here when all are asleep. *(CEO exits. Aliyeh at the entrance.)*

ALIYEH

Ali! Aalleee! Where are you? *(Marji enters, goes up to Alyeh.)*

MARJI

What is it, my lady?

ALIYEH

Ohh baba-re-baba, that husband of mine! Never around when you need him!

MARJI

Tell me what need, my lady. I may be able to help you.

ALIYEH

We have an honoured guest at home. A rich oil sheikh.

MARJI

An oil rich sheikh.

ALIYEH

A sunflower oil sheikh.

MARJI

Big market for that nowadays. People are getting smart about good cholesterol, bad cholesterol, and all that.

ALIYEH

The least I can do is give him a good, hot meal, as humble as the dish might be.

MARJI

Ohhh, my lady, we are out of cooking oil in the house!

ALIYEH

Exactly! And just at this moment, when you want him to run an errand and get some oil from the grocer, where do you think that husband of mine is?

MARJI

Not here.

ALIYEH

Not anywhere in sight! What am I going to do now?

MARJI

Why don't you leave it to me, my lady. I will take care of the cooking oil – and the cooking. Go in and get some rest.

ALIYEH

Are you sure?

MARJI

Of course, my lady. Leave it to me.

ALIYEH *(Leaving)*

Don't cut corners. We must give the rich merchant a really good meal.

MARJI

Yes, my lady. *(As Marji ponders over the next move, Don ambles along and nudges her)*

Hello, sweetie-pie! *(Don, pleasantly surprised, rubs his head against her)*

Are you hungry? They make you work really hard, don't they? *(Don reacts)*

Now, tell me, if you were in my place, what would you do to get some oil for cooking a quick meal? *(Don points to the audience)*

Ask them? All right, what would you do? *(Gets some responses)*

Borrow some oil? Borrow from...? *(Don nudges her in the direction of his cask)*

I suppose it should be all right to take some from there. I can always put it back later. When the lady and Ali and the oil sheikh are enjoying their dinner, I will slip into town and get the oil from the grocer, and put it back into the cask. *(Don approves)*

And I can always say I had your permission. *(Marji goes up to the first cask, opens the lid, takes out a measure of oil. She turns to Don.)*

This much all right? *(Don does a little tap dance, seven steps. A head pops up from another cask.)*

THIEF 3

Is it time already? *(Marji and Don exchange winks)*

MARJI

Not quite. Just a test drill. *(Don tap dances seven steps again. Another head pops up from another cask.)*

THIEF 4

Time already? What about dinner?

MARJI

Haven't you had dinner? Poor thing!

THIEF 4

Not a bite since we left the forest. It's work, work, work all day.

MARJI

Would you like some hot soup? *(Two other heads pop up)*

THIEF 5

Mulligatawny!

THIEF 6

Now, that's what I call service!

MARJI *(To all four)*

Shhh. Not so loud! You are on a secret mission, remember? Get back in. You will get your soup right where you are. Leave it to Room Service.

(The thieves pop back into the casks. Marji and Don do a high ten. Marji picks up the first cask on her head and leaves. The first thief pops his head out again.)

THIEF 3

Who was she?

(Don pushes him back into the cask.

The stage darkens. Ominous music. Marji in silhouette in dance like steps. Voice of Aliyeh off stage.)

ALIYEH

Marji! Are you done with the cooking?

MARJI

I am, my lady.

ALIYEH

What did you make for our honoured guest?

MARJI

Hot soup as an appetiser, my lady.

ALIYEH

Enough I hope. What if the guest asks for some more.

MARJI

I made enough for an army, my lady.

ALIYEH

Good! I hope you made it nice and rich.

MARJI

It took a lot of oil, my lady.

ALIYEH

Have you tasted it?

MARJI

I am testing it out now, my lady.

(Through this she is pouring steamy, boiling oil into the casks one by one. Fade out. Crescendo to the music. In the dark, the gleeful braying of Don.)

•

SCENE 9

Ali's house. A rug on the floor has a large satin covered cushion on it.(A seat?) Aliyeh and Marji enter, bowing and kowtowing to let CEO in and guide him to his place on the cushion. There is much ceremony in seating CEO, through which Marji notices a bulky scabbard under his robe. She jokes lightly about it.

MARJI

What a large sword, my lord!

CEO

Ah, this...for self defence, really. You never can tell nowadays.

MARJI

That is wise, my lord. You are surely not one who lives by the sword. For then –

ALIYEH

Marji! Look into the meal, please. Our guest must be hungry. *(Marji exits with a sweet smile, holding the CEO's gaze.)*
Sir...?

CEO

Uhunh...Where is the master of the house?

ALIYEH

What can I say, sir? He is hardly home. He is a good man, but... you know... He has sent a message that he will join us by and by, and most certainly before our honoured guest departs.

CEO

It is of utmost importance that we meet before I depart. Meanwhile, many thanks for your kind hospitality.

ALIYEH

We do what little we can, sir.

CEO

You will be suitably rewarded...very soon.

ALIYEH

We shall bow our heads to receive what you choose to bestow upon us.

CEO

You...and your family...your household...hmmm...surely you deserve lasting peace after all your toil.

ALIYEH

You are too kind. *(Marji enters with a large ornamental tray, empty, and places it before CEO.)*

MARJI

My lord, are you ready for your meal?

ALIYEH AND CEO *(Together)*

Marji, what is the meaning of...What do we have here?

MARJI

My lord, it is an ancient custom in our land to entertain an honoured guest before the meal is served. And the honour of entertaining our guest today has been conferred upon me. Shall we begin? *(CEO signals she may)*

It always begins with a few riddles. Here is the first.

There was a man with seventeen camels, blessed with three sons. Just before he died, he called all his sons and –

CEO

Gifted the camels to them. He requested them to share the camels peacefully, as instructed in his will, and da-da-da-da-da.

MARJI

You are well informed, my lord. You win this round. Let us try another. A man tells his two sons to race their camels to a distant city to see who will inherit his fortune.

CEO

The one whose camel is slower will win. So, the boys mount their camels and da-da-da-da-da.

MARJI *(To Aliyeh)*

Another win. Our guest this evening is truly learned.

CEO

You are allowed only one more riddle. After that it will be my turn to provide some really out of the ordinary entertainment.

MARJI

My lord, It is plain to see that this evening we are entertaining an out of the ordinary guest.

CEO

These riddles are commonplace in every corner of our land. Do you think this is the court of the stupid king in the Arabian Nights?

MARJI

Perhaps we should move on to the one thousand and first night.

CEO

Get a riddle from elsewhere. For a change. Enough of camel tales.

MARJI

My lord, it is said that the wisest riddles originated in the land of India, beyond the Hindukush mountains to the East.

CEO *(Rising)*

Hah! I have yet to hear one clever riddle from the stupid people of that land. But hurry. There are other plans I have for the rest of the evening.

MARJI

A simple question, my lord.

CEO

Get on with it.

MARJI

Allow me to ask you, my lord...which is the one question for which you do not have an answer?

(The CEO looks for an answer, and realises he is stumped. Don ambles in and hee-haws CEO's plight. CEO stamps his foot in anger. Don imitates him. CEO makes another wild gesture, stamping his foot more. Don imitates him again. CEO then decides the time has come for action.)

CEO

You think you are very clever, don't you? Well, let me show you who you are dealing with. My turn to fox you now!

(CEO taps the code with his feet. Don imitates him. CEO tries again, tapping louder. Don imitates him again, doing a tap dance. CEO goes to the casks kept upstage and does the tapping routine again, nice and loud. Don does an elaborate dance step. In rage, CEO opens the lid of a cask and gasps. He rushes to the other casks, opening their lids.)

CEO

They are empty!

ALIYEH

Empty, sir?

MARJI

What was in them, my lord?

CEO

My men?! Where are they?!?

MARJI

Were they your men, my lord. What a pity! Poor souls!

CEO

Where are the men?!

MARJI

Six feet under the ground, my lord.

CEO

WHAT?!!

ALIYEH

Marji, what is all this blabbering?

MARJI

The least we can do for any soul, my lady. A decent burial is the right of every god sent creature, so that the soul may rest in peace.

CEO

ENOUGH!! The time has come for the last act in this evening's entertainment. Prepare yourselves as best as you can!

(CEO draws his sword and swishes it menacingly. Marji immediately picks up the large tray and places it at CEO's feet. She claps her hands in glee.)

MARJI

Look! Everybody, look! Our honoured guest wishes to entertain us with a sword dance! We must do him the honour of joining in the dance. Get everybody to join in!

(Marji claps hands and hollers, getting the neighbourhood in. Aliyeh joins her in gathering all on to the stage. Don chips in hee-hawing. Girl, Boy and Leader also come on, seating themselves opposite Aliyeh. Marji gets CEO to join her in the dance, cleverly taking away the sword from him and placing it on the tray.

Choreography with music.

Marji has clearly taken charge, getting CEO to join her in the dance, moving around the tray. She dances with abandon [a Bollywood number?], swaying and swirling around CEO, who is quite dazed at the sudden turn of events.

Every time CEO tries to pick up the sword, Marji has a clever move by which she has beaten him to it. The third [or fourth] time he tries, she picks up the sword herself. She plays with the sword tantalizingly around CEO, a mock executioner, seductive.

A gradual transition to ominous lighting as the music builds up. At near crescendo Marji has the sword held high over CEO. Sudden freeze in sound and all movement. A beat.

Leader and Don go up and hold a sheet covering Marji and CEO. Crescendo.)

ALIYEH AND BOY *(Together)*
MARJI!!

BOY
What are you doing?

ALIYEH
He is our honoured guest! *(Black out)*

SCENE 10

Lights come on to reveal Don and Leader holding the sheet as in the last scene. The sheet is lowered slowly to reveal... an empty area.

DON
Can't stand the sight of blood.

LEADER
Too much violence nowadays. As if we don't have enough of it on TV already. We can't be accused of adding to it.
(Crossfade Girl and Boy. She is reading the book.)

GIRL
The story ends there.

BOY *(Approaching her)*
That's it? What about Ali?

GIRL
What about Ali?

BOY
I suppose Ali...

GIRL
He gets home and finds a crowd there, all the townsfolk buzzing and milling about.

BOY

I mean – it was all on account of him, wasn't it?

GIRL

Maybe. Maybe not.

BOY

What if he had been in the house when Aliyeh called?

GIRL

But he wasn't. And that was that. Nothing lost.

BOY

And the story ends.

GIRL

Not only does the story end, there are no more stories to be told.
(Crossfade to Sheherazad, with Duh-King.)

DUH

That's it? The CEO dies, and the story ends?

SHEHER

He meets his fate...

DUH

He meets who?

SHEHER

His fate. His end, as it was written.

DUH

Ah, yes, His fate, his final mate.

SHEHER

That is so profound, my lord.

DUH

What you mean is that he goes there and dies, doesn't he?

SHEHER

At the hands of a woman, my lord.

DUH

A very clever woman, if you ask me.

SHEHER
Thank you, my lord.
(Crossfade to Girl and Boy.)

GIRL *(Closing the book)*
The end of the one thousand and first story.

BOY
At the end of the one thousand and first night.

GIRL
When the sun rises it will all be over.

BOY
You mean...

GIRL
The lovely Sheherazad will have told her last tale, and she will have to prepare herself for her fate.

BOY
If only we could find a way to keep it going.
(Crossfade to Sheherazad and Duh-King.)

DUH
I thought the story could go on a little longer. Don't you think the cobbler deserved another appearance on stage?

SHEHER
The bug has bitten, my lord?

DUH
Well, it is a pity it couldn't go on just a little longer.

SHEHER
Look there, my lord. The eastern sky is glowing, as the sun prepares to rise once again. We must stop now.

DUH
One thousand and one nights, what?

SHEHER
Exactly, one thousand and one at the end of this night.

DUH
What comes next?

SHEHER

It ends here, my lord. There is no more.

DUH

No more? How can that be? *(A pause)* We make such a fine pair keeping the tales going!

SHEHER

A truer word was never spoken, my lord.

(Crossfade to Girl and Boy)

BOY

You know what I am thinking... ?

GIRL

I am thinking...that you are thinking of a way to keep the stories going. Maybe your Ali has found a way?

(Sheherazad and Duh-King DR)

DUH

You know what I am thinking... ?

SHEHER

I am thinking, my lord, that you are thinking of a way to keep the stories going. Perhaps, in your wisdom you have found the way?

DUH

Hmmm...Is it possible that you and I are thinking of the same thing? A drama company in which you write the stories for me, and I act in your stories?

SHEHER

It might work, my lord.

DUH

It usually works when the pair are married.

SHEHER

My lord...

(Girl and Boy)

GIRL

Duh-King realises that he is in love with Sheherazad, and that she is smart after all and, what's more, she is not bad looking...

BOY

Deliciously plump and all.

GIRL

So... why not take the plunge?

BOY

He springs a surprise on Sheherazad.

GIRL

As if she did not know what was happening to him through the last story. But she must act surprised anyway.

(Sheherazad and Duh-King)

DUH

Let it be known that on this night, the one thousand and first since the lovely Sheherazad –

SHEHER

Who, my lord?

DUH

You heard me.

SHEHER

It was not clear, my lord. Important announcements should be loud and clear.

DUH

Hmmm...Dictating already! *(Clearing his throat)*

Let it be known that the lovely Sheherazad shall henceforth be known by the title, Her Royal Highness, the Queen of Baghdad, and thereby the Queen of Queens.

SHEHER

And shall henceforth be known as the Artistic Director of BLT.

DUH

BLT?

SHEHER

Baghdad Little Theatre. You have your empire to look after, my lord, and I have mine.

DUH

And I will be President of BLT, I suppose?

SHEHER

Honorary President, my lord.

DUH

And I will have a say in casting.

SHEHER

Naturally, my lord.

DUH

You know, it might be a good idea if henceforth you can stop saying My Lord, and change to something more sweet sounding.

(Girl and Boy)

GIRL

And on the one thousand and second night since they first started seeing each other, Duh-King and Sheherazad were...how shall we put it?

BOY

United in wedlock.

GIRL

Invitations for the wedding were sent to all lands in all directions.

BOY

No flowers, no presents please. Gold not unwelcome.

GIRL

It included the land beyond the Khyber pass and the Indus river in the east, the enchanted land of Hindustan.

(As they speak, there is festivity on stage. The Chorus enters in a procession as at the start of the play. A Brahmin in the procession is carrying an aarati tray and garlands. The procession reaches Sheher and Duh King. The Brahmin blesses them. The garlands are given to them to be exchanged. The couple lead the procession towards the Boy and Girl, who join the procession. As it winds their way around the stage – and the front of the auditorium – the rest of the cast joins the procession.)

OPTIONAL: EPILOGUE

At the end of the last scene the procession led by the Brahmin leaves the stage, but without Girl and Boy, who remain in their corner.

Girl is sniffing.

GIRL
She was so beautiful!

BOY
No, I am not going to say anything. But this is no time for tears. They are going to be happy.

GIRL
I can't help it. I always cry in weddings.

BOY
We do have a problem, though. *(Girl looks up)* That was the last story. What do we do now? *(Boy gives Girl the story book, closed. Don and Leader enter and join them.)*

LEADER
Chin up, chin up.

GIRL
That was the last story from Baghdad.

DON
Hum hain na!

LEADER
You will have stories till the end of time. As long as we are here, there will be no end to stories.

BOY
You have something in your mind for the next one?

LEADER
Stories from ancient India. *(Don takes out a story book identical to the book in Girl's hand and gives it as a present to Boy.)*

BOY *(Opening the book)*
'The court Jester: Tales of Tenali Rama.' Hmmm...Is this for our next story?

LEADER
Could be, could be.

GIRL
When do we begin?

LEADER
Whenever you say!
(The four of them celebrate the start of the next tale.

Looking at the drum DR Girl makes a grand gesture as before. The drum starts to beat by itself. The four of them break into a peppy jig.

The wedding procession re-enters to its own music, preparing for the curtain call. At the end of the line are Girl, Boy, Leader and Don.

Group tableau.)

Close of play.

The Court Jester

Tales of ***Tenali Raman***

A play by ***Vijay Padaki***
with additions by ***Sridhar Ramanathan*** *and* ***Aliyeh Rizvi***

FOR
SRIDHAR RAMANATHAN

CHARACTERS IN THE PLAY

A SCHOOL TEACHER
A SMALL GROUP OF SCHOOL CHILDREN
YOUNG TENALI RAMAN
THE INSPECTOR OF SCHOOLS
GODDESS KALI (GIANT PUPPET)

THE PRINCIPAL MINISTER
MINISTER OF FINANCE
MINISTER OF FOREIGN AFFAIRS
CHIEF OF POLICE
GENERAL OF THE ARMY
ROYAL PRIEST AND ASTROLOGER
EMPEROR KRISHNADEVARAYA
TENALI RAMAN

AN ENSEMBLE OF ACTORS FOR VARIOUS PARTS INCLUDING
RAMAN'S WIFE
KRISHNADEVARAYA'S WIFE
A CONSTRUCTION WORKER
A HORSE
A PACK OF ASSES
CLERKS IN OFFICES

The stage setting is meant to be multi-functional and is made up of three rostra arranged as steps upstage. The top most rostrum may have more depth, perhaps four feet, while the two others will need a minimum depth of three feet. The width of the three rostra may be the same, say, two-thirds of the stage width. Alternately, they may be progressively wider from top to bottom. The three rostra have two pillars each, placed Left and Right The top rostrum may have bright carpeting, suggesting a regal character. The pillars there are golden. The other two rostra and their pillars are dark stone. Behind the pillars are stools, richly upholstered, that will bc drawn forward to serve as seats for the actors.

There are two carved stone entrances Left and Right. The rest of the stage is bare, and serve as a variety of locations for the stories to be acted out.

INTRODUCTION

READERS IN SOUTH India will not need any introduction to the tales of Tenali Rama. They would have heard innumerable stories from innumerable sources, they would have heard him quoted and would have quoted him themselves in all kinds of situations – at work, at play, in social gatherings, in family gatherings, in train journeys, in bus rides, in pubs, in places of worship and as much as places of mourning. The best introduction to the tales is in a short scene in the play itself. Two narrators are engaging the audience. They comment:

- There are more stories of Tenali Raman than all the people gathered out there.
- You can go on and on the whole day, and still not have them all.
- He is sometimes known as the Birbal of the South.
- Considering that the reign of Krishnadevaraya was nearly a hundred years before Emperor Akbar, Birbal should really be called the Tenali Rama of the North.

It was not easy selecting the tales to be included in a stage performance. The compilation in this play script followed the same method as in the script of *The Magic Drum*. Although the adaptation project prepared fifteen scripts from the stories for performance on stage, this volume is presenting only ten stories and a prologue – the most popular ones from the set. Other stories to be included in other combinations are available on request. These include an alternative Prologue, done in the style of traditional Indian theatre.

The script in this volume has a running time of two hours, requiring one intermission. A performing group can mix-and-serve any combination of stories for presentation, depending on the time available and the composition of the audience. The recommendation of the authors is to:

- Retain Scene 2 as the start, making that the Prologue if needed.
- Retain the Interlude (Scene 7)
- Retain the Epilogue (Scene 11) at the end

In keeping with the tradition in several BLT Children's Theatre productions, a group of children appears as narrators (or a Chorus). They are accompanied by a Teacher, who bridges the past and the present as best as s/he can.

The play was developed in the Summer Project on Theatre (SPOT 2010) specially for celebrating the 500th anniversary of the coronation of Emperor Krishnadevaraya, in whose court all the stories of the clever Tenali Raman unfold. Most of the stories included here are renditions of well known Tenli Raman stories. The sources are many and in the public domain. A small number grew out of the exploratory workshop exercises, but retained the spirit of Tenali Raman stories. The extended prologue included here was meant to set the historical context for the audience: a group of school children learning about the Vijayanagar kingdom, Krishnadevaraya and, of course, Tenali Raman.

The first production of *The Court Jester* opened the same year. There have been other productions of the play, using other styles of presentation, other combinations of stories, but retaining the basic script developed in the project. More recently a two-actor version has been performed as storytelling in BLT's Courtyard Theatre programme.

FIRST PRODUCED

By Bangalore Little Theatre. Opening at Ranga Shankara in August 2010.

Sutradhar/ Rama Sastry........................VIKRAM MAHESHWARAN
Krishnadevaraya.............NAVEEN TATER, SANTOSH KUMAR VR
Queen...PREETI MAHESHWARAN,
RAMALAKSHMI, SHWETAMBARA
Raj Guru..ANSHUL PATHAK
Chief of Police....................................MOHAMMED SHAMEER,
NAVEEN MUNDURU
Foreign Minister.............................ASTHA GUPTA, VISHAL JAIN
Principal inister..............SUREKHA SHETTY, MAYANK RUNGTA
Tenali Raman.................RAVI CHARI, SRIDHAR RAMANATHAN
Wife / Ghosts...................................SUNITHA RAJAGOPALAN
Teacher...PRUTHVI BANWASI
Young Raman...PRANAV RAO
Raman's son......................MAYANK TATER, BS PRITHVI KUMAR
Kali.....................................DHRITI RAO, REHA CHANDRESH
Inspector of Schools.............................MOHAMMED SHAMEER
Assistant 1 / Guard..................................AMIT SHARMA, VASU
Assistant 2 / Guard................................ANUSHA MAJUMDAR
Thief 1...ARJUN SASHIDHAR,
MOHAMMED SHAMEER
Thief 2..VASU
Leader of minstrels...............................ARJUN SASHIDHAR,
MOHMMED SHAMEER
Ensemble leader...PRUTHVI BANWASI
Percussion....................................ARJUN SASHIDHAR, RAM
Village children...............REHA CHANDRESH, MAYANK TATER,
RAJEEV RAO, BS PRITHVI KUMAR,
SARTHAK KEJRIWAL, DEVDUTT S, AMIT SKANDA

Lights...PRADEEP BELAWADI,
SHASHANK PURUSHOTHAM
Art direction....................................ALIYEH RIZVI, PRIYA RAO
Costumes..ALIYEH RIZVI, PRIYA RAO
Stage management..................................RAGHU T, PRIYA RAO
Publicity design.........................THE OTHER DESIGN COMPANY

Directed by.................ALIYEH RIZVI, SRIDHAR RAMANATHAN

PROLOGUE

The play opens to a dark stage. It has the look and feel of a large, dark underground chamber. It is quiet. Presently we hear the voices of a group of children off stage. The group, led by a Teacher with a flashlight, enters and gathers down-left.

TEACHER

Shhhh! Quiet, please. All of you! Here, everybody here. Raju! Join the group. Don't go off by yourself.

ALL

Raju!!

A BOY

This is the place! This is where it happened!

ALL

Shhhh!

TEACHER

Maybe. Maybe not. It is not one hundred per cent pukka where exactly the coronation took place. Some people say it was here. Maybe.

A GIRL

A royal coronation, here! Wow!

A BOY

Five hundred years ago!

A GIRL

Right here, in this room!

There is much excitement in the group.

TEACHER

Shhhh! Quiet, please. Remember, where you are. This is not the school canteen.

A GIRL

Can we look around? *(The group is excited again. 'Yes', 'This way', 'No, let's go up there', 'Wait', etc. They see that the Teacher is looking annoyed. They quieten, and...)*

ALL

Shhhh!

TEACHER

We must stay quiet.

(They move quietly in a group, Teacher leading with the flashlight. We see a human-like figure before each of the pillars, covered in muslin cloth.)

TEACHER

There is a lot of restoration work going on. Here...these are the statues of the great ministers and scholars in the court.

(He lifts the cloth on the first statue a bit and lights it with the torch.)

A BOY

This looks like a General in the army.

A GIRL

How do you know?

A BOY

He is armed, can't you see?

ALL

Ahhh ...

TEACHER

They are there to remind people for hundreds of years what a great kingdom it was in those days.

A GIRL

And what great men there were serving in his court.

A BOY

Can we look at the other statues?

TEACHER

Yes, but –

ALL

But quietly!

(They move in twos or threes from statue to statue, quietly, lifting the cover and peering at the form underneath. They recognise some of the personages. 'A priest', 'A minister', 'This is the musician', etc. Suddenly, there is the sound of a trumpet fanfare echoing in the hall. The group is frightened and scurries down-right into a huddle.)

A BOY

Sir! I'm scared!

TEACHER

Scared of what?

BOY

I don't know. I thought it was a ghost.

A GIRL

Thoo, boys! Always scared of something or the other!

(The sound of troops marching and coming to a halt. The group dashes across to down-right. Another huddle. The Girl holds her ground. A Boy in the group speaks up.)

A BOY

You know what? I think they are putting together a sound and light show. It must be for the special occasion.

TEACHER

You could be right. Five hundred years! A very special occassion.

(The sound of a huge crowd cheering)

Right, we can sit here and continue our lesson.

(The group sits. The Girl joins them, but gestures to the group that there is an audience out there.)

We will begin with a little quiz. *(Noticing the Girl)*

Yes? Ah, them? Well, they can join us too. *(A Boy whispers in his ear)*

For them? A quiz for them? Hmmm...Why not? *(To group)*

Why don't you ask them the questions?

A GIRL *(Rising, positioning herself, speaks to the audience)*

You are welcome to join us in a little history quiz. Are you ready for the first question? Yes? Everybody ready? All right, here is the first question:

WHO WAS THE FAMOUS KING IN INDIAN HISTORY WHO WAS CROWNED FIVE HUNDRED YEARS AGO?

(The questions can be presented in any manner found approriate – on a flipchart board a projection, placards, etc.

The group joins in priming the audience, keeping answers coming in. Finally, they concede the correct answer: KRISHNADEVARAYA. A round of applause.)

A BOY

All right, all right, good, are you ready for the second question now? Everybody ready? Right, here is the question:

WHAT WAS THE NAME OF THE KINGDOM OR DYNASTY OVER WHICH KING KRISHNADEVARAYA RULED?

(The group joins in priming the audience, keeping answers coming in. Finally, they concede the correct answer: VIJAYANAGARA. Caution: some may give the answer as Tuluva dynasty, which is also correct. A round of applause.)

A BOY

Let's bring in the audio section of the quiz now. Please listen carefully. We will sing the first line of a song...that's right, a song. We will sing the first line. What you have to do is to tell us which movie it is from. Yes? Everybody ready?

A GIRL *(Stepping in, scolding the Boy)*

No, no, no, skip the movie business. *(To audience)*

Ignore him, please. We will make it a bit easier for you this time. We will sing the first line of a song, and you have to tell us...the name of the composer of the song.

BOY

Composer?!

GIRL

Composer. That means the person who wrote the song. Here is a clue. The composer was a famous musician in the court of Krishnadevaraya.

(The group sings the first line of any Purandaradasa song. The answers come in. The group concedes the answer: PURANDARADASA. A round of applause.)

TEACHER *(To the group)*

Good! You have done your homework!

(To the audience) And what a lovely audience we have here today. You had all the answers to their little quiz! Now, tell us, would you like to know the rest of the song? Yes? Yes?

A BOY

Better still, would you like to join us and sing the rest of the song?

A GIRL

It's very simple. We will sing the first line, you repeat it. We will sing the second line, you repeat it. And so on. Soon we can sing the whole song all together.

TEACHER

Let's go!

(The group leads the audience in the song. Clapping, percussion may be added as felt necessary. There may be a projection of the lyrics [perhaps with a translation] while the group is singing.)

Thank you, thank you! That was lovely! You brought Purandaradasa alive. Most fitting! You can just imagine the scene five hundred years ago at the court of Krishnadevaraya...the music of Purandaradasa...

(If there is not enough time, the scene may fade out with the opening bars of a song. When the lights return we are at the scene once again.)

A GIRL

I suppose you know where we are just now, the name of this city...

A BOY

That sounds like the fourth question? I thought the quiz business was over. Everybody knows where we are!

GIRL

Everybody knows?

BOY

Everybody knows.

GIRL

Everybody knows we are where?

BOY

Everybody knows we are in Hampi.

GIRL

Thank you. Just wanted to remind you where we were. We are not in Russell Market. Not Doddakallasandra, not Guruppannapalya.

BOY

And...this is where it was all happening, five hundred years ago.

TEACHER

Krishnadevaraya had great respect for poets, artists and scholars. They were always welcome at his court. He called his court Bhuvana Vijayam. In that court he had eight highly respected scholars.

A BOY

The greatest scholars in the land were honoured as the eight great pillars of his kingdom

A GIRL

Known as Ashtadiggajalu.

A BOY

Was Purandaradasa one of the eight pillars?

TEACHER

Maybe. Maybe not. It is not one hundred per cent *pukka* who all were actually named as the eight pillars. They were certainly those very dear to the king.

A GIRL

One of them might even have been the Court Jester.

TEACHER

Ah, the Court Jester! The eternal jester! The jester at the Vijayanagara kingdom of Krishnadevaraya!

(There is the sound of high pitched laughter echoing in the hall. The group huddles down-left once again.)

A BOY

It sounds like a ghost.

A GIRL

Thoo, boys!

A BOY

It sounds like a friendly ghost.

A GIRL

Maybe...maybe it is the ghost of the Court Jester.

ALL

Tenali Ramakrishna!

GIRL

(Ahem) Tenali Ramalinga.

BOY

Ramakrishna.

GIRL

Ramalinga

BOY

Krishna

GIRL

Linga

GIRL AND BOY *(together)*

Tenali Raman!

TEACHER

Tenali Raman... Raman from the town of Tenali...Tenali Raman for short...Sometimes just Raman...sometimes just Tenali. What a package he was!

(The sound of the laughter again.)

A BOY

Maybe...it's Tenali Raman...

A GIRL

Maybe...he wants you to tell them *(the audience)* the stories...the stories of Tenali Raman.

TEACHER

We need somebody to play the part of Tenali Raman.

ALL

Me! Me! I'll be Tenali! Let me play Tenali Raman!

TEACHER

Shhhh!

ALL

Shhhh!

TEACHER

You know, there are hundreds of stories of Tenali Raman. Nobody knows the exact number.

GIRL AND BOY *(together)*

It is not one hundred per cent pukka!

TEACHER

That is pukka! Even if every one of them there *(the audience)* has one story to tell, there would still be that many more!

A BOY

So, who is going to play the part of Tenali Raman?

A GIRL

You, I suppose!

TEACHER

I'll tell you what! Every one of you can play the part of Tenali Raman, each in a different show. How about that?

A BOY

And the girls?

TEACHER

What about the girls?

A GIRL

What about the girls?!

TEACHER

And there's the king, Lord Krishnadevaraya.

A GIRL

Well...the king is a bit slow on the uptake in these stories. Tenali Raman is always showing him how stupid he is...

A BOY

Who shall we have playing the king?

GIRL

It must be a grown up.

BOY

He must be a bit stupid. *(The Teacher glares)*

A GIRL

Well, not stupid, exactly. Krishnadevaraya is known in the history books as a wise king after all.

A BOY

Not stupid, no. But not as smart as Tenali Raman, that's all.

GIRL

There are lots of actors who are just right for that. We will find one.

(A roar of approval from the group and they march off, taking the Teacher with them.

Brief blackout)

SCENE 1: THE RIVALS IN COURT

When the lights come on the stage is a deep blue, dimly held. We see the statues in front of the pillars, covered. The covers on the statues slip off one by one, revealing characters in Krishnadevaraya's court. The lights brighten. The statues come to life.

They are: the General of the royal army, the Prime Minister, the Royal Priest and Astrologer, the Minister of Finance, the Minister of Foreign Affairs, and the Chief of Police. The group steps DC.

Suggested line up stage right to stage left:

Police, Foreign, General, PM, Finance, Priest.

GENERAL *(To audience)*

Gentlemen! *(Noticing that some of them are women)*

Gentlemen and ladies! This is going too far!

PRIME MINISTER (PM)

Really! Too far!

GENERAL

Far too far!

PM

That's what you just said! Too far!

FINANCE MINISTER (FINANCE)
By far too far!

FOREIGN MINISTER (FOREIGN)
We are the ones so dear to the king.

PRIEST
So near to the king.

ALL
So near, and yet so far!

POLICE
Who is this Raman fellow? A joker, really!

PM
A joke, really!

POLICE
That's what I just said! A joke!

PRIEST
We do all the hard work, we give it all we have –

FINANCE AND FOREIGN *(Together)*
Our brainpower –

GENERAL AND POLICE *(Together)*
Our muscle power –

PRIEST
And he ...?

ALL
He always has the last laugh!

PM *(To audience)*
You are wondering...

PRIEST
They must already know ...

FOREIGN
They look the intelligent kind...

FINANCE
The educated kind ...

POLICE AND GENERAL *(Together)*
The trouble-making kind ...

PM
You are wondering who we are. Allow me to introduce ourselves.
(Turning to the General) This distinguished looking person on my right is...
(Finance Minister nudges and objects)
Ah, yes, a matter of protocol and seniority...This distinguished person on my left is our honourable Minister of Finance. He looks after the royal treasury and is therefore a very important person.

FINANCE
Thank you. *(Pointing left at Priest)* And it is my pleasure...
(Foreign Affairs and general both cough) yes, it is my pleasure to introduce to you...*(General steps forward)* the distinguished Minister of Foreign Affairs.
(General retreats)

FOREIGN
Thank you. It is an honour to serve the noble Krishnadevaraya as the Minister of Foreign Affairs, and in that capacity to travel to many foreign lands for attending conferences, signing treaties, launching exchange programmes, inaugurating cultural festivals –

POLICE
And so on and so forth.

FOREIGN
And this weighty personality on my right is the kingdom's Chief of Police. As you may well appreciate, it is a very important position and a very sensitive position. We can never imagine the number of rich and famous people in this land who wish to be introduced to him and be in his good books.

PRIEST
I looked into his horoscope and cleared his appointment. The king was very pleased.

GENERAL *(Stepping forward)*
And lest we forget –

POLICE

And lest we forget, the person who matters most in all matters of state policy and all royal proclamations of far reaching significance, ladies and gentlemen, let me present to you the state astrologer and priest!

(The General clears his throat to make a speech. Police repeats)

The state astrologer and priest!

GENERAL *(Continuing anyway)*

Thank you. Ladies and gentlemen –

POLICE AND PRIEST *(Together)*

The state astrologer and priest!

GENERAL

Ladies and gentlemen –

PM, POLICE AND PRIEST *(Together)*

The state astrologer and priest!

GENERAL

Ladies and gentlemen –

ALL FIVE *(Together)*

The state astrologer and priest!

PRIEST

I thank you for acknowledging so vociferously the significance of my office, although I must admit that I remain a small man, carrying out a humble duty. And now, allow me to introduce to you the one person who has almost single-handedly made the empire of Vijayanagara as vast and far-flung as it is today. Ladies and gentlemen, our national hero, the General, the Commander of the Vijayanagara army!

GENERAL *(Satisfied but not pleased)*

That's me! And here, on my left, is the Principal Minister. Thank you.

PM

Thank you. As you can see, we are the ones making Vijayanagar what it is.

GENERAL AND POLICE *(Together)*
We made the kingdom click.

FINANCE, FOREIGN AND PRIEST *(Together)*
We make the kingdom tick.

PM
And yet...

ALL
That Tenali Raman!

The group sings

Ooh! Tenali Raman!
Aargh! Tenali Raman!
He's here, he's there, he's everywhere
He turns the court upside down without a care.

He's a great big pain in the you know where
That Raman!
That Tenali Raman!

Ooh! Tenali Raman!
Aargh! Tenali Raman!
When the king has a bee in his bonnet up there
We give him our expert advice threadbare
Then he comes along and we're tearing our hair
That Raman!
That Tenali Raman!

Ooh! Tenali Raman!
Aargh! Tenali Raman!
He and the king are a pair so rare
But to break the bind, we hardly can dare
We can't bear it! It's not fair, it's not fair, it's not fair!
That Raman!
That Tenali Raman!

Ooh! Tenali Raman!
Aargh! Tenali Raman!

Just you wait, dear Raman!
We'll show you, Tenali Raman!
We'll show you, dear Raman!
Just you wait, Tenali Raman!

(Fade out)

SCENE 2: THE CHILD PRODIGY

The group of children is seated for a lesson.

TEACHER
Imagine yourself in a village school five hundred years ago. The teacher is taking a class in arithmetic. What do you think they are learning there?

A BOY
Multiplication tables!

TEACHER
All right, multiplication tables.

A GIRL *(Kicking off)*
Six fives are thirty.

GROUP
Six fives are thirty.

TEACHER *(Picking up)*
Six sixes are thirty six.

GROUP
Six sixes are thirty six.

TEACHER
Six sevens are forty two.

GROUP
Six sevens are forty two.

RAMAN *(Loud)*
Seven twelves are eighty four

Twelve sevens are eighty four
Nine twelves are a hundred and eight
Twelve nines are a hundred and eight

TEACHER
Raman!

RAMAN
Eleven twelves are a hundred and thirty two
Twelve elevens are a hundred and thirty two.

GROUP *(Stopping him)*
Ohho! Raman, stop!

A BOY
You have got us mixed up!

A GIRL
As usual! Stop your mischief now!

TEACHER
Where were we?

A GIRL
Six sixes, I think.

A BOY
Seven sixes, I think.

A BOY
No, it was six sevens.

RAMAN
Six sevens and seven sixes are the same.

A GIRL
How do you know? We haven't gone into seven times yet!

RAMAN
I know!

(There is argument and commotion in the group, with the Teacher trying to bring order, when the Inspector of Schools makes a grand entrance into the room. The children sit still. The Inspector walks about and stops next to the Teacher.)

INSPECTOR

Hmmm....

TEACHER *(To the audience)*

The Inspector of Schools.

(To the group, prompting) What do you say when we have a visitor?

GROUP

Good morning Uncle! (Aunty)

INSPECTOR

Hmmm....I am going to ask the class some questions.

TEACHER

Yes, of course...Sir!

INSPECTOR

Who is the most intelligent child in this class?

(There is no response. He repeats.) Who is the most intelligent child in this class?

(There is no response. He decides to ask another question.)

All right... who is the most mischievous child in this class?

(Slowly, one by one, all in the group are pointing at Raman)

You...come up here. *(Raman steps forward)*

Your name?

RAMAN

Raman.

INSPECTOR *(Takes out a silver coin and holds it in his palm)*

This silver coin is yours if you answer all the questions I ask you. Are you ready to start?

RAMAN

As soon as you have answered one question of mine.

TEACHER

Raman!

INSPECTOR *(Cutting in)*

Ask your question.

RAMAN

You asked me to answer all your questions. Is that all? Or do I have to answer them correctly as well?

INSPECTOR

My first question was: Are you ready to start? You have answered the question already. You are ready. Now, the next question. What is your favourite hobby?

RAMAN

I like to sleep under a tree next to the pond.

INSPECTOR

You like to...Why do you like sleeping under the tree?

RAMAN

I dream. I get ideas.

TEACHER

I am sorry about this, but Raman is a lazy boy. He is also very mischievous. Shall I suggest another student for asking questions?

INSPECTOR *(Cutting in)*

Next question!How can a child be a dreamer and good in studies at the same time?

RAMAN *(Taking the coin from the Inspector's hand)*

The two sides of this coin are different, sir. But they are on the same coin.

INSPECTOR

Keep the coin! *(To the Teacher)*

See what you can do to have more dreamers in this school. God knows the kingdom needs them badly!

The Inspector strides out. The Teacher continues his lesson.

TEACHER *(To the audience)*

And so it was that Tenali Raman discovered what his life was going to be. Oh, of course he knew the multiplication tables. He knew them well ahead of all the children in the whole village.

(To the group) He was different, wasn't he? Even as a child he was different.

A BOY

How else was he different? Tell us more!

A GIRL

How did he get that way?

TEACHER

One day a wise sage showed him how to reach such deep concentration that he could have the goddess Kali visit him privately. He sat in meditation and recited a thousand and one praises to the goddess.

(The Teacher and the others leave the stage quietly, leaving Raman seated in a state of deep meditation.

A giant figure – puppet? – in the form of goddess Kali descends from above and stops in front of Raman. The goddess coughs. Raman opens his eyes, sees her, and prostrates himself before her.)

KALI

Rise, Raman. *(He does)* You have passed the test. But tell me, how on earth did you find a thousand and one names for me when even the gods in heaven struggle with barely six or eight?

RAMAN

Seven times a hundred and forty three –

KALI

Seven times a hundred and forty three?

RAMAN

Are a thousand and one.

KALI

Ahh...you know your seven times table I can see. So, now you want some boon from me, I suppose. What will it be?

RAMAN

I want to know.

KALI

You want to know! You want to know what? You want to know where the king hides his gold? You want to know how to conquer the universe in three simple steps? Where to dig a hole in the ground to get the biggest, brightest diamonds?

RAMAN

I want to know...

KALI

Out with it! What treasure are you after?

RAMAN

I want to know why the cock crows at break of day. I want to know why the flame of the candle feels hotter as I take my hand closer to it, but it gets colder as we climb higher and higher towards the sun. I want to know why worms become butterflies.

KALI

Hmmm...no gold and diamonds?

RAMAN

I want to know why you have four hands.

KALI

Don't get too personal, boy! Nobody has asked me that question before, you know.

RAMAN

Why four?

KALI

Well, actually I have a thousand hands. You look surprised.

RAMAN

Eight times a hundred and twenty five.

KALI

Yes, a thousand. But the sculptors and painters on this earth don't know how to show that clearly enough, so everybody has to be satisfied with four hands.

RAMAN

What do you do with four hands?

KALI

Much more than what you can with two hands.

RAMAN

Show me.

KALI

Show me, what?

RAMAN

Show me, please.

KALI

That's better. Well, suppose I showed you two things with my two hands, and asked you to choose one of them.

RAMAN

Like a bowl of milk in one and a bowl of curd in the other?

KALI

How did you...? Who told you about this riddle?

RAMAN

It is an old story, everyone knows!

KALI

So, what is the answer?

RAMAN

Why one? I would find a way to take both of them.

KALI

Hmmm...We have to think of something else for you. Suppose –

RAMAN

Suppose you brought things in four hands?

KALI

You say so. Here goes... As you can see, my hands are empty. That is because I have already given the things I brought to four children out there.

(Raman looks at the audience) Yes, they are out there. Now, what you have to do is guess what the four things are, and who has them.

RAMAN

I have to get these things from the children out there?

KALI

Yes, of course. Let me warn you. The things I have given them are not what you will see around you in your village. They are from foreign lands and are from another age, five hundred years from today. You must find your own way to get those things from the children out there.

(Raman takes out four sweets wrapped in silver foil like coins and addresses the children in the audience)

RAMAN

Now, here's a fine spot the goddess has put me in! I hope this works. All right, I have four sweets with me, blessed by goddess Kali herself. I will give them to whoever has what I am looking for. Is that a fair exchange? I will not take away what you have. I will ask you only to bring them here and show them to the goddess. I will then give you this sweet wrapped in silver, and you can go back. All right? You help me, and I give you a sweet. Are you ready?

The first thing I want....

(Raman calls out one item after another, making sure the person brings it to the stage to be shown to Kali, giving the child a sweet, and going on to the next item. The items can change from show to show, and can include things like:

chewing gum, a safety pin, a one rupee coin, a black ball point pen, a biscuit, a pencil with a broken point, a sock with a hole, an empty purse, a pocket comb, a watch showing 12 o'clock, and so on.

After four items have been successfully presented to Kali, and the owners suitably rewarded, Raman prostrates before Kali once more.)

KALI

Well done, boy! You are destined for greatness that is beyond the reach of ordinary mortals. You can attain this greatness only by remaining true to yourself. Wherever you are, whatever the challenges thrown at you, you will never be at a loss, because you have the most powerful weapon ever known, gifted to you by the gods. You have laughter. You will laugh at all adversities, and in the end you will make even your worst adversaries laugh with you. Use the weapon without hesitation. You can win wars without shedding a drop of blood.

RAMAN

Where do I begin?

KALI

In the city of Hampi is a king with his heart in the right place. What he needs is wise counsel from one who has no need to please him, agreeing to all his whims and fancies. He has mastered the skill of building his empire, but has not yet learned the art of laughter. Seek him out.

(The goddess ascends, leaving Raman alone on stage, still prostrate.
Fade out.
The sound of a high pitched laughter echoing in the hall.)

SCENE 3: RAMAN'S ENTRY INTO THE COURT

There is more than one version of the story of Tenali Raman making his way into the court of Krishnadevaraya. This play script has chosen two. Both are charming! They are given below. The performing group can choose either one.

Version 1

The lights return to reveal Raman, now grown up, still prostrate down-centre. Upstage is the court of the emperor Krishnadevaraya. He is seated on a throne. At the next two levels are his advisors left and right, The Principal Minister, the Priest, the Finance Minister, The Minister of Foreign Affairs, The General and the Chief of Police.

KRISHNADEVARAYA (KRISHNA)
You say he has been lying there at the entrance since daybreak?

POLICE
My lord, it could not have been earlier. The night patrol ends at the break of day. My men would surely have –

PRIEST
Picked up anybody lying suspiciously at the entrance to the palace!

FOREIGN AND GENERAL *(Together)*
He could be a spy from an unfriendly kingdom.

FINANCE
He could be a beggar playing on your lordship's sentiments.

KRISHNA
He could be –

POLICE

He could be drunk.

PRIEST

He could be dead.

PM

He could be this, he could be that. What has anybody done to find out who he is and what he wants?

POLICE

Exactly! My men would have found out in less than a minute had the honourable Minister taken the trouble to inform us in time.

PM

The question remains. Who is he?

PRIEST

I think ...

FOREIGN AND FINANCE *(Together)*

All thought, no action!

GENERAL

What would your Highness have us do?

KRISHNA

Why not ask him?

(The group is caught unprepared. They exclaim in agreement: 'Ah, yes', 'Of course', 'Just what I was going to say', etc. They all approach the prostrate Raman.)

KRISHNA

Wait! *(Walks up to Raman and kneels at his head)*

Young man...O stranger...are you dead?

(Raman raises his head and shakes it left to right) Are you drunk?

(Raman shakes his head left to right again) Then how dare you lie there in front of the royal court if you are neither drunk nor dead?!

(Raman sits up. The king stands. Raman kneels before the king and replies.)

RAMAN

O illustrious son of the Tuluva dynasty, most revered ruler of the land, king of three kings, emperor of emperors, blessed by Lord Krishna himself at your coronation, I wish to only seek your audience for the humblest of requests that seeks no material favours.

(Krishna looks at the others, who nod their approval, not without some reluctance.)

KRISHNA

Ask without fear.

RAMAN

My lord, I wish to compose some poetry for you.

KRISHNA

Poetry!

RAMAN

Yes, my lord, poetry, some songs. They will be my humble offerings for you. I ask for no gifts in return.

(The courtiers mumble protests. Krishna cuts in.)

KRISHNA

We have the greatest poets and musicians of the land already here in Hampi, you know.

RAMAN

I am aware of that, my lord.

KRISHNA

And the wisest men in my Council. *(The courtiers are pleased)*

RAMAN

You are indeed fortunate, my lord.

KRISHNA

So, what can you do that is not already done in this court?

RAMAN

I can compose even as you speak, my lord. And I can compose even as you are in thought, my lord.

KRISHNA

How so? For instance, if I turn towards the court astrologer and priest here, and –

RAMAN

And you are wondering how you may benefit from his council without being crushed by the weight of the opinion.

KRISHNA

Why, that is absolutely –

RAMAN *(Continuing)*

Oh venerable owl perched high
You see in the dark what no other creature does
By day or by night

If we could fathom the depth of your hoot
There would be no room for fear of the stars
By day or by night

A moment of silence. Krishna is stunned.

KRISHNA

Wah! Did you all see that? Instant art!

(Krishna claps. The others follow. The Priest is not sure.)

Your name, young man. Tell us about yourself.

RAMAN

Raman, my lord. From the little town of Tenali.

KRISHNA

Raman! We will call you Raman in my court. And when people wish to know for certain that it is you we are talking about, we shall say Tenali Raman.

RAMAN

I am honoured, my lord.

KRISHNA

Where did you learn such exquisite Telugu and such rich Sanskrit? And your ready wit, where did that come from?

RAMAN

It came to me, my lord. I never sought it or bent my back for it.

KRISHNA

And now, allow me to take you for a walk through our garden. I am going to put your talents to further test. I wish to see what music comes to your lips as you see things in the garden.

Krishna leads Raman out. The group watches them leave and then gathers down-centre.

Version 2

The lights return to reveal Raman, now grown up, seated down-centre facing the audience. Upstage is the court of the emperor Krishnadevaraya. He is seated on a throne. At the next two levels are his advisors left and right, The Principal Minister, the Priest, the Finance Minister, The Minister of Foreign Affairs, The General and the Chief of Police. They remain frozen.

Two guards are posted below the tableau, stage left and stage right.

The Teacher and the children's group enter, survey the scene and stand behind Raman, facing the audience.

TEACHER

Aah, but Tenali Raman was not part of Bhuvana Vijayam from the start. He was a late inclusion. His entry was theatrical, to say the least.

BOY

Desperately wanting to enter the king's court Tenali Raman found himself stopped at the gates by one sentry or the other.

GIRL

He then saw a group of wandering minstrels who were going to perform for the king. They had permits to enter the court area.

(The group enters the court area, going past one of the sentries. They bow deep to Krishnadevaraya and sit down. Raman rises, looks left and right, sees the sentries, returns to down-centre.)

RAMAN

Aha! I should be able to slip in by joining the group there. I can be one of the actors.

(As Raman tries to go past the sentry he is stopped.)

GUARD 1

Oy! Did I not send you back just a moment ago?

RAMAN

Shhh! This is just between you and me. I have been invited to perform Krishna-Leela for the king by this group.

GUARD 1

Hmmm ... so you will begin by putting on this natak for me now?

RAMAN

You are a very clever guard, you know.

GUARD 1

And the king will reward you for your natak there?

RAMAN

I suppose so.

GUARD 1

All right, you may go in. But on one condition. You must give me half of whatever you are awarded.

RAMAN

Done! Now let me go in, quick. *(Guard 1 points in the direction of the other sentry. Raman speaks to the audience as he moves there.)* It is not easy getting in anywhere these days. You can be sure I will be stopped by a second sentry.

GUARD 2

Oy hoy! Did I not send you back just a moment ago?

RAMAN

Shhh! Just between you and me...I have been invited to perform Krishna-Leela for the king by that group there.

GUARD 2

Good try! Next you will say the king is going to reward you for this natak you are putting on!

RAMAN

Yes, of course!.

GUARD 2

All right, you may go in. But on one condition. You must give me half of whatever you are awarded by the king.

RAMAN

Done! Now let me go in, quick. *(To audience, as he makes his way to the group)*

So far, so good. But just as the Krishna-Leela was being given an interesting new twist in the tale by me, the cast members stopped the play.

(The group rises and points together at Raman)

TEACHER

There is an intruder in the party!

GROUP

Raman!

(The king rises in fury. He is joined by the courtiers.)

BOY

The king was furious. He ordered that Rama be punished immediately.

KRISHNA

A hundred lashes! I order that this intruder be given a hundred lashes immediately!

RAMAN *(Laughing)*

Thank you, my lord. My profuse thanks!

GIRL

Naturally the king and all the courtiers present were mystified–this stranger laughing at the award of a hundred lashes.

RAMAN

My lord, please call the two sentries at the gate. They have let me into the court under the condition that I give away whatever I receive as an award from you to the two of them – exactly half and half! All I wanted was your audience, to be able to make a humble offering in song to you. I have got much more than that. I may please be permitted to leave now.

(A moment of silence. Krishna is stunned.)

KRISHNA

Wah! Did you all see that? Instant wit! Instant hit!

(Krishna claps. The others follow. The Priest is not sure.)

Your name, young man. Tell us about yourself.

RAMAN

Raman, my lord. From the little town of Tenali.

KRISHNA

Raman! We will call you Raman in my court. And when people wish to know for certain that it is you we are talking about, we shall say Tenali Raman.

RAMAN

I am honoured, my lord.

KRISHNA

Your singing is quite good too. And your ready wit, where did that come from?

RAMAN

It came to me, my lord. I never sought it or bent my back for it.

KRISHNA

So, what can you do that is not already done in this court?

RAMAN

I can compose even as you speak, my lord. And I can compose even as you are in thought, my lord.

KRISHNA

How so? For instance, if I turn towards the court astrologer and priest here, and –

RAMAN

And you are wondering how you may benefit from his council without being crushed by the weight of the opinion.

KRISHNA

Why, that is absolutely –

RAMAN *(Continuing)*

Oh venerable owl perched high
You see in the dark what no other creature does
By day or by night

If we could fathom the depth of your hoot
There would be no room for fear of the stars
By day or by night

KRISHNA

And now, allow me to take you for a walk through our garden. I am going to put your talents to further test. I wish to see what music comes to your lips as you see things in the garden.

(Krishna leads Raman out. The group watches them leave and then gathers down-centre.)

TEACHER

Of course Krishnadevaraya did not permit him to leave. He persuaded Rama to stay back. And thus began a long and enduring friendship between the two men.

(The group exits. The courtiers rush to take their place down-centre.)

Continuing after either version 1 or version 2

PM

This does not look good.

FINANCE AND FOREIGN *(Together)*

Not good, not good.

GENERAL AND POLICE *(Together)*

A troublemaker

PRIEST

It does not look good at all.

PM

Did you see how he mocked the good Priest?

GENERAL

Oh, that was clever, I thought. Perched high! Ha ha ha!

POLICE

Just what I was going to say, clever. He hoots! Hoo hoo hoo!

PRIEST

Yes, clever! That is the problem, my friends. He is clever.

FOREIGN
Today it's the priest, tomorrow...

FINANCE
That's right, tomorrow it could be you...or you.

PM *(To Finance)*
Or you.

FINANCE *(To PM)*
Or you.

ALL
This does not look good at all.
(Reprise: the song chorus)

ALL
Just you wait, dear Raman!
We'll show you, Tenali Raman!
We'll show you, dear Raman!
Just you wait, Tenali Raman!
(Krishna enters without Raman. The group repositions itself.)

KRISHNA
Gentlemen, you should have been there! The song of the brinjal! Exquisite!

PM
The song of the ...?

PRIEST
Brinjal?

KRISHNA
Badanekaayi! Egg plant, aubergine, as the traveller from across the seas called it. Our own Vankaaya!

FOREIGN AND FINANCE *(Together)*
My lord, we do not understand ...

PM
Your prized brinjals, my lord –

POLICE
Nobody is allowed to pluck them except your cook! And only under your supervision! Did he dare to –

GENERAL
I would never allow a stranger –

KRISHNA
I allowed him to look from a distance. He burst into song!

PM
A song on the brinjal, my lord?

KRISHNA
In chaste Sanskrit! He sang of the power of the brinjal over men in all civilisations. The verses were metered as in vedic hymns, of men in search of perfection in mortal existence, finding it in the gastronomical delights of the brinjal. He sang of the timelessness of its sensuous appeal, to men and women alike, to grandparents and grandchildren.

FOREIGN
Sire, it is known that the brinjal in your garden is very special, and there is none like it in any other part of the world.

GENERAL
Spies from many lands have been sent on high powered missions to extract the secret of your brinjals. They have never returned alive.

POLICE
No, we have never let them return alive.

FOREIGN
The secrets of gardening this brinjal shall remain the property of the royal household alone.

PRIEST
Questions will be asked, your highness. Eyebrows will be raised.

KRISHNA
What questions?

PRIEST
About knowledge of gardening being treated as property.

FINANCE
One may own the brinjal, but can one own knowledge of the brinjal?

GENERAL

That is not for us to worry about.

FOREIGN

Five hundred years hence they may even enact a law that gives a gardener the right to own all the knowledge about growing his brinjal.

PRIEST

They will give it a respectable name, call it intellectual property.

POLICE

And they may declare it a right to own intellectual property.

GENERAL

And defend the rights to the property – with force, if necessary.

PM

Perhaps your Highness recalls the story of the royal princess who was abducted for her secret recipe of stuffed brinjal curry.

KRISHNA

That is what Raman sang about! Five hundred years ago was there a fascination with the brinjal, and five hundred years hence will there be a confrontation between warring groups on the sanctity of the brinjal.

(By now the group is a semi-circle around Krishna)

ALL

We must guard the royal garden from suspicious strangers!

POLICE

Tighten security!

GENERAL

Scale up the vigil on the borders!

ALL

Before it goes too far!

(Fade out)

SCENE 4: LESSONS FROM A BOTTLE

The Teacher is seated with the group of children down-left. There is a bottle at the centre of the circle.

A BOY

Do you think the people in the court are going to create trouble for Tenali Raman?

TEACHER

What do you think?

A GIRL

They look mean.

A BOY

But they are great men, aren't they?

A GIRL

The king can't be so stupid. He can't have people in his court who are no good.

A BOY

They may be good in their work, but they can still be no good in some other ways.

TEACHER

That is human nature. Everybody has some good things, they have some weaknesses as well. What about you? Are you one hundred per cent *pukka* good?

A GIRL

That's right. No one is perfect.

TEACHER

And nobody –

ALL

Is one hundred per cent *pukka* bad.

A BOY

Poor Tenali Raman! They will make life difficult for him.

A GIRL

But he is smart! He will outwit them.

TEACHER

He may even knock some sense into the king's courtiers. Shhh! I think they are on their way here. Quiet!

(The courtiers enter and take their places before the six pillars. A trumpet fanfare. Krishnadevaraya enters and takes his place UC. The courtiers pay their respects.

Krishnadevaraya looks around, disappointed.)

KRISHNA

Where is our Raman? *(Silence)*

Has anybody seen him this morning? *(No response)*

Has there been a death? Why is everybody looking so glum?

PM

Sire, On our way here we saw Raman walking in the opposite direction.

POLICE

We asked him where he was going.

GENERAL

Why he was not coming to the court.

FINANCE AND FOREIGN *(Together)*

We reminded him that your Highness is very particular about punctuality.

PRIEST

He said he had business more urgent than being at court in time.

KRISHNA

He said what?!

PM

Business more important...

KRISHNA

How dare he! I want him here immediately.

(Everybody looks at the Chief of Police. He is unprepared.)

POLICE

Ah, yes! *(To PM)* He should be brought here immediately!

PM *(To General)*

He should be picked up!

GENERAL *(To Finance)*
And marched here!

FINANCE *(To Foreign)*
Immediately!

FOREIGN *(To Priest)*
Carried here, if necessary!

(A short pause, as they look at each other. Krishna points to the exit. All six of them dart to the exit, but are stuck there as they cannot all go out at the same time. Just then we hear the sound of the laughter echoing in the hall. Raman enters, a bottle in his hand, identical to the one with the group of children. The courtiers return to their places, looking accusingly at Raman.)

RAMAN *(Entering)*
Oh, what a beautiful morning! Oh, what a beautiful day! *(Seeing the courtiers)* Don't you agree?

KRISHNA
What is so beautiful about a day when my courtiers are not all present in full strength – and on time?! Where were you?!

RAMAN
I was visiting a glass blower in your kingdom, my lord. It is a beautiful day, because the blower taught me wonderful things about the world.

KRISHNA
And what could the glass blower show you that is more important than matters of state? I hope you remember that you are appointed a member of the court, and that you have a duty here.

RAMAN
You may consider me on duty this morning, my lord.

KRISHNA
At picnic with a glass blower! We have matters of governance to attend to here, and you while away your time at a glass blowing furnace. And what is that toy you have in your hand?

RAMAN
A clever toy, my lord. Also a tool for wiser governance.

PM

Playing games in official work hours!

KRISHNA

Enough! Taking to the bottle first thing in the morning!

RAMAN

Allow me to show you the wonders of this humble bottle, my lord.

PM

Your highness, this is going too far.

ALL

Too far! Way too far!

KRISHNA

All right, Raman. Here is your chance on a beautiful day to make an ass of yourself with an empty bottle. Show us what we can learn from the bottle.

RAMAN

Your highness, you will not be disappointed. May I ask the honourable members of the court to gather in a circle around this bottle?

(Raman places the bottle on the floor, and waits. The courtiers hesitate. Krishna nods, suggesting they go along. They gather in a circle around the bottle, with Raman outside the circle.

Cross fade to down-left.

The Teacher has the group in a circle, with the bottle at the centre. The children laugh out loud and clap their hands in glee.)

A BOY

Did they have glass bottles in those days?

ANOTHER BOY

The must have been there! We had everything even in our Harappan civilisation!

TEACHER

Actually no, I am afraid. Glass came into use in India about two thousand years after that.

GIRL

The first use of glass was in ancient Syria and Egypt, right?

BOY

It doesn't matter when! India had glass long ago, that's all.

GIRL

At least two thousand years before Krishnadevaraya's time! That's what matters.

TEACHER

Shall we try it out here? With them? *(Referring to the audience)*

ALL

Yes! Let's!

TEACHER *(Rising, to audience)*

Tenali Raman was playing a game with the six wise courtiers of Krishnadevaraya. Would you like to know what the game was? Yes? You would like to know? Would you like to play the game yourself? Yes?

All right, let's give it a go.

Now, how many wise persons were there in the court?

(Gets the number from the audience) Right, six of them. Now, to play the game as Raman played it at the court we will need six volunteers. That's right, six volunteers. They must come up here on stage. Who would like to play the game? Up here. Quick!

(The Teacher gets the six volunteers to form a circle down-left where the group was, while the children shift off stage in the auditorium area.

Optional: the boy and girl may also conduct the game – or assist the teacher in the conduct.

The Teacher then takes out six lengths of string, with a sweet or toffee attached at the end of each string. Each volunteer is given one string with a sweet attached. The teacher asks each volunteer, one by one, to drop the sweet into the bottle, but hold the end of the string in one hand. All six volunteers do this.)

TEACHER

Now...let us see how quickly you can take out the sweet. Who is the cleverest to take out the sweet fast? Are you ready? Right, go!

(The volunteers try to work fast. The sweets cannot come out all together. They struggle. The meaning of the word 'bottleneck' is established.

Cross fade to court area. Raman has the group of courtiers in a circle with the bottle at the centre, They are holding strings with sweets inside the bottle.)

RAMAN

Now... let us see how quickly you can take out the sweet. Who is the cleverest to take out the sweet fast? Are you ready? Right, go!

(The courtiers try to work fast. They struggle.

Cross fade to down-left. The Teacher intervenes.)

TEACHER

Wait! Let us not struggle so much. Would you not like all six strings to come out? So that all six of you get the sweets? What will you do then? *(Engages the children)*

That's right. We take them out one at a time. It does not matter who is first and who is last. It is more important that all strings are out. *(He turns to one child)*

Now, let us start here. You can pull out your string – while all the others loosen their strings and let the sweets stay down. That's right...You got it. *(Turning to others)*

Now, you next ...

(He gets the children to take out their sweets one by one.

Cross fade to court area. Raman invites the king to intervene, who takes charge. The king does exactly what the Teacher has just done.)

KRISHNA

Wait! Let us not struggle so much. Would you not like all six strings to come out? So that all six of you get the sweets? What will you do then? *(Engages the group)*

That's right. We take them out one at a time. It does not matter who is first and who is last. It is more important that all strings are out. *(He turns to one courtier)*

Now, let us start here. You can pull out your string – while all the others loosen their strings and let the sweets stay down. That's right...You got it. *(Turning to others)*

Now, you next...

(He gets the children to take out their sweets one by one.

Cross fade to down-left. The volunteers have all got their strings out.)

TEACHER

Thank you! Good job! Well done! *(Guides the volunteers back.)* You may now return to your seats.

(The children's group joins the Teacher. They march out happily. Cross fade to court area. The courtiers have all got their strings out.)

KRISHNA

At last! Thank you! I thought you would never get done!

RAMAN

My lord, thank you for allowing us the game. And even more for taking part yourself.

KRISHNA

It was such a simple task. Yet they were struggling so much!

RAMAN

Governance, my lord! You may have the most skilled and the most knowledgeable persons of the land to serve you, but if they have not learned how to work together, their hardest efforts go to waste.

KRISHNA

And one more thing, dear Raman.

RAMAN

Yes, my lord?

KRISHNA

You need somebody to show them how to work together!

RAMAN

You are indeed a fast learner, my lord!

Fade out

SCENE 5: GIVING AND TAKING

The script for this story about the rooster that Tenali Raman used to drive home a message, was greatly aided by the discovery of the Norwegian tax system. Every year in October, the annual tax returns of Norwegian citizens are posted online on the Norwegian Tax Administration's official website, and anyone can go and have a look. This tradition of publicly sharing everyone's earnings is not new, but it is very telling about the kind of society, and tax system, that the citizens wish to have.

When the lights fade in we see the courtiers in a huddle. Krishnadevaraya is pacing angrily. He speaks finally

KRISHNA

It is an established tradition in this kingdom. The more money you make, the more Income Tax you pay. If you are rich, you pay. The more tax you pay, the more you can expect from the kingdom.

FOREIGN

Absolutely in order, your Highness.

POLICE

Just what I was saying.

KRISHNA

There shall be no secrecy about it. Everybody will have the right to know what anybody else pays as tax.

FINANCE

Everybody, your Highness?

KRISHNA

Everybody.

GENERAL

But many do not pay taxes, because they are poor, your Highness.

KRISHNA

They may not pay Income Tax, but they are entitled to know what Income Tax others have paid.

PRIEST

We can issue a Palace Gazette and have the list of tax payers kept in the Finance Minister's office, your Highness.

KRISHNA

It will not do. We must make it public. We shall have the list kept at the great assembly hall for all to see. We can paste them on the walls of the market square if needed.

PM

A rather bold step, your Highness.

KRISHNA

We shall lead the way. We shall set an example for other lands to follow, even if it is to be five hundred years later.

(Cross fade to down-right, Raman's humble home. He is seated with his wife at dinner. She is serving him.)

WIFE

Did you hear that? The list will be displayed at the great assembly hall for all in the land to see.

RAMAN

It is called Right to Information.

WIFE

They also have a separate list of fifty persons who pay the highest tax in the year.

RAMAN

It is called High Net Worth hit list.

WIFE

Why would anybody wish to be on that list? For all to see?

RAMAN

It is Krishnadevaraya's incentive scheme. The more tax you pay, the more privileges you are entitled to in the kingdom's banking system.

WIFE

Are you in the list? *(Pause)* Are you?

RAMAN

You know that I get paid the least among all the people the king has gathered in his court.

WIFE

You have not answered the question. Are you in the list of people who pay the highest taxes?

RAMAN

Yes, I am.

(Trumpet fanfare. Cross fade to court area. The courtiers are in their places. Krishnadevaraya is seated.)

PM

On behalf of all your loyal courtiers, may I offer my congratulations, your Highness? Your innovative scheme of listing the highest tax paying citizens is an outstanding success.

GENERAL

However...

KRISHNA

However!

FINANCE *(Approaching him, scroll in hand)*

Sire, take a look at the list. Do you see anything peculiar in it?

KRISHNA

Well, the ink does not go with the gold border of the scroll. It should have been a deep indigo.

FOREIGN

How very observant, your Highness.

POLICE

True, true. We must not neglect the colour of ink in the list.

PM

Your Highness, you will notice that at the head of the list, at the very top, is the name of...?

KRISHNA

Tenali Raman. He should be proud of his place there. We shall ensure the right order of rewards for that.

FINANCE

But sire, is it not strange that the person who gets paid the least in court is at the top of the list in paying taxes? He shows his total earning in the year as more than all our six salaries combined.

GENERAL

Now, where could he be getting all this income from?

PM

Do we get the distinct smell of some fish here, my lord?

POLICE

Definitely something smelly here!

PRIEST *(Correcting him)*

Something fishy.

POLICE

That's what I said, something fishy.

KRISHNA

If there is something out of order here, Raman will indeed be punished. It will be without any special consideration. But he must be given a chance to explain. Since he is a member of this court –

PM

Of course, your Highness. He must be given a chance to explain.

POLICE

And we can see how he finds a way out of the evidence staring him in the face.

(Cross fade to Raman at his meal.)

WIFE

The whole town is talking about it.

RAMAN

Very soon the whole kingdom will be talking.

WIFE

What if the king asks for an explanation?

RAMAN

I will have to give it.

WIFE

What do you get by paying so much tax? We are still eating the same humble rice with the same humble daal. And do you have any idea of the price of daal these days?

RAMAN

Who knows, one day the king may give me a brinjal from his garden!

WIFE

You'd better have a proper explanation for your top bracket Income Tax. Or else we may not even have this daal-rice at your meal.

RAMAN

What is simple to understand is that the higher the income, the higher the tax. What is not easy to understand is that higher income need not have any connection with higher spending on food. Your daal is dearer to me than the king's kesari bhath.

WIFE

Flatterer! You will still have to convince his Highness.

RAMAN

When the cock crows the hens also wake up from their slumber.

(A heavy knocking on the door. Before Raman or his wife can move, the Chief of Police has entered.)

POLICE

Well, well, well! A happy family meal! I am sorry to disturb your peace, but I am here at the direction of our beloved king. He has sent me to convey his wish to meet you.

RAMAN

As soon as we have –

POLICE

Immediately!

RAMAN

I was expecting this invitation from his Highness.

POLICE

His invitation! Ha ha ha. I suppose you think it is a garden party.

RAMAN

And I have a gift to be taken to the party.

(Raman rises and picks up a bag from a corner and gives it to Police.)

Please carry this to the king's court ahead of me as a token of my acceptance of his invitation. I will join you there as soon as my good wife and I have cleared the dishes.

(Cross fade to the court area. Krishnadevaraya and the courtiers are in their places. Police enters with the bag and places it at the centre. He opens it and takes out a basket-cage in which there is a rooster. Police takes his place. The sound of the high pitched laughter echoing. Raman enters and offers his respects to the king.)

KRISHNA

Raman, this is serious business. You have been summoned for an enquiry about our Income Tax returns. This is not the time to be playing cock-a-doodle-do jokes. Why have you sent this rooster here?

POLICE

With the Chief of Police, no less!

RAMAN

My lord, I thought I should show you this rooster myself. It has been a cause of great stress for the entire household.

FINANCE

Your Highness, this is needless digression.

PRIEST

We are gathered here –

RAMAN

To decide what to do with a rooster that is compelled to do more than crow every morning at dawn.

KRISHNA

To the point, Raman!

RAMAN

My lord, I have a few hens in the house alongside this rooster. There are sundry pigeons and mynahs too. They all keep themselves busy, doing what they are accustomed to doing, strutting about the courtyard.

PRIEST

No bulls? For a cock and bull story?

RAMAN *(Smiling, unperturbed)*

I throw a fistful of grains every now and then into the courtyard. But this rooster, my lord, he eats up his own grains and then eats into the shares of the six hens as well.

GENERAL

That is because he has a bigger appetite!

POLICE

He works harder, so he eats more!

PM

Perhaps he deserves more than what is given to him!

RAMAN

No matter, my lord. The appetite of the rooster is my problem. It should not come in the way of your business in court today. Which is...? *(Krishna bursts out laughing. Seeing him, the courtiers laugh too, tentatively.)*

KRISHNA

Tenali Raman, it is simple. You are the one rooster among the bunch of birds! He that gives more must get more, and he that gets more, gives more.

Fade out

SCENE 6: AN INTERLUDE OPTION

This may be done as a musical interlude between Scenes 5 and 7. (After Tenali Raman's income tax story and before his wife's complaint about his absence.)

The decision to perform it or not will depend on the ability of the children's group and the time available. The rest of the play is constructed to be performed in one stretch, without an intermission. This interlude may add three minutes to the duration.

The passage below is written for a pair of children, preferably a boy and a girl. It can be choreographed. Parts of it can also be set to tune if thought fit.

A GIRL

You know what the Teacher said at the start?

A BOY

There are more stories of Tenali Raman than all the people gathered out there.

GIRL

You can go on and on the whole day, and still not have them all.

BOY

My grandmother told me that when she and all her cousins sat down for dinner every evening the real treat was a Tenali Raman story.

GIRL

Everybody would be there bang on time! Lined up in the family courtyard, hands and feet washed.

BOY

At a signal from an aunt they would all sit in a little semi-circle, waiting to be served.

BOTH

Tenali Raman stories!

GIRL

Rolled chapati with Tenali Raman, Daal-bhat with Tenali Raman.

BOY

Hot steaming rice and ghee with menthye hittu and Tenali Raman.

GIRL

It didn't matter who served the kayi-thuthoo, it was always with a Tenali Raman story.

BOY

Sumana kaki

GIRL

Kamalu mausi

BOY

It didn't matter who. They all had a bag full of stories.

BOTH

Tenali Raman stories!

GIRL

And you know what? The bag never ran out of stories!

BOY

How many dinners in that courtyard? How many evenings, how many years? How many stories?!

GIRL

There were stories about beggars, real beggars, fake beggars, greedy merchants, honest merchants, humble folks with lofty minds, rich folks with petty minds, small men with large hearts, big men with small hearts, brave women, clever women, godly rascals, ungodly godmen, woodcutters, stone cutters, diamond cutters, bone cutters, bone setters, hair setters, head setters, tail setters, locksmiths, ironsmiths, coppersmiths, goldsmiths, grain millers, oil millers, crowing cocks, cawing crows, hooting owls, howling jackals, chattering mynahs, parroting parrots, laughing rivers, laughing winds, laughing rain showers, laughing jackasses, not to forget laughing children.

BOY

You can go on and on for years, and still not have them all.

BOTH

Tenali Raman stories!

SCENE 7: THE ANCESTORS

Tenali Raman's house. His wife is looking for him.

WIFE

Ohho! Where is he?? *(To audience)* Who, you ask? Why, HIM, of course! Yes, him.

The court is in session, so you think he must be there, at the court. His Highness, of course, expects him there all the time.

But he is not there! And his Highness is upset. Upset and cross! This is not the first time he is absent at court. Either absent or late, he hasn't changed one bit from his school days. He must be taking a nap under the tree next to the pond. What else?!

(Cross fade to DL. Raman is taking a nap. The Priest approaches. Seeing Raman asleep, he smiles to himself.

Cross fade UC. Krishnadevaraya is with the courtiers. The Priest enters and takes his place.)

KRISHNA

Where is he?

GENERAL

Who, sire?

KRISHNA

HIM!

GENERAL

Oh, him, sire ...

KRISHNA

Yes, him!

PM

The court is in session, your Highness. He must be here, at the court, your Highness. Perhaps on his way ...

KRISHNA

He is not here! And his Highness is upset. Upset and cross! This is not the first time he is absent at court. Either absent or late, he hasn't changed one bit. Does he think this is like his school days? Taking off and taking a nap under a tree?!

GENERAL

The tree next to the pond. Where else?!

KRISHNA

What did you say?

GENERAL

The tree next to the pond, sire. He is there, taking a nap, as you correctly guessed.

PM

Not the first time, your Highness, as you correctly observed.

FINANCE

Your Highness, if I may be so bold as to remind you, Raman has a habit of falling asleep even in court.

FOREIGN
He is often seen yawning in court.

FINANCE
He even snores in court.
(Light on Raman DL)

RAMAN
What to do! Sometimes the jabber jabber at court is so boring.

PM
Do you remember, sire, when all proceedings stopped, and our noble Priest whispered in Raman's ear that your Highness was staring at him? He had the most audacious explanation.

RAMAN
I am not asleep! I am concentrating!

POLICE
Or that time when I had to tap him on the head.

RAMAN
I am never asleep. I am day dreaming. There is a difference.

KRISHNA
What do you think he must be dreaming of now at the pond?

GENERAL
Your Highness, may I suggest that we take an excursion to the pond and catch him in the act?

KRISHNA
What a marvellous idea! Let us get there straight away.

PRIEST
May I ask the royal kitchen to pack an excursion lunch for all of us?

KRISHNA
Forever the Brahmin!
(The group exits, as the upstage area fades out.
Raman stirs DL and addresses the audience.)

RAMAN
Let me tell you what has agitated my mind for a long time. It's like this. I have often thought about how noble our king is, how

prosperous our land is, how vast the empire is under his rule ... And so on. And yet, there is one serious problem that we have not been able to overcome in all these years. I find that we have lived with this problem for centuries. My fear is that the country will have the problem for centuries more. Can you tell me what I have in mind?

(Raman engages the audience in a guessing game: What is the one serious problem that this land has not been able to shake off over hundreds of years? Finally...)

RAMAN

That's right! We believe deep in our hearts that some people are superior to others by birth. Not by what they accomplish in life, but by birth! How do you like that? Does it make sense?

Not just that, we believe that those born inferior must stay inferior. Ohhohoho – that is going too far. But what do we *do* about it??!! I can tell you I have lost many waking hours agitated by this. It forces me to walk down here and take a nap! How can I tell the good king that I am actually working?! I feel very sad every time this problem raises its head.

And do you know what? Even among the Brahmins in this land, those who are supposedly the learned, there are different classes of – what can you call it – classes of pedigree. Much seems to depend on how the lines on the forehead are worn. Is it one line or three? Is it horizontal or vertical? At what angle from the bridge of the nose? No laughing matter, it is very serious! Each group of Brahmins thinks it is superior to another group!

We may pride ourselves in all that we have accomplished as a kingdom, people in many foreign lands may look upon our kingdom with admiration, the learned scholars, the gold reserves, the art and culture, and so on and on, the list can be endless. But as long as we put hundreds of thousands of our own people in an enclosed space and say they must remain there, can we really claim to be a civilised people? How many more centuries of this must we put up with? (*A construction worker walks on stage with a group of asses – actors in donkey masks. The donkeys are carrying gunny sacks filled with construction material – What looks like sand. The Worker shouts a greeting.)*

WORKER

Ram Ram Ramanappa!

RAMAN

Ram Ram Hanumappa! Where are you off to?

WORKER

I am building a great big temple of god! I am on my way there!

RAMAN

A temple? Which god?

WORKER *(Sending the donkeys ahead, stops for a chat)*

I don't know! Who cares? It is a great big temple, and I am building it!

RAMAN

Why, that is wonderful, Hanumappa! How long will it take to complete the temple?

WORKER

I don't know! Who cares? It is a great big temple, and I am building it!

RAMAN

Keep it up, Hanumappa! I hope to see you again.

WORKER

I pass this way every half an hour. I will see you, even if you don't happen to see me.

(The Worker starts to leave. Just then the Priest enters. On seeing the Worker he covers his face with end of his top cloth and steps out of his way. The Worker looks down and exits. The Priest approaches Raman.)

RAMAN

Pray, why did you cover your face when you saw the man?

PRIEST

Is that a question to ask? The man is of a low caste?

RAMAN

But he is building a temple!

PRIEST

He is not 'building the temple'. The royal architect is building the temple. And the royal architect is a Brahmin! This man merely crushes stones and is an assistant to the mason.

RAMAN *(To audience)*

This mere mason's assistant is named after god Hanuman, and is capable of wonderful feats with his hands.

PRIEST

That may be, but the temple will be dedicated to the gods by a Brahmin. In all likelihood the king will ask me to perform that important duty.

RAMAN

Hmmm...may I ask another question? What if you happened to catch his face? Or if he happened to look you in the face?

PRIEST

Unthinkable! I would be born as a donkey in my next birth! Unthinkable! But enough of this diversion. You should know that our royal Highness is on his way here. He has expressed a special desire to catch you in the act of taking a nap – daydreaming and concentrating on state affairs, as you choose to put it.

(Krishnadevaraya and the courtiers enter, riding puppet horses. After a circuit around the stage they 'park' their horses on one side and walk up to Raman, who rises and pays his respects. Krishna stands staring, arms akimbo, wondering where to begin. Just then the pack of donkeys crosses the stage on its way back. Raman rushes forward to the pack and starts paying respects to the donkeys, prostrating.)

RAMAN

Oh, venerable Narasimhachar! Oh, lord Garudachar! Ah, the saintly Tatachar! And you too, Venkatachar and Srinivasachar! I bow to you all and seek your blessings!

KRISHNA

Raman! Have you gone mad?! What is the meaning of this?! Control yourself! This is what comes of being out in the sun so long!

RAMAN

My lord, what a great event this is turning out to be! First, your Highness graciously visits me at my seat of meditation. And then this! The venerable ancestors of our royal Priest are here with us! They are all reborn, and have come here now to bless us with their presence. Join me, my lord. Such an opportunity will not come our way again in this birth.

(Unsure of himself, Krishna joins Raman in prostrating before the donkeys. The other courtiers cannot help following. Only the Priest remains apart. He then slaps his forehead and storms out.

The donkeys do a little jig, enjoying the spectacle. The Worker enters, takes in the scene and cautiously leads his donkeys away.

Raman rises and seats himself DL at his meditation spot. The king and the courtiers rise, pick up their parked horses, ride around the stage and exit.)

Fade out

SCENE 8: BUYING AND SELLING

This story, a riddle, appears in more than one form in folk tales and is not a trade mark Tenali Raman tale. The riddle is common in several cultures, probably originating in the Middle East. It is a tale of buying and selling around a horse. It was included in the play mainly for the children's group.

Another version is included in the play ROBI'S GARDEN, but with the horse replaced by an ass.

Fade in DL on the Teacher and the children's group.

TEACHER

My students have really been bitten by the Tenali bug! They are cooking up Tenali Rama stories now!

A GIRL

We want to tell you a story about a horse.

TEACHER

From asses to horses!

A BOY

The horses in the kingdom were the very best. They came from a long line, sired by champion horses from all parts of the world.

GIRL

But the best of the best were Arabian horses, brought specially to the Vijayanagar kingdom by Portugese traders from across the Gulf. These traders brought horses, and took back spices and the precious sandalwood for which Hampi was most famous.

TEACHER

Ah, but not everybody could own an Arabian horse, oh no. It was only Krishadevaraya who had the authority to buy Arabian horses, and to do what he liked with them after they were brought into the kingdom.

BOY

Most of them went into the royal cavalry.

GIRL

A few very special ones remained with Krishnadevaraya in his personal stables.

TEACHER

So, you see, if you owned an Arabian horse, you had to be somebody of very high rank in the kingdom.

BOY

Or... you had to be very close to the king.

GIRL

Or... you knew a trick or two to get that horse without being either close to the king or holding a high rank.

(The General enters, leading a horse – an actor in a horse mask. The Teacher and children are frightened.)

GENERAL

Don't be frightened. He looks ferocious, but he is very gentle.

TEACHER *(To audience)*

He thinks we are frightened of the horse!

BOY

Sir, if I may ask, where did you get this magnificent ass from?

GENERAL *(With pride)*

He is a horse! And he is Arabian.

GIRL

It is said that only lord Krishnadevaraya may own an Arabian horse!

GENERAL

Chup! Impudent girl! This horse is mine! I have earned the right to own him! I don't suppose you know who I am in the king's court.

BOY

A horse trader?

GENERAL

Hmmphh! Try again.

GIRL

I know, a horse doctor!

GENERAL *(To audience)*

We will have to do something about the text books in our schools! Maybe look into the medium of instruction.

(The Chief of Police walks on.)

Ah, here he comes. I knew he was following me.

POLICE

A hundred salutations, General!

GENERAL *(To group)*

Here it comes.

POLICE

What a fine morning!

GENERAL

And...

POLICE

Lovely blue sky!

GENERAL

And...

POLICE
Birds singing in praise of this paradise on earth.

GENERAL
And...

POLICE
What a magnificent ass!

GENERAL
Ah, you are referring to this horse, I believe.

POLICE
The one I behold –

GENERAL
My horse!

TEACHER *(To audience)*
The Chief of Police wants that horse!

BOY
How would Tenali Raman have handled this situation?

GIRL
He would have had some fun at the expense of the General and the Chief of Police.

BOY
He would get the two to open a negotiation.

GIRL
We will have to help. You can take part too. Just listen carefully.

(A Girl positions herself on the side of the General, speaking on his behalf. A Boy positions himself on the side of the Chief of Police, speaking on his behalf. During the negotiation below the General and Chief of Police go along with the game.)

BOY
Oh General, I have admired that horse of yours for a long time. I am wondering if you would care to sell him to me.

GIRL
Perish the thought. He is too dear to me.

BOY

I will make it worth your while.

GIRL

He is too precious. You can't buy him.

BOY

How about five thousand silver coins?

GIRL

Well... no, sorry, he is –

BOY

Ten thousand!

GIRL

Well, all right, since you insist!

(The horse crosses over from the General's side to the Chief of Police.)

TEACHER

A few days passed, and the General began to miss his horse. He decided to talk to the Chief of Police.

GIRL

Ahem...I say, I hope all is well with you, my good friend...and my horse

(Police raises his eyebrows) I mean your horse. *(No response)*

You know, I really miss that horse. He was so dear to me. I am wondering if you would consider giving him back to me...? *(No response)*

I can make it worth you while! *(Police looks at General at last)*

Say, twelve thousand silver coins?

BOY

Well, all right, since you insist!

(The horse crosses over from Police to General.)

TEACHER

It was now the turn of the Chief of Police to feel lost without the horse. He had to get him back.

BOY

I say, my old friend, I was wondering...

GIRL

Sorry, I am busy! Can't take your call just now.

BOY

I can make it worth you while! Say –

GIRL

Sorry!

BOY

Fourteen thousand silver coins?

GIRL

Well, all right, since you insist!

(The horse crosses over from General to Police.)

TEACHER

Then, what happens? You guessed right! The General simply had to get his horse back. He pulled in his tummy, stuck out his chest, and approached the Chief of Police.

GIRL

I say, old friend, I know we have been through all this before, but –

BOY

No!

GIRL

But –

BOY

Sixteen thousand silvers?

(The Chief of Police allows the horse to cross over to the General's side.)

TEACHER

So, there we have it. *(The Boy and Girl join him)*

BOY

The Chief of Police buys the horse for ten thousand silver coins.

GIRL

The General buys the horse back for twelve thousand.

BOY

The Chief of Police buys him once more for fourteen thousand.

GIRL

The General buys him back once more for sixteen thousand.

TEACHER

Now... at the end of all this buying and selling, who has ended making a profit?

(The Group gets the audience to give the answer. We see the General and Chief of Police calculating frantically. The horse dances in glee and trots off. The General and the Chief of Police run after the horse.)

Fade out.

SCENE 9: THE BRINJAL CURRY

There are many stories around Krishnadevaraya's fabled brinjals. At least two of them have Tenali Rama's wife coveting the royal brinjals and dreaming of cooking a curry with them. Both have been scripted. Only one of them is included in this volume.

Raman's wife is seated down-right.

WIFE

Any minute now he will walk in here, as if nothing had happened, happy as a goat after a bellyful of hay. He will give me the most absurd story of how the king was so pleased with him for his clever counsel, and how he rewarded him with a box full of gold coins. Again! Now you know why he pays the highest Income Tax. Lowest salary, highest Income Tax. Gold, silver, diamonds, rubies... why can't he get a brinjal from the king's garden? Something more exciting for a change!

'Hello, my darling wife, guess what happened at court today?' He will hand me the box of gold coins, and start off on his story, sitting down to eat – as if sitting down is some sort of switch, and the food will just drop into his plate! Will he even notice what I am wearing? This sari, for instance, he got it for me when he accompanied his Royal Highness on a mission to Utkala, the land they will one day call Odisha. Gave me the sari and forgot all about it afterwards. Forgot all about me, you could say.

I simply have to get that brinjal from the king's garden! And I have to get it by hook or by crook. Knowing that husband of mine, it will most likely be a hook. Knowing that king of ours, It will have to be a very clever hook indeed.

(Raman sweeps in, hands the Wife a box of gold coins and takes his place at dinner.)

RAMAN

Hello, my darling wife, guess what happened at court today?

WIFE

You solved the case of the Portugese trader and the Arabian horse.

RAMAN

How did you...?

WIFE

And the king was pleased to gift you a box of gold coins. Again!

RAMAN

Shall we give it away to charity? Again?

WIFE

I wish the king would stop giving you boxes of gold coins.

RAMAN

It is just the gesture, my dear.

WIFE

I wish he would give you a brinjal instead.

RAMAN

You know that is never going to happen.

WIFE

Well, you may be the cleverest man in Lord Krishnadevaraya's court, but you can't even get me one brinjal from his garden!

RAMAN

Now, don't start on that again! The king's brinjal is his brinjal, and our brinjal is our brinjal.

WIFE

What would I not do for one single brinjal from his garden?

RAMAN

What are you willing to do?

WIFE

I'll do anything.

RAMAN

Anything?

WIFE

Anything!

RAMAN

Hmmm... one brinjal, that's all?

WIFE

One brinjal from his garden!

RAMAN

If I did bring you the brinjal, how would you know it was from his garden?

WIFE

I would know straight away.

RAMAN

How?

WIFE

I would know blindfolded! Only one who loves to cook brinjal can tell the difference. You will never understand!

RAMAN

All right, here is an offer. I will get you two brinjals. You will have to tell me which one is the brinjal from the king's garden.

WIFE

And if I do?

RAMAN

You must never ask me for another brinjal from his garden! Done?

WIFE
Done!

RAMAN
I will get it as soon as possible.

WIFE
Promise?

RAMAN
So that I don't have to hear you ask for the brinjal again.

WIFE
But tell me, how will you get your hands on one of king's brinjals?

RAMAN
Leave it to me.

(Cross fade to the Queen seated down-left.

A short dance interlude may be introduced here.

The stage is bathed in blue light with a full moon above. Four maidens dance across the stage, setting up the king's moonlight dinner. They keep two floor level tables and place silver thalis with elaborate spreads on the tables. They escort the queen to the tables and dance their way out.)

QUEEN
Another moonlit night, another moonlight dinner in the garden. Any minute now he will walk in here, as if nothing had happened, happy as a mule after a bellyful of hay. He will give me the most absurd story of how Tenali Raman solved the most complicated state litigation with his clever counsel, and how he rewarded him with a box full of gold coins. Again! Now you know why everybody in court is so jealous of Tenali Raman. Why can't he come in with something more exciting for a change!

'Hello, my darling wife, guess what happened at court today?' He will start off on his story, sitting down to eat – as if sitting down is some sort of switch, and the food will just drop into his plate! Will he even notice what I am wearing? This sari, for instance, he got it for me when he took his military campaign to Utkala, the land they will one day call Odisha. Gave me the sari and forgot all about it afterwards. Forgot all about me, you could say. Would he ever take me out on one of his trips? Never! I have to stay back and make his favourite brinjal curry! It has to be brinjal only from his own garden!

(Raman is seen standing obediently at the edge. The Queen notices him, and bids him enter.)

QUEEN

Why, it's Raman. At this hour?

RAMAN

My apologies, my lady. It is indeed late.

QUEEN

Please come in. The good king is delayed in the garden. He should be here soon.

RAMAN

I have just seen him in the garden, my lady. I gave him a poem to read.

QUEEN

A poem? In the garden?

RAMAN

It is a beautiful moonlit night. I thought I should do my little bit to build the atmosphere for your monthly moonlight dinner.

QUEEN

Why, that was so very thoughtful of you.

RAMAN

My lady, I realise that matters of state often keep his Highness away from your side. If there is something I can do...

QUEEN

What can you do, Raman? Unless you know an exotic brinjal recipe!

RAMAN

My lady! That is indeed something I can do for you! The recipe my wife has for stuffed brinjal curry is at least six hundred years old, and is guaranteed to set the diner's heart on fire!

QUEEN

I have heard of this secret recipe, but had no idea that your wife –

RAMAN

GUTTI VANKAAYA PULUSU KURA!

QUEEN

Ah, but it can only be with the brinjal grown in the king's private garden, you know.

RAMAN

I know, my lady. I am also informed that the brinjals are plucked and kept in a silver basket, which in turn is kept in a cupboard and locked.

QUEEN

That is correct. You are well informed.

RAMAN

My lady, I have with me a specimen of a brinjal grown in our own humble garden, tended lovingly by my wife. *(Takes out a plump aubergine)*

May I suggest a little temporary arrangement? An innocent switch? My wife shall then cook the curry with a brinjal from the cupboard, and nobody need know that a brinjal has been replaced. Temporarily!

QUEEN

Ah, but your brinjal must not get mixed up with the others in the cupboard.

RAMAN

My lady, I have already thought of that. Here, if you look closely at the bottom of this brinjal, you will see a tiny black dot. You will know which one to throw out from the cupboard after the curry from my wife has been delivered and eaten.

QUEEN

Hmmm... Wait outside at the entrance. I will bring a brinjal from the cupboard personally.

(Raman leaves. The Queen, in a happier mood, sits at her place. The king sweeps in.)

KRISHNA

Hello, my darling wife, guess what happened at court today? I simply must tell you about this clever Tenali Raman. Not only did he solve a complicated state litigation at court, he gave me a wonderful poem to read in the garden.

QUEEN

A poem, my lord?

KRISHNA *(Moving close to her)*

A poem about the magic of moonlight... a romantic poem...

(Cross fade to Raman and Wife down-right)

RAMAN

Well, here we are! We have two brinjals here, one from the king's garden, and one from our own garden. *(He keeps juggling them)*

First, you have to tell me which is which. Then, you have to make two plates of stuffed brinjal curry, one from this one, and one from this one. Only I know which one came from the king's garden.

WIFE

I am ready. You can blindfold me now.

(Raman takes out a scarf and blindfolds the Wife, and gives her the two brinjals. She handles them with great care, feels the surface, passes them under her nostrils, weighs them in her palms, and so on. Finally, she announces her verdict.)

WIFE

This one!

RAMAN

Well! How did you know?!

WIFE

Ah, men! You will never understand. Ours smells of cow dung manure. Theirs smells of horse manure.

She dashes off.

RAMAN *(To audience)*

She is wrong, of course!

(Calling after her) Don't' forget to cook two separate dishes of curry! *(To audience)* Nobody will really know which curry has

which brinjal! But everybody happy! She will think her curry is with the king's brinjal. The king will think his curry is made from our brinjal! All our taste buds will tickle with delight because we will believe what we want to believe.

(Cross fade to Krishnadevaraya and the Queen down-left)

KRISHNA

Delicious! Simply divine! This Tenali Raman has a knack for turning everything he touches into something sublime. I have never had stuffed brinjal curry as heavenly as this.

QUEEN

Of course, it would be seventh heaven if the curry was made with brinjal from your own garden, my lord.

KRISHNA

Of course, of course. No doubt about that.

QUEEN

You must reward him, my lord. Him and his wife.

KRISHNA

Yes, we must. We could invite them to join us at next month's moonlight dinner.

QUEEN

With stuffed brinjal curry?

KRISHNA

With their brinjals!

Fade out

SCENE 10: ALL IS WELL

The sound of soldiers marching, coming to halt. Lights come on upstage. The Chief of Police strides to up-centre and speaks.

POLICE

All quiet in the streets. Law and Order situation fully under control. Lord Krishnadevaraya's royal garden completely protected. Not a single brinjal unaccounted for!

The Ministers of Finance and Foreign Affairs join Police.

FINANCE
Tax collections reach a record level in the last month.

FOREIGN
Exports to neighbouring countries exceed targets by thirty per cent.
(The General and Prime Minister join the three.)

PM AND GENERAL *(Together)*
The sun shall never set on the Vijayanagar empire.
(The Priest joins the group.)

PRIEST
The stars are auspiciously aligned. The gods are more than pleased with the collections in all their temples.

ALL
ALL IS WELL!

FOREIGN
All is happiness!

FINANCE
It is all around us!

GENERAL AND PM
It surrounds us!

POLICE
That's what I was saying, it is fully rounded.

PRIEST
But.... We have one unsolved problem.

ALL
Tenali Raman!
(Song interlude)

Ooh! Tenali Raman!
Aargh! Tenali Raman!
Just you wait, dear Raman!
We'll show you, Tenali Raman!
We'll show you, dear Raman!
Just you wait, Tenali Raman!
(Cross fade to children's group down-left)

TEACHER

And so, my friends, it was clear that all in the kingdom were happy and at peace in the reign of king Krishnadevaraya.

A BOY

Travellers from many lands were amazed at the prosperity in the Vijayanagar kingdom.

A GIRL

More important, the happy faces in the kingdom.

BOY

Everybody knew that it was because of the wise king Krishnadevaraya.

GIRL

And the wise jester in the king's court, Tenali Raman.

TEACHER

But... there was one little unsolved problem. The courtiers!

BOY

They simply could not accept that Tenali Raman was so close to Lord Krishnadevaraya.

GIRL

But they simply had to accept that Tenali Raman was actually smarter than them!

TEACHER

Time to close now! We hope you have enjoyed this small packet of Tenali Raman stories. *(A boy tugs at the Teacher's sleeve. He brushes it off.)*

We have certainly enjoyed learning about Tenali Raman and Lord Krishnadevaraya from this visit to Hampi.

(A girl tugs at the Teacher's sleeve. He brushes it off. She tugs gain. The teacher looks at the girl. She gestures that we could have one more story. He turns to the boy. He repeats the gesture.)

TEACHER

There is no time for any more stories!

BOY

Just one more!

TEACHER
We must close now. The bus to Hospet starts in half an hour!

GIRL
One last story! Please!

TEACHER *(To audience)*
What do you say? One more story? Suppose we miss the bus? Are you sure you want one more story? *(He gives in)*
All right! One last story!

ALL
PUKKA!

SCENE 11: EPILOGUE: HOPE FOR HAMPI

PRIEST
What? One more chance?!

PM
We have one more chance!
(The courtiers tiptoe into a huddle. There is much buzzing, interspersed with hee hee hee. They break the huddle and are giggling. Krishnadevaraya enters. The courtiers hastily reposition themselves.)

KRISHNA
I have some questions this morning for my learned courtiers. *(An air of suspense)*
The first question. What is the entrance tax for a horse drawn cart to come into the city of Hampi?

FOREIGN
Why, my lord, it is known all over the land. The tax is a mere single silver coin.

ALL *(Eager voices)*
Yes, of course. A mere silver coin. Easy entry.

KRISHNA
Next. What is the cost of a bag of ragi grain in the market?

FINANCE

My lord, nobody goes hungry in your kingdom. Everybody has enough to eat because ragi and other grains are so affordable.

KRISHNA

The question again. What does a bag of ragi grain cost?

FINANCE

A mere two pieces of silver, my lord.

ALL *(Eager voices)*

That's right. Just two pieces of silver. That's what I was saying.

KRISHNA

What is the fee for building one's own house within the city walls?

PM

We declared this the Year of Housing for All, my lord.

KRISHNA

What is the fee?

PM

There is no fee, my lord. We make loans available at easy rates for all in the kingdom to have roofs over their heads.

(The sound of laughter echoing. Raman enters.)

RAMAN

And what is the distance between your middle finger and your nose?

KRISHNA

Welcome, Raman. Late again!

RAMAN

My lord, I was –

KRISHNA

Daydreaming at the pond, I suppose.

RAMAN

I was measuring the distance people have between the middle finger and the nose.

KRISHNA

And is that pertinent to this morning's council proceedings?

(The courtiers are delighted that Raman is being put in his place.)

RAMAN

It seems so, my lord.

KRISHNA

It seems so!

RAMAN

You see, my lord, some people touch their noses this way. *(Demonstrating)* Others insist on touching it the roundabout way, from around their heads.

(Cross fade to children's group down-left.)

TEACHER

Have you heard stories of wise kings who went about the countryside incognito to see what the people were really thinking and saying about the kingdom?

A BOY

What is in-cog-ni-to?

TEACHER

Incognito? Well, it means... let's ask them. *(Points to the audience)*

A GIRL

Do you know what incognito means? You do? You don't? Well, maybe you should google it when we get home.

TEACHER

It is just possible that king Krishnadevaraya invented the practice of mingling with the people incognito – wearing a disguise, as a beggar or an old man or any other commoner, and just listening to what people had to say.

BOY

Tenali Raman sometimes kept the king company on these trips, both of them going about in disguise.

GIRL

This time, Tenali Raman wanted to show the king how the government departments actually worked.

TEACHER

Shhh! Here they come. Let's watch from out there.

(The group withdraws off stage.)

(Through the passage above we see Krishna and Raman don cloaks and taking a journey' upstage, perhaps silhouetted.

The three journey episodes below are best done rapidly.

They reach an 'office' down-right. It is the check post at the city entrance. There is an officer at a floor level desk, whose face is not clearly seen. Next to him is another person at another desk, whose face is also not clearly seen. The two parts here and in the next two scenes may be played by the courtiers if there is a shortage of actors.

The desk has a prominent sign that says WE ARE CLOSED. Krishna and Raman reach the desk. The person at the neighbouring desk coughs.)

RAMAN

My good man, we have come from the neighbouring town. Where do we pay the entrance tax for our horse drawn cart?

(The man points to the desk with the sign)

And what is the tax, may we ask?

(The man shows two fingers)

Two silver coins? Is it not supposed to be one silver coin?

(The man shows three fingers. Krishna tries to protest, but Raman restrains him.)

Three silver...

(The man shows four fingers)

Well, I suppose four is better than eight.

(Raman gestures to Krishna to cough up. He does, reluctantly. The person at the first desk turns the sign around to show WE ARE OPEN.

Raman and Krishna continue the journey, a circular path, bringing them back to the two desks down-right. The sign at the first desk is now OUT FOR LUNCH.

Krishna and Raman reach the desk. The person at the neighbouring desk coughs.)

RAMAN

My good man, we have walked all the way from the other side of town. We wish to buy a bag of ragi grain.

(The man points to the desk with the sign)

And what is the price for a bag of ragi, may we ask?

(The man shows four fingers)

Four silver coins? Is it not supposed to be two silver coins?

(The man shows six fingers. Krishna tries to protest, but Raman restrains him.)

Six silver...

(The man places two bowls of grains on the table. He pushes one bowl forward, showing two fingers.)

This one is for two silvers? But this is mostly sand!

(The man pushes the second bowl forward, showing six fingers.)

The real ragi! And this is for six silver coins?

(The man shows eight fingers.)

The price has gone up! Well, I suppose eight is better than ten.

(Raman gestures to Krishna to cough up. He does, reluctantly. The person at the first desk turns the sign around to show BON APPETIT.

Raman and Krishna continue the journey, a circular path, bringing them back to the two desks down-right. The sign at the first desk is now ROOF UNDER REPAIR.

Krishna and Raman reach the desk. The person at the neighbouring desk coughs.)

RAMAN

My good man, we come to this city to work every day from the other side of the river.

We wish to have a house in the city, so that we can work harder for the kingdom.

(The man points to the desk with the sign)

May I ask what we must do to get a housing loan?

(The man shows eight fingers)

Eight silver coins? Is it not supposed to be a free loan?

(The man shows ten fingers. Krishna tries to protest, but Raman restrains him.)

Ten silver ...

(The man places one foot on the table and rests two hands with ten fingers next to the foot)

Ahh, I see. A service tax for the free housing loan!

(The man grins)

Service with a smile!

(Raman gestures to Krishna to cough up. He does, reluctantly. The person at the first desk turns the sign around to show ROOFS FOR ALL.

Raman and Krishna continue the journey, a circular path, bringing them down-left. Krishna is fuming. They take off their cloaks.)

KRISHNA

Raman, Raman! This is unbelievable!

RAMAN

But completely true, my lord!

KRISHNA

In my kingdom!

RAMAN

Under your very nose, my lord.

(He gestures touching his nose from around the head)

KRISHNA

What do we do?! What do we do?!

RAMAN

My lord, when all else fails, it is customary for mortals to turn to god for divine intervention!

KRISHNA

Do you think that will help?

RAMAN

It is indeed worth a try.

(They don their cloaks and undertake another journey, ending down-centre. The goddess Kali has descended from above. At the feet of the goddess is a priest, lying down.)

RAMAN

We wish to offer a prayer to goddess Kali.

(The priest puts up five fingers. Krishna tries to protest, but Raman restrains him.)

You see, it is a rather special request from ...

(The priest puts up ten fingers)

KRISHNA

Aaarghh!!

(Krishna storms out right in a rage, Raman following.)

RAMAN

My lord!

(The priest picks up his to cloth and exits.)

KALI

What can I do? All my hands are tied!

(Goddess Kali ascends.)

KRISHNA

In my kingdom! In my kingdom!! Where did I go wrong?!

RAMAN

Do not blame yourself needlessly, my lord. You will still be known for centuries to come as a just and wise emperor.

KRISHNA

How can we go about policing everybody in every corner of the city?

RAMAN

We cannot, my lord.

KRISHNA

There will be more policemen than people!

RAMAN

It cannot be so, my lord.

KRISHNA

Is there no solution? No hope?

RAMAN

Perhaps in a future generation, my lord. Perhaps good sense will descend on mankind, and people will change.

KRISHNA

What can we do in the remaining years of our lives to make it happen?

RAMAN

We can listen to our children.

KRISHNA

The children?

RAMAN

There is hope there, my lord.

KRISHNA

We can hope, I suppose.

RAMAN

My lord, allow me to suggest one more journey. I would like to take you to my old school in the town of Tenali.

KRISHNA

Well, if you say so....

(Cross fade to Children's group down-left.)

TEACHER

We are back in the village school five hundred years ago. The teacher is taking a class in arithmetic. What do you think they are learning there?

A BOY

Multiplication tables!

TEACHER

All right, multiplication tables. Who will be Tenali Raman?

(All in the group point to one boy.)

ALL

Krishnan!

TEACHER

All right, Krishnan. You know what to do in this scene.

A GIRL *(Reciting)*

Sixty-six fives are three hundred and thirty.

GROUP

Sixty-six fives are three hundred and thirty.

TEACHER *(Picking up)*

Sixty-six sixes are three hundred and ninety six.

GROUP

Sixty-six sixes are three hundred and ninety six.

TEACHER

Sixty-six sevens are four hundred and sixty two.

KRISHNAN *(Loud)*

Sixty-seven twelves are eight hundred and four. Twelve sixty-sevens are eight hundred and four.

TEACHER

Krishnan!

RAMAN

Sixty-eight twelves are eight hundred and sixteen Twelve sixty-eights are eight hundred and sixteen.

GROUP *(Stopping him)*

Ohho! Krishnan, stop!

A BOY

You have got us mixed up!

A GIRL

As usual! Stop your mischief now!

TEACHER

Now, where were we?

(There is argument and commotion in the group, with the Teacher trying to bring order, when Krishnadevaraya and Raman enter.)

KRISHNA

Hmmm....

TEACHER *(To the audience)*

Great heavens! Emperor Krishnadevaraya himself! *(To the group, prompting)* What do you say when we have a visitor?

GROUP

Good morning Uncle!!

KRISHNA *(To Raman)*

What is this Uncle business?

RAMAN

It can't be helped, my lord. We opened up the education system. There have been some foreign influences.

KRISHNA

Hmmm... I am going to ask the class some questions.

TEACHER

Yes, of course...Sir!

KRISHNA

I can see you know your multiplication tables well enough.

RAMAN

Much more than in my times, my lord.

KRISHNA

Now, tell me what you would like to have most in your life in this village.

A BOY

We want to know.

KRISHNA

You want to know! You want to know what? You want to know why the cock crows at break of day, I suppose.

A GIRL

We want to know why men are greedy.

KRISHNA

You don't want to know why worms turn into butterflies?

BOY

We want to know why people never seem to have enough.

KRISHNA

You want to know...

ALL

Why do grown-ups always think they know everything?

(Krishna takes Raman aside.)

KRISHNA

Raman! I think there is hope!

RAMAN

Indeed, my lord, there is much hope.

(Krishna turns to the audience)

KRISHNA

Time to close!

RAMAN

My lord, you can rest assured that the good work started by you in Vijayanagar will always be carried forward.

KRISHNA

Always?

RAMAN

As long as we have children going to school in Tenali town!

KRISHNA *(Turns to the group)*

You know what? I think it would be most fitting to have you teach the gathering here a thing or two. You can lead us. Show us the way.

TEACHER

Your Highness, what better way to show the way than by a song?

KRISHNA

As you wish. Your group has a song in mind already, I can see.

TEACHER

Not a song of our own, your Highness. It is one composed by the saintly Purandaradasa of your court.

KRISHNA

Most fitting! Most fitting!

RAMAN

We shall all join in. You lead, we follow.

(Concluding song of Purandaradasa here. The children's group leads the audience in the song from its position down-left. The king and Raman are with the group.

As the song reaches its end, the courtiers enter and watch from down-right. The King walks across to down-centre, Raman following, and gives the courtiers an admonishing glare. They grin sheepishly.

The last stanza of the song ends. There is a reprise of the courtiers' chorus, but with changed wording.)

Ooh! Tenali Raman!
Dear old Tenali Raman!
You're's so precious, dear Raman!

We all know, Tenali Raman!
We all need you, dear Raman!
Ooh, Tenali Raman!

(The last stanza of the song and courtiers' chorus alternate a few times...as the cast assembles on stage to join in.

A procession....tableau..curtain call.)

Close of play

BANGALORE LITTLE THEATRE

Six Decades of Wholesome Community Theatre

In 1960, a small group of committed persons in Bangalore sought a theatre experience that could be a genuine alternative to the order of the day that was called BBC Theatre – British Bedroom Comedy. The group included the talented couple, Scott and Margaret Tod, and at least four other expats, along with a handful of Bangaloreans. They had a vision of a Community Theatre best described by the slogan invented 25 years later: *Think Globally, Act Locally.* Bangalore Little Theatre came into existence with a play reading in the last week of September that year. The first production on boards in December 1960 was Moliere's *The Prodigious Snob*, more commonly known as *The Would-be Gentleman*

In 1962, within a year of inception, BLT arrived at a character and identity for itself: to maintain pride in its strictly amateur status, but to conduct its affairs in a thoroughly professional manner. The group gave itself a constitution and, through that, a participatory style of functioning. The group was seen as belonging to a membership, and therefore to be managed transparently by a elected management committee. The founding members were the first to give way to younger members to take the group forward.

Way back in 1963, BLT produced its first Indian play in English, an original adaptation of *Mrichhakatika* (The Toy Cart of Clay) by a founder-member, Prof B Chandrasekhara. Since then, the group has maintained the conscious policy of producing Indian plays periodically – translations, adaptations, original scripts, by its own members and others. Not surprisingly, two of the six awards for contemporary playscripts instituted for the first time by *The Hindu* in 1993 landed in BLT. The first prize was for the play by Vijay Padaki, *Credit Titles,* a political satire on intellectual property rights for patenting life forms. A Special Prize was awarded to another member, Ambika (Poile) Sengupta

Old-timers of BLT have often been asked the secret of the group's long life when, in contrast, we see hundreds of cases of groups starting with a bang and dropping by the wayside in a couple of years. The difference, it seems, is in the simple fact that BLT is a community-based organisation and, therefore, a membership driven group. From this fact has followed a number of guiding principles that appear to have served BLT well over the years. For instance:

- The participatory and transparency principles in management (with all financial transactions completely open and made available to the entire membership)
- The highly open leadership structure around an elected Managing Committee (rather than being founder-centric or personality-driven)
- The constant development of new talent, including new directors (rather than being dependent on the same old hands or breeding star complexes)
- The pursuit of the higher purpose, the constitutionally-enshrined objective of promoting the theatre and related arts in Bangalore (rather than the attitude of 'let's do another play')

All of this actually makes it far more difficult to 'manage' the organisation. It is so much easier to let a charismatic leader take charge and 'run' the group as he (or she) wishes.

The significance of these principles is understood better when we see that a sizeable majority of the theatre talent in Bangalore, including the more recognised names, has been in BLT productions, workshops and training programmes earlier. They continue their affiliation with BLT even if they perform under other banners.

Related to this point is one other indisputably important feature of BLT. It is the only English-language theatre group in Bangalore (perhaps anywhere in India) with strong links to the local-regional theatre, building bridges across language divides.

Many of the stalwarts on the Kannada stage and screen have been either life members of BLT or have been prominently involved in some capacity or the other. After all, among the founders were personalities like Prof B Chandrasekhara, Nani, Shivaram, Seetharam, V Ramamurthy and S Ramaswamy. Then there were CR Simha, Vimala Rangachar, SG Ramachandra, KC Sekhar, Suresh Heblikar, Paddu, Shankar and Arundhati Nag, Ashok Rao.... And many many more – including some who went on to become Presidents of Karnataka Nataka Academy! Indeed, BLT has been a substantial support to Kannada theatre groups in their start up stages.

BLT has invested heavily in training and outreach activity. In the late 1970s, BLT introduced for the first time in Bangalore a comprehensive introductory programme for newcomers to the theatre, based on the Stella Adler system. Since the mid '80, the group has made its Summer Project on Theatre (SPOT) a regular training event. It has come to be recognised as the most prestigious training event in the city, because of the quality of inputs provided. And it continues to be a part of BLT's social commitment. Other groups and productions snap up the talent from these training projects.

In 1993, the group initiated an annual Festival of Short Plays (SHORTS), aimed at promoting theatre activity among the college and youth population. With the audience response as enthusiastic as seen, the scale of the Festival may well be enhanced considerably in the coming years.

As a socially-responsible theatre society, BLT has readily taken on many a fundraising production for worthy causes. In 1970-71, BLT's production of the new play by Badal Sircar, *Evam Indrajit*, was the first fundraising event to contribute to the Prime Minister's Fund for the Bangladeshi (then East Bengal) refugee crisis. An original script, *Head Start*, by Vijay Padaki, was produced for CRY in January 1996. Since then BLT has made a constitutional commitment to dedicate one production for a charity every year. The group also provides various kinds of help to theatre projects in colleges, schools, clubs and other institutions.

With the high repute in training and outreach activity, it was only logical for BLT to set up an Academy of Theatre Arts in 2008. The stated mission of the Academy is to enrich the theatre institutional system through the thrust programme of *Theatre Education,* thus building the societal base for the true appreciation of the theatre and, indeed, all of the performing arts.

THE SERIES EDITOR

Vijay Padaki is a Theatre Educator based in Bangalore. He has worn two caps for most of his life with equal facility. He has been active in the theatre for sixty years. He has been a management professional for over forty-five years.

Vijay is a psychologist and behavioural scientist by training, and founder-director of The P&P Group, a management resource centre that has programmes of research, consulting and training in the areas of Organisation and Institutional Development. A good part of the work of The P&P Group is devoted to the effectiveness of large development programmes. Among his earlier assignments he headed the Human Resources Division of India's oldest cooperative R&D institution, Ahmedabad Textile Industry's Research Association (ATIRA), which also helped set up the first Indian Institute of Management in Ahmedabad. Later, he was a member of the founding faculty at Indian Institute of Management, Bangalore, the founder of a Centre for Management for the textile industry in Ahmedabad, and a Visiting Professor at Indian Institute of Science, Bangalore to initiate a programme in R&D Management. He was a Senior Associate at the National Institute of Advanced Studies in its early years.

Vijay joined Bangalore Little Theatre in 1960, the year of its inception, and later served the company in many capacities – as actor, director, trainer, writer, designer and administrator, including two stints each as Secretary and President. In 2008, the institutional set up was restructured. Bangalore Little Theatre Foundation was created as a Public Charitable Trust. It was done with the purpose of reinforcing the organisation's strengths in outreach activity, and thus *rededicating the commitment to social development goals beyond performance.* The Trust requested Vijay to provide the leadership to a newly-created Academy of Theatre Arts in its formative years. The Academy is developing a long term programme thrusts to strengthen the institution of theatre education and practice in India.

Vijay has been responsible for institutionalising several activities of BLT, such as the annual summer workshop for newcomers to the theatre (SPOT), from which has emerged a large number of the theatre personalities in Bangalore, the History of Ideas programme of biographical plays, the Courtyard Theatre programme, and the Children's Theatre programme, which includes the annual flagship children's play as a partnership production to support a charity. Vijay conceived and initiated the highly successful Trainer-Training programme and the Directors Training programme in Bangalore.

He has forged several international partnerships with BLT over the years. The John F Kennedy Centre for Performing Arts in Washington invited him to serve as an advisor to the India Festival in 2011. The same year, he gave the Harold Clurman lecture at the Stella Adler Studio in New York. More recently, the Ministry of Culture invited Vijay to initiate a programme of Arts and Heritage Management in India.

Vijay has written over 50 original plays. He has also adapted or translated several play scripts. Seagull Books has published a volume of two Gujarati plays translated by him. In 1993, Vijay won the award for the best contemporary play script instituted by *The Hindu* for the play *Credit Titles.*

PUBLICATIONS IN THE SERIES

This edition commemorates the 60th year of Bangalore Little Theatre.

Volume 1: FOUR CLASSICS on the Indian Stage

Contains original English language adaptations of Indian classics. These include ***The Toy Cart of Clay***, an adaptation of the Sanskrit Classic ***Mrichhakatika*** by Sudraka; ***The Anklet***, an adaptation from Ilango Adigal's Tamil Classic *Silappadikaram*; ***Kurukshetra Burning!*** based on *Smashana Kurukshetra* in Kannada by Kuvempu; ***The Echo,*** an adaptation of *Chomana Dudi* in Kannada by Shivaram Karanth.

Volume 2: THE HISTORY OF IDEAS Programme of new plays

From BLT's highly acclaimed History of Ideas programme, plays include ***The Prophet and the Poet,*** based on the Gandhi-Tagore exchanges; ***Finding Ananda***, rediscovering the life and work of Swami Vivekananda, with the Bengal Renaissance as the backdrop; ***Tiger! Tiger!*** revealing the humanistic side of Tipu Sultan; ***Monsters in the Dark,*** an original adaptation of the Pulitzer award book *The Emperor of All Maladies* by Siddharyha Mukherjee, sub-titled A Biography of Cancer; ***Einstein's Dreams,*** an original dance theatre adaptation of the novel by the same title by Alan Lightman.